Power of...
Word 2 for Windows

Mike Lottridge
Vicky Stevens

MIS:
PRESS

A Subsidiary of
Henry Holt and Co., Inc.

First Edition—1992

ISBN: 1-55828-200-9

Printed in the United States of America

10 9 8 7 6 5 4 3 2 1

MIS: Press books are available at special discounts for bulk purchases for sales promotions, premiums, fund-raising, or educational use. Special editions or book excerpts can also be created to specification.

For details contact: *Special Sales Director*

    MIS: Press

    a subsidiary of Henry Holt and Company, Inc.

    115 West 18th Street

    New York, New York 10011

Acknowledgments

Many thanks to Steve Berkowitz, Bruno Quinson, and Bob Williams of MIS: Press for giving us this opportunity.

We especially appreciate Kevin Latham's professionalism in handling complex layout issues and Joanne Kelman's fine layout work. Cary Weinberger's direction and words of encouragement are always appreciated.

Our cats, Xanadu and Bastet, rarely complained when supper was late so many nights while we worked on this book. We thank them.

Finally, we acknowledge each other for this and the many other adventures we plan together (and for working closely in small quarters and still staying married)

CONTENTS

INTRODUCTION

About 25 years ago, a graduate student proudly presented his English dissertation for defense. "You'll have to type it all over again," his advisor said. "The margins and the indentations for quoted material are all wrong." With that, a downtrodden Ph.D. hopeful went back to his study, sat down at the typewriter, and retyped 400 pages.

Even 12 years ago, we developed computer documentation using text processing programs that required the author to "code" text, even for simple things like underlining words. We stopped in the middle of a sentence, entered the macro to turn on underlining, typed the word to be underlined, and turned off the macro with another code. If we forgot type in the code to turn off the macro, the remainder of the document would be underlined! What a mess. And the computer printers were down the street in another building.

Needless to say, creating a small document took an incredible amount of time. Just talk to anyone who created documents in a technical business environment more than 10 years ago, and they will offer you a great story about how difficult it was to write with a word processor. (And the laser printer was always three blocks away, and they had to crawl on icy sidewalks at midnight to get their printouts, but they never missed a deadline.)

That was then. Today, using a powerful word processor like Word for Windows 2.0, you can create a long document and change the way it looks easily — sometimes with only a few keystrokes. Like Microsoft's many other fine products, Word for Windows makes many tasks easy and fun to perform.

This book will help you to learn Word's powerful capabilities and feel confident about creating all kinds of documents for business and personal use.

WHO NEEDS THIS BOOK

This book serves users with a variety of word processing and desktop publishing experience. If you are an intermediate word processing user, who has a basic knowledge of Word for Windows, you will appreciate the time-saving power information. You will learn how to create style sheets and macros and increase productivity in document design.

If you are a novice user, you will gain a basic understanding of working with text in the Word for Windows environment before moving to those more sophisticated techniques. Even long-time users can benefit from the "brush up" on the basics and the information about using the WordBasic language.

WHAT YOU WILL LEARN IN THIS BOOK

The Power of Word for Windows 2.0 presents a logical sequence of tasks and information that move from simple to complex so you can gain increasing skill at each level. The book is organized as follows:

Chapter 1

Mastering the Word for Windows Environment explains the Word for Windows environment, how to navigate in it, and how to use the "tools" of the work area. You will learn about the Title bar, the Menu bar, all the buttons of the Toolbar and the Ribbon, the Ruler, the workplace, and the Status bar. The chapter also explains the different page views and to use them, quick navigation, use of the Clipboard for cutting, copying, and pasting text.

Chapter 2

Setting Up a Word Document shows you how to set up all the elements of a Word document. You will learn about page setup, section breaks, page breaks, headers and footers, footnotes, annotations, and bookmarks.

Chapter 3

Formatting Characters and Words shows you multiple ways to apply and change the look of the fonts you use. You will learn multiple ways to apply attributes, such as bold, italic, underlines, hidden text, superscript and subscript characters. The chapter also covers use of hyphens, nonbreaking spaces, character spacing, copying and repeating formats, and working with special characters and symbols.

Chapter 4

Formatting Paragraphs and Objects explains the use of line spacing, tabs, indentations, paragraph alignment, numbered and bulleted lists, tables, columns, and borders.

Chapter 5

Formatting Tutorial provides two structured lessons for applying formatting to text. You can use the text on the disk to format a letter and a business proposal.

Chapter 6

Creating a Template shows you how to define styles based on the formatting you apply and how to create a new template that you can use for similar documents.

Chapter 7

Tables of Contents and Indexes shows you how to build and generate tables of contents, lists, and indexes using headings and field codes.

Chapter 8

Microsoft Draw and WordArt show you how to use Word's powerful graphic capabilities. The chapter explains how to use the tools and menus, and how to import graphics from other applications.

Chapter 9

Microsoft Graph shows you how to create many different types of graphic charts from numerical data, making the presentation of numeric data far more interesting.

Chapter 10

Equation Editor shows you how to enter and customize equations for simple to complex mathematical expressions.

Chapter 11

Macros teaches you how to automate and simplify repetitive operations by saving them as macros that you can run with a few keystrokes.

Chapter 12

WordBasic gives you access to the programming language macros are saved in, allowing you to fully customize macros and even create your own WordBasic applications from scratch.

Chapter 13

Print Merge shows you how to create your own mailing lists, form letters, and form documents.

WHAT YOU NEED TO USE THIS BOOK

This book assumes that you have at least a 286 processor, the Microsoft Windows operating environment, and the Word for Windows 2.0 package. It also assumes that you have installed the packages and that you have some working knowledge of the Windows environment and features.

CHAPTER 1

MASTERING WORD FOR THE WINDOWS ENVIRONMENT

In this chapter you will learn about the working environment in Word for Windows, and some navigation methods for working in a document, including:

- *the title bar*

- *the menu bar*

- *the Toolbar*

- *the ribbon*

- *the ruler*

- *the workplace*

1

- *the status bar*

- *page views*

- *the Clipboard*

- *the insertion point*

- *the Find command*

- *the Go To command*

- *text selection*

Learning all the ways you can move around in a document will help you become a more efficient (and more powerful) user. Word provides an interface that gives you a variety of ways to choose options, select and change text, and move from one area to another. Many users find that they never stick to just one method of moving around in the document. After they learn all the navigation techniques, they just do whatever seems right for the moment.

THE OVERALL WORD WORK AREA

When you launch Word for Windows, the program displays the default work area, which is the *workplace*. This area is the foundation upon which you can build many document types, using all of Word's features. The following sections describe the parts of the work area.

The Title Bar

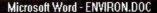

The title bar shows the document name. Word assigns your document a temporary name until you save it with the name you choose. The leftmost area of this bar contains the button for the Application Control menu, which you click to display commands that let you size and move a window, switch to other applications, and close Word. The rightmost area of this bar shows the minimize and maximize buttons that you click to either fill the screen with Word or shrink Word to an icon.

The Menu Bar

| ▭ | <u>F</u>ile   <u>E</u>dit   <u>V</u>iew   <u>I</u>nsert   Forma<u>t</u>   T<u>o</u>ols   T<u>a</u>ble   <u>W</u>indow   <u>H</u>elp | ▲▼ |

You use the menu bar to choose all commands while working in Word. The leftmost area of the bar contains the button for the Document Control menu, which displays the commands for sizing, moving, splitting, and closing the document window and for moving the insertion point between windows. The rightmost button is the Restore button, which returns the window to its previous size. Word displays this button when you click the maximize button.

The Toolbar

The Toolbar lets mouse users quickly access some of Word's commands without having to use a pull-down menu. The following table describes the Toolbar options, and gives hints for using each one.

Table 1-1

Tool	Description
▢ New	Opens a new document, named Document N, where N equals the number Word assigns. The document has the default settings. You name the document when you save it.
▢ Open	Displays the Open dialog box, which lets you type the name of a document to open or select one.
▢ Save	Saves the active document. If you have several documents open, make them active, one at a time, to save them.If you have not named the active document,Word displays the Save As dialog box when you select Save.

Table 1-1 (continued from previous page)

Tool	Description
Cut	Removes the selected text or object and places it on the Clipboard, where you cannot see it. If you cut another item and place it on the Clipboard, then you lose the first one you cut. Always paste the text or object in the Clipboard before you cut another one.
Copy	Copies the selected text or object and places it on the Clipboard, where you cannot see it. If you copy another item and place it on the Clipboard, then you lose the first one you copied. Always paste the text or object in the Clipboard before you copy another one.
Paste	Inserts whatever is stored on the Clipboard at the location of the insertion point. You can paste the text or object multiple times until you cut or copy another item to the Clipboard.
Undo	Reverses the latest action you took. If you cannot undo an action, then the Edit menu either displays **Cannot Undo** or the Undo option will be dimmed, indicating it is unavailable.
Numbered	Gives selected paragraphs consecutive numbers and applies hanging indents to List text.You can change a numbered list to a bulleted list by selecting the paragraphs in the list and choosing the Bulleted List button.

Table 1-1 *(continued from previous page)*

Tool	Description
Bulleted List	Gives selected paragraphs bullets and applies hanging indents to text. You can change a bulleted list to a numbered list by selecting the paragraphs in the list and choosing the Numbered List button.
Unindent	Moves selected indented paragraphs left to the previous default tab stop. If you decide to remove bullets from paragraphs, select the paragraph and choose this button, and then delete the bullets. (You may have to reapply the chosen style for paragraphs.)
Indent	Moves selected paragraphs right to the next tab stop.
Table	Inserts a table where you have postioned the insertion point. You can select the number of rows and columns you want by dragging the cursor over the sample table in the drop-down box. Then, you can add more columns and rows, if necessary, from the Table menu.
Text Columns	Formats the current section with columns. You do not have to select the entire section to format it with columns. You can select the number of columns you want by dragging the cursor over the sample columns in the drop-down box.

Table 1-1 *(continued from previous page)*

Tool	Description
Frame	Places a nonprinting frame around selected text, tables, or graphics or inserts an empty frame. A *frame* is a formatted space. As you type in a frame, text wraps to fit inside it. You work with the text in a frame almost in the same way you work with any other text. You can apply formatting, move the frame, or size it.
Draw	Starts the Microsoft Draw program. You can create a drawing and insert it in your Word document at the location of the insertion point. For more information about using the Draw program, see Chapter 8.
Graph	Starts the Microsoft Graph program. You can create a graph and insert it in your Word document at the location of the insertion point. For more information about using the Graph program, see Chapter 9.
Envelope	Formats an envelope that prints along with the active document. Depending on the kind of printer you have, you may need to feed the envelope manually. You can print an envelope by itself, or when you print the entire document. You can choose envelope setup and printing options with the Create Envelope command from the Tools menu.

Table 1-1 (continued from previous page)

Tool	Description
🔤 Spelling	Checks the spelling of all Words in your document or any selected word or line.
	You can check spelling from any point in a document. Word checks from the insertion point to the end and then asks if you want it to check from the beginning.
	Word flags any word that it does not recognize and allows you to ignore the word, change it, ignore or change all identical entries, or to enter it in a custom list.

Choose custom additions judiciously. If you enter the wrong spelling of a word by accident, Word will ignore the misspelled word in the future.

N O T E

Tool	Description
🖨 Print	Prints all pages of the active document.
🔳 Zoom Whole Page	Shows the active document in page layout view. The size is reduced to show the entire page. Use this view to see how your pages will look when you print them.
🔲 Zoom 100%	Shows the active document in full size and in normal view. Work in this mode when you type and edit. If you are working in multiple columns, you will see them in their actual widths, but they will not appear side-by-side.

Table 1-1 (continued from previous page)

Tool	Description
▦ Zoom Page Width	Displays the full width of a page, even if you have set margins wider than the workplace shows.

The Ribbon

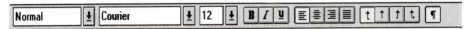

The ribbon contains quick formatting options for which you need a mouse.

The three leftmost ribbon options (from left to right) let you apply styles, fonts, and font point sizes. Click on the down arrows beside the options to select them.

The next three ribbon options let you apply bold, italic, and underline attributes to characters, words, or paragraphs.

The next four ribbon options let you apply text alignment for left, centered, right, and block (right-justified).

The next four options let you apply tab alignment for left, centered, right, and decimal tabs The last option button on the right is for displaying or hiding nonprinting characters, such as paragraph marks.

The Ruler

The ruler lets you change paragraph indents, margins, and column widths for text and tables.

To make the Ruler active, press **Ctrl-Shift-F10** or click it anywhere with the mouse. Word displays the ruler cursor at the left margin of the ruler.

Everything you can do from the toolbar, ribbon, and ruler can also be done by choosing commands and options from the menu bar. However, the opposite is not true.

N O T E

The Workplace

The workplace is where you type text, use all formatting features, and open other windows. To open another document in a window, choose **Open** from the File menu, (**Alt-F, O**) and open a document. You can view and work between the two documents by choosing **Arrange All** from the Window menu (**Alt-W, A**). Only the window in which you are working is active.

The workplace also includes the vertical and horizontal scroll bars that let you move around in the document. For more information about using the scroll bars, see "Using the Mouse to Move the Insertion Point" later in this chapter.

The Status Bar

The status bar displays the page number, section number, the number of pages in the document, the insertion point position from the top of the page, the line and column numbers, the level of magnification, the status of keys on your keyboard, and whether you are recording macros.

You cannot type anything in the status bar.

PAGE VIEWS

The page views that Word allows help you to get a better idea of how the pieces of a document are coming together. There are four ways that you can view your document while you are working:

- Normal
- Page Layout
- Print Preview
- Outline

You use each view for a different purpose, and you will probably find each type useful during the development of any document. All view modes, except for Print Preview, allow you to reduce and enlarge the view and edit just as you would in the normal size.

Normal View

Normal is Word's default view. Usually, you will do most of your work in this view, where you can perform all typing, editing, and formatting, including styles, fonts, and spacing. You can open other panes, such as headers and footers, in Normal view. Also, you can open and work in more than one document (for example, cutting and pasting text from one document to another). When you add a header or footer, you must be in Normal view; however, when you close the header or footer pane, you can look at your document in another view.

If you are not working in Normal view, and you want to be, choose **Normal** from the View menu **(Alt-V, N).**

Draft Mode

While Word lets you create very long documents, there is the possible disadvantage of a decrease in the speed of the display. Draft Mode speeds the display because it "strips" most formatting and graphics from the document, requiring less processing for display. When you choose Draft Mode **(Alt-V, D)**, Word displays the text in one font and size,using underlining to show any character formatting you might have added. When you return to Normal view, all of the original formatting in the document is intact.

Page Layout View

Page Layout view can help you save a lot of time and paper. Instead of printing your document to see how the parts look together, you can see how the page is laid out before you print. Choose **Page Layout View** from the View menu **(Alt-V, P)**. This view is particularly useful if you are building a document that has multiple formatting elements, for example, headers, footers, columnar text, and graphics. However, line numbers and lines between columns are not available in Page Layout view. The following illustration shows a page in Page Layout view, with the Zoom Whole Page option applied to reduce it. A discussion of enlarging and reducing documents is included in this section.

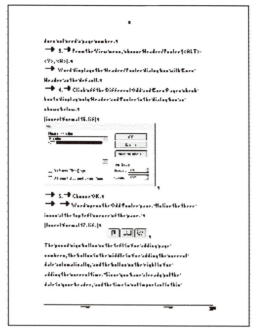

Figure 1.1

Page Layout View versus Normal View

While you are working in this view, you can edit and format your document much like you can in Normal view. However, there are a few things that you cannot do in Page Layout view that you can do in Normal view and vice versa. For example, in Normal view, you cannot drag a framed item to another position on the page, but Page Layout view allows it. You can also adjust headers and footers in Page Layout view without having to open the header or footer pane.

You will probably find it easier to make most formatting changes while working at 100 percent of the size of the document, instead of at 50 or 200 percent. The 100 percent size is the one in which most people are accustomed to typing and formatting.

N   O   T   E

When you scroll in Normal view, you can scroll to the bottom of one page and continue scrolling so that the bottom of one page and the top of the next are both displayed at one time. However, in Page Layout view, when you scroll past the bottom of a page, Word displays the top of the next page on the screen. You cannot look at the bottom of one page and the top of another at the same time.

Page Layout view also allows you to display dotted lines around the different blocks of text or graphics on a page. This is particularly useful in pointing out how a page will look in regard to where text and graphics are positioned. If you have a page with a header, text, a graphic, and a footer, Word draws a dotted line around each of the elements. To display the dotted lines, choose Options from the Tools menu (**Alt-O, O**). Then, select the View category and select the Text Boundaries check box under Show Text With.

You can see that the zero mark on the ruler on top of the workspace is not aligned with the left margin in Page Layout view. This is because the zero mark aligns with the left boundary of the paragraph that contains the insertion point.

N O T E

Print Preview

The Print Preview feature, like Page Layout, lets you see how your document will look when you print it. However, Print Preview can show you any elements you added to the printable area, whereas Page Layout cannot always show elements that you placed outside of the margins. Additionally, Print Preview can display two whole pages at a time, as shown in Figure 1.2.

To invoke the Print Preview, choose **Print Preview** from the File menu (**Alt-F, V**). The four options across the top of the screen allow you to print the document, display or hide margins, display one or two pages, or close the window without printing. If you are working with a document that has landscape orientation, you may find that the one-page option is more useful because the two-page view may be too wide to display in the view area.

Making Adjustments in Print Preview

Word lets you make some adjustments to your layout in Print Preview. This is a very powerful, time-saving feature; however, you cannot type or reformat text. In this section in which you are working, you can adjust the margins, reposition headers and footers, and insert, move, and delete page breaks.

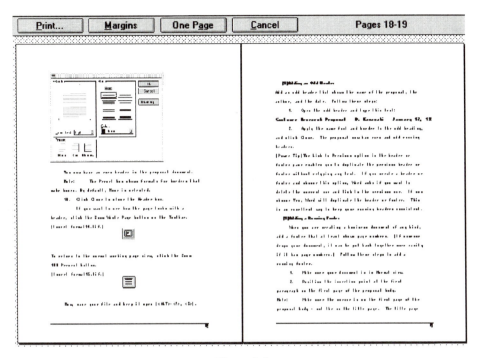

Figure 1.2

Using the Mouse

To change your margins, headers, or footers using the mouse, follow these steps. Keyboard instructions follow this procedure.

1. Choose Print Preview from the File menu (Alt-F, V) and choose the Margins button.

2. Click on the page for which you want to display the margins.

3. Point to a margin handle or to the item you need to move.

4. Drag the margin handle (small black square) or item to the new position and release the mouse button. Watch the upper-right corner of your screen. Word displays the distance from the item to the edge of the page.

5. Click off the page to update the display.

You cannot use the Undo feature from the Edit menu if you decide to undo the change. You have to manually reposition the item again, using the same method described above, to move it back where it was.

N O T E

6.   Choose **Close** from the Control menu to return to the previous view or double-click anywhere off the page to return to Page Layout view.

Using the Keyboard

To change your margins, headers, or footers using the keyboard, follow these steps.

1.   Choose **Print Preview** from the File menu
        (Alt-F,V), and choose the **Margins** button.
2.   Press **Tab** until you select the item you want.
3.   Move the item with the arrow keys, and press **Enter** when you reach the new location.
4.   Press **Enter** to update the display.
5.   Choose **Close** from the Control menu to return to the previous view or double-click anywhere off the page to return to Page Layout view.

Outline View

Outline view is much more than just another view mode in Word. In addition to allowing you to look at the structure of your document, it lets you completely reorganize topics with a few simple steps.

Outline view is particularly useful if you designate headings within a template. When you switch to Outline view, all headings and paragraphs are marked with symbols that show the whether there is subordinate text and point out body text.

The following illustration shows the Outline view for a section of a chapter. Notice the bar above the outline. You can choose to display from one to nine levels or all levels of headings and text in your document.

```
┌──────────────────────────────────────────────────────────────────────┐
│ [←] [→] [↑] [↓] [⇥]   [+] [−]   Show: [1][2][3][4][5][6][7][8][9][All] │
├──────────────────────────────────────────────────────────────────────┤
│  ✛  Chapter 9: The Equation Editor                                     │
│      ✛  Using the Equation Editor to Create an Equation                │
│          ✛  Invoking                                                   │
│      ✛  Key Features                                                   │
│          ✛  Embedded Object                                            │
│          ✛  The slot                                                   │
│          ✛  The insertion point                                        │
│              ✛  moving the insertion point                             │
│              ✛  Selecting an item                                      │
│              ✛  Deleting selected items                                │
│              ✛  Nudging Text                                           │
│              ✛  Vertically Aligning Equations (Piles)                  │
│              ✛  Status Bar                                             │
│      ✛  Symbol and Template Palettes                                   │
│          ✛  Relational Symbols                                         │
└──────────────────────────────────────────────────────────────────────┘
```

Figure 1.3

The following table describes the symbols you see in outline mode.

Table 1-2

This symbol...	Indicates...
✛	There is subtext associated with the heading.
▭	There is no subtext associated with the heading.
▫	Body (or paragraph) text.

You use the buttons on the outline bar (above the view area) to reorganize information. The following table shows how to use the buttons. They are described as they appear from left to right as they appear on the outline bar.

Table 1-3

Select this button...	To do this...
Right arrow (**Alt-Shift-Right arrow**)	Move a selection down one level.
Left arrow (**Alt-Shift-Left arrow**)	Move a selection up one level.
Up arrow (**Alt-Shift-Up arrow**)	Move a selection above the preceding heading.
Down arrow (**Alt-Shift-Down arrow**)	Move a selection below the preceding heading.
Right arrow with shadow (**Alt-Shift-keypad 5**)	Convert a heading to body text.
Plus sign (**Alt-Shift-+**)	Expand subheadings or body text under a heading.
Minus sign (**Alt-Shift- -**)	Collapse subheadings or body text under a heading.
1 through 9 (**1** through **9**)	Display headings up to nine levels.
All(**Alt-Shift-A**)	Show all headings and text.

Reducing and Enlarging Page Views

You can display a whole-page view by clicking the Zoom Whole Page button (third from the right) from the Toolbar or by choosing **Zoom** from the View menu **Alt-V, Z** and choosing Whole Page button. The Zoom dialog box gives you more options for enlarging and reducing the view. Returning to 100 percent is just as simple; click the **Zoom Page Width** button (second from the right) on the Toolbar or choose **Page Width** from the Zoom dialog box.

Working in an enlarged view (such as 200 percent) is often very helpful if you are examining a graphic more closely to see if it needs refinement.

N O T E

THE CLIPBOARD

The Clipboard is a temporary storage area within Word that you cannot actually see. However, this area functions much like a clipboard that holds loose pieces of paper. Whenever you use the Cut, Copy, and Paste commands, you activate this storage area. You can even cut and paste or copy and paste information from one Word document to another and to and from other applications, for example, a Microsoft Excel worksheet.

Using the Clipboard

You can copy or move text to the Clipboard using the Toolbar, the Edit menu, or the from the keyboard. To cut, copy, or paste text or graphics, you have to select all of what you want to move, and position the insertion point where you want to place the text. The following table shows the different ways that you can cut, copy, and paste text using the mouse or keyboard.

Table 1-4

To...	*Do this...*
Cut text	Choose Cut from the Edit menu **(Alt-E, T)** or Press **Ctrl-X** or Click the Cut button on the Toolbar.
Copy text	Choose Copy from the Edit menu **(Alt-E, C)** or Press **Ctrl-C** or Click the Copy button from the Toolbar.
Paste text	Choose Paste from the Edit menu **(Alt-E, P)** or Press **Ctrl-V** or Click the Paste button on the Toolbar.

Bypassing the Clipboard

Even though the Clipboard is a convenient feature, you can bypass it entirely when moving and copying text. You do this by using the Drag and Drop feature, clicking with the mouse, or using the keyboard.

Dragging Text with the Mouse

Word's Drag and Drop feature makes it easy to move text. To do so, select the text to move with the left mouse button, click inside the selected area until you see the small dotted box and insertion point, and drag the dotted insertion point to the location where you want to move the text. Word moves the text.

WARNING After you drag text, it remains selected. Therefore, you need to deselect it immediately, as any keystroke will cause Word to delete the selected text and replace it with any text you type. If you forget this and accidentally press a key before you deselect the text, choose Undo Typing from the Edit menu (**Alt-E, U**) to restore the moved text before you do anything else.

Using the Keyboard to Bypass the Clipboard

You can also move and copy text using other keys to bypass the Clipboard. Follow these steps:

1. Position the insertion point where you want to move or copy text.

2. Press the Move Text key (**F2**) to move text

   or

   press the Copy Text key (**Shift-F2**) to copy text.
   Word displays one of the following messages, depending on which key you pressed, in the lower-left corner of the status bar:
   Move from where? or **Copy from where?**

3. Scroll to the text or graphic you want to move or copy, and select it. Word places a dotted underline under the text you selected.

4. Press **Enter.**

The text you selected moves or is copied to the insertion point.

MOVING THE INSERTION POINT

Moving the insertion point means a lot more than just using the arrow keys, spacebar, or mouse functions to go to the next word or line. If you are working in a large document, you need to be able to navigate in it quickly so you can work more efficiently.

Using the Keyboard to Move the Insertion Point

Even if you become a die-hard mouse user, you need to know all the quick ways you can move around using keystrokes. The following table shows you which key or key combination to use to move the insertion point.

Table 1-5

To Move the Insertion Point...	*Press...*
Back one character	Left Arrow
Forward one character	Right Arrow
Up one line	Up Arrow
Down one line	Down Arrow
To the previous word	Ctrl-Left Arrow
To the next word	Ctrl-Right Arrow
To the beginning of the line	Home
To the end of the line	End
Up one paragraph	Ctrl-Up Arrow
Down one paragraph	Ctrl-Down Arrow
To the window's first character	Ctrl-Pg Up

Table 1-5 (continued from previous page)

To Move the Insertion Point...	Press...
To the window's last character	Ctrl-Pg Dn
To the previous window	Pg Up
To the next window	Pg Dn
To the beginning of the document	Ctrl-Home
To the end of the document	Ctrl-End

Using the Mouse to Move the Insertion Point

Word's scroll bars allow you to use the mouse to move vertically and horizontally through your documents. The following two illustrations show you the vertical scroll bar and the horizontal scroll bar.

The Vertical Scroll Bar and Box

The vertical scroll box (shown at left) lets you see your relative positioning the document. If you move the box near the top of the bar, you are closer to the beginning of the document. If you move the box near the bottom of the bar, you are closer to the end of whatever amount of information you have entered. The distance that the scroll box moves is relative to the length of your document. The longer your document, the less the scroll box moves when you click above or below it.

Table 1-6 shows where to click the mouse button to move to certain places in your document.

The Horizontal Scroll Bar and Box

The horizontal scroll box lets you see the position of the page on which you are working. Scrolling left takes you toward the left margin; scrolling right takes you toward the right margin. This feature is particularly helpful if you are working on a multiple-column document or on a document that you have given wide margins and a longer line length.

Table 1-7 shows where to click the mouse to move to certain places on your page.

Table 1-6

To scroll here...	Do this...
Up one line	Click on the up arrow one time
Down one line	Click on the down arrow one time
Up one window	Click on the scroll bar above the scroll box one time
Down one window	Click on the scroll bar below the scroll box one time
To any position you choose	Hold down the mouse button and scroll up or down

Table 1-7

To scroll...	Do this...
Left a few columns	Click on the left arrow
Right a few columns	Click on the right arrow
Left into the margin	Hold down **Shift** and click on the left arrow
One window to the left	Click on the scroll bar left of the scroll box
One window to the right	Click on the scroll bar right of the scroll box
To any position you choose	Hold down the mouse button and drag the scroll box left or right.

Moving the Insertion Point to the Previous Location

Word lets you move the insertion point to the last location where you performed an action in a document. Even if you save and close a document, then open it again, you can move the insertion point where it was when you last saved the document.

To move to the point where the last action took place, press **Shift-F5**.

N O T E

You can only move back to three prior insertion point locations. For example, if you delete a word, go to the next line and type a word, and save the document, you can press the key sequence to go back where you saved, then where you typed, and finally where you deleted the word. If you press Shift-F5 a fourth time, the insertion point moves where it was before you first pressed this key sequence.

USING THE FIND COMMAND

The Find command from the Edit menu **(Alt-E, F)** lets you search for a string of characters.

You can enter a maximum of 255 characters in the Find What box. As you type, the text scrolls horizontally in the box.

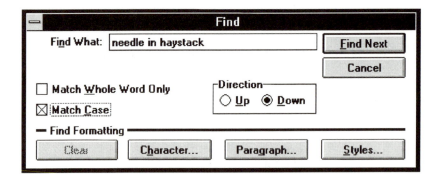

Figure 1.4

There are several options for finding text:

Table 1-8

Select this option...	To find...
Match Whole Word Only	Whole separate words in the document. For example, Word would find the word **text,** but would not stop at **context.**
Match Case	Words that have certain uppercase and lowercase letters. For example, in Figure 1.4, Word would find **needle in haystack**, but not **Needle in Haystack** or **NEEDLE IN HAY-STACK**.
Up or Down	Words either up or down (backward or forward) from your current position.
Find Next	The next occurrence of the text.
Cancel	No text. Return to the text and edit it.

You can also find text with specific character formatting, paragraph formatting, and defined styles. Choose any of the options at the bottom of the Find dialog box and select options for text that has formatting and styles that you want to search for in the document. This is a very powerful feature. Some desktop publishing packages do not allow any searching for formatting styles.

You use the Replace command and dialog box much the same way. The main difference is that you can enter the text and styles that you want to replace.

N O T E

Finding Special Characters

In addition to finding words and strings of text with the Find command, you can find (and replace) special characters, such as paragraph marks and tabs, that are represented by special codes. For example, you could use this feature to replace all double tabs with single tabs. The following table shows elements you can find and replace and the codes you would use.

Table 1-9

Find or replace this character...	By typing this code...
Any character	**?**
	For example, type ?ike to look for all occurrences of Mike, bike, like or any other words ending in "ike."
Tabs	**^t** (SHIFT-6) You can replace multiple tabs with one tab and vice versa.
Paragraph	**^p**
	You can replace multiple paragraph marks with one paragraph mark and vice versa.
Hard page break (entered by pressing **Ctrl-Enter**)	**^d**
Line break (entered by pressing **Shift-Enter**)	**^n**
Column breaks (dotted line across the column)	**^14**
Section breaks (inserted with the Break command from the Insert menu)	**^d** (also finds hard page breaks)
Footnote reference marks	**^2** You can find but not replace these.

Table 1-9 (continued form previous page)

Find or replace this character...	By typing this code...
Annotation mark	**^5** You can find but not replace these.
White space (including normal and nonbreaking spaces and tab characters)	**^w**
Graphic	**^1**
Optional hyphen	**^-**
Nonbreaking hyphen	**^~**
Fields	**^19**
Question mark	**^?**
Carets	**^^**
Clipboard contents	**^c** Use with Replace only if you want to replace the search text with the contents of the Clipboard.
ANSI characters	**^0nnn** (where **nnn** equals the ANSI code for the character)
Search text	**^m** For example, you can type **Ashley** in the Find What box and **^mHardee** to replace all occurrences of Ashley with Ashley Hardee.

USING THE GO TO COMMAND

The Go To command gives you yet another way to move the insertion point where you want to work.

You can display the Go To dialog box three ways:

- Press **Alt-E, G**
- Press **F5** twice
- From the Edit menu, choose **Go To.**

This is the **Go To** Dialog box.

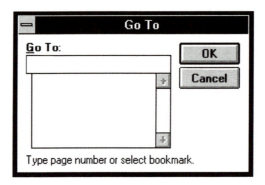

Figure 1.5

Additionally, you can press **F5** once to display a Go To prompt on the status bar, as shown below.

Go To:

Choosing a Location

Once you display the Go To dialog box or status bar prompt, you can choose several target locations, including

- Line
- Page
- Section
- Percentage of document
- Annotation
- Bookmark
- Footnote

You can also use a combination of these targets.

Going to a Line

You can use the Go To prompt or dialog box to go to a line two ways: to go to a specific line or to jump forward or backward a certain number of lines. Word calculates the line number from the beginning of the document, no matter how many pages or sections you have put in your document.

To go to a specific line, type **L< *line number*>**, for example, **L7**.To jump forward a particular number of lines, type **L+<*line number*>**, for example,**L+7.**

To go backward a particular number of lines, type **L-<*line number*>**, for example, **L-7**.

Do not add any spaces between the letter L and the line number.

N O T E

Going to a Page

Word makes it easy to jump to another page in the document, no matter where you are working, without having to scroll or repeat the **Pg Up** or **Pg Dn** keys. For this feature to work, you have to paginate the document first. Word calculates from the beginning of the document, and considers the first page of the document to be page 1 no matter what page numbers or sections you have assigned.

To go to a page, type the page number or **p <*page number*>** in the Go To prompt or dialog box, for example **p22**, or just **22**. You can also jump forward or backward a certain number of pages without entering a specific page number. To go forward, type **p+<*number of pages*>**, for example, **p+10**. To go backward, type **p-<*number of pages*>**, for example, **p-10**.

Do not add any spaces between the letter p and the page number.

N O T E

Going to a Section

You can go to another section, provided you have section breaks in the document. To go to a section, type **s<*section number*>**, for example **s2**. To go forward a given number of sections, type **s+<*number of sections*>**, for example, **s+3**. To backward a given number of sections, type **s-<*number of sections*>**, for example **s-3**.

Moving through a Given Percentage of the Document

In addition to navigating to a specific page or section, Word lets you move forward or backward a given percentage of the document. To move to a place that is a given percentage of the document, type **%<*percentage number*>**, for example, **%40** would display the page that is at 40 percent of the document in length.

Going to an Annotation

If you have added annotations to your document, you can use the Go To command to move to specific ones. You can also go forward or backward a given number of annotations. Word ignores any specific numbers that you might have assigned to the annotations, and considers the first annotation to be annotation 1. Refer to Chapter 2, "Setting Up a Word Document," for information about adding an annotation to a document.

To go to an annotation, type **a<*annotation number*>**, for example, **a4**. To go forward a given number of annotations, type **a+<*number to go forward*>**, for example, **a+4**.

Going to a Footnote

You can go to a footnote, much in the same way you go to a page, section, or annotation. You can also skip forward or backward a given number of footnotes. As with annotations, Word ignores any numbering you have given the footnotes. Refer to Chapter 2, "Setting Up a Word Document," for information about adding a footnote to a document.

To go to a footnote, type **f<*footnote number*>**, for example, **f5**. To go forward a given number of footnotes, type **f+<*number to go forward*>**, for example **f+5**. To go backward a given number of footnotes, type **f-<*number to go backward*>**, for example, **f-5**.

Going to a Bookmark

If you have added bookmarks to your document, you can go to a specific one, but you use the Go To command differently than you do in the previous examples. You type the actual name of the bookmark in the Go To prompt. Refer to Chapter 2, "Setting Up a Word Document," for information about adding a bookmark to a document.

SELECTING UNITS OF TEXT

Selecting text means that you highlight it so that it is displayed in reverse video (generally, light text on a dark background). After you select text or an item, you can perform actions on the entire block of selected text, such as cutting and pasting, copying, and deleting. You can select text in Word with the keyboard or the mouse.

Using the Mouse

You can select with the mouse by holding down the left mouse button and dragging the mouse cursor over the area you want to select. Or you can use the selection bar, the unmarked area that runs vertically down the left side of document's window. Follow these steps to select whole units of text with the mouse.

Table 1-10

To Select...	Do this...
A word	Double-click on the word
A sentence	Hold down **Ctrl** and click anywhere in the sentence
A line of text, regardless of whether it is a sentence	Position the pointer in the selection bar, point to the line, and click. (The selection bar is an unmarked area on the left side of the window were you can select text with a mouse.)

Table 1-10 (continued from previous page)

To Select...	Do this...
A line of text, regardless of whether it is a sentence	You can select multiple lines by dragging in the selection bar beside the lines.
A paragraph	Position the pointer in the selection bar, point to the paragraph and double-click.
	You can select multiple paragraphs by dragging in the selection bar beside them.
An entire document	Hold down **Ctrl** and click anywhere in the selection bar.

N O T E It's easy to go a little too far when you select text with the mouse. If you do, you don't have to cancel and start over. You can hold down **Shift** and click where you want to end the selection. However, if you selected text by unit, then the selection changes by the amount of that unit. For example, if you selected an entire paragraph when you wanted to select only one sentence, then holding down **Shift** and clicking at the end of the sentence will deselect the entire paragraph.

Using the Keyboard

If you don't have a mouse, or simply prefer using the keyboard, you can use key sequences to select text.

Table 1-11

To select this unit...	*Press this key sequence...*
One character to the right	Shift-Right Arrow
To the end of a word	Ctrl-Shift-Right Arrow
To the beginning of a word	Ctrl-Shift-Left Arrow
To the end of a line	Shift-End
To the beginning of a line	Shift-Home
One line down	Shift-Down Arrow
One line up	Shift-Up Arrow
To the end of a paragraph	Ctrl-Shift-Down Arrow
To the beginning of a paragraph	Ctrl-Shift-Up Arrow
An entire table	Alt-5 (on the keypad)
One screen down	Shift-Page Down
One screen up	Shift-Page Up
To the end of a document	Ctrl-Shift-End
To the beginning of a document	Ctrl-Shift-Home
An entire document	Ctrl-5 (on the keypad)

If you press **Del** while text is selected, *you delete everything that is selected.* If you accidentally delete the text, choose **Undo** from the Edit menu **(Alt-E, U)** to restore it before you do anything else.

SUMMARY

Now you know some of the basics of working in Word, including how to navigate in a document; how to use the menu bar, the Toolbar, the ribbon, and the ruler; and how to view a document. In the next chapter you will learn to use some of the powerful features that help you to easily create complex and professional-looking documents every time.

CHAPTER 2

SETTING UP A WORD DOCUMENT

This chapter explains the optional "peripheral" pieces of a Word document that you can set up, including:

- *page setup*

- *section breaks*

- *page breaks*

- *page numbers*

- *headers and footers*

- *footnotes*

- *annotations*

- *bookmarks*

- *file attachments*

When you open a new document in Word, you see only the blank workspace on which you can begin working. However, underneath this simple facade lie the powerful features that you can use to create a very complex, professional-quality document.

PAGE SETUP

You can choose your page settings at any time while you are working in a document; however, if you go ahead and use this feature as soon as you open your document, you will know the exact length and look of your document as you work. You can prevent a lot of rework if you organize your document with the correct page setup. (A document that is five pages long at the standard settings may turn out to be seven or eight pages when you convert to a smaller page or expand the margins.)

Word's default template, Normal, assumes that you are working on an $8\frac{1}{2}$-by-11-inch page with top and bottom margins of one inch, left and right margins of $1\frac{1}{4}$ inches, and no gutter. This is acceptable for a variety of documents. However, if you are building a document that will be printed on a different size of paper (such as this book), you need to use the Page Setup feature to set the corresponding margins, page orientation, and paper source or printing setup.

Setting Margins

To set up the margins, orientation, or paper source for printing, choose **Format** from the menu bar, and select **Page Setup (Alt-T, U)**. Word displays the Page Setup dialog box, with the default margin options displayed.

Click the up or down arrowheads beside the top, bottom, left, right, or gutter buttons to change the margins and gutter.

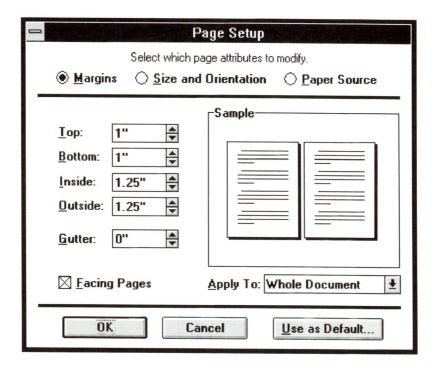

Figure 2.1

Margin settings affect the headers and footers in a document. If headers and footers are several lines long, Word will automatically adjust the top and bottom margins. To prevent Word from making that adjustment, type a minus sign in front of the top or bottom margin setting. If you do this, however, you can have a header that overlaps the text, and you will need to have less information in the header or footer.

N O T E

If you have not used a gutter before, it is an extra space in the margin to allow for binding. If you are working on a document that will not be bound, then leave the gutter width at zero.

N O T E

The Facing Pages option is for documents that will be printed on both sides of the paper. Word automatically adjusts your margin settings to accommodate facing pages. The inside margins are the same width on both pages, and the outside margins are the same width. If you choose to have a gutter, then that space is also added to the margin.

The Apply To option lets you apply the margin setup either to the whole document or forward from the point where you are working.

The Sample box shows a sample layout for all changes that you make in this dialog box.

Even after you set your margins, you can place information so that it will print in the margin. By default, Word prints page numbers, headers, and footers in the margins. You can set a negative indent for headings and text to print them in the margins, where you can also place graphics. See Chapter 4, "Formatting Paragraphs and Objects," for more information about placing text and graphics in the margins.

N O T E

Setting the Page Size and Orientation

The Page Setup dialog box also allows you to set up the size and orientation of your page. At the top of the dialog box, press **S** or click the button for Size and Orientation to display the following option boxes.

Figure 2.2

The Paper Size option gives you choices based on paper sizes that your printer can use. The Custom option in the list lets you set the page size of your choice and is generally used for nonstandard paper sizes. Word assumes you will be printing on the paper size you enter, even if you print on letter-size or legal-size paper. For example, if you set up your page to be 10-by-15, and you are printing on 8 1/2-by-11 inch paper, then the text will print incorrectly—the text and graphics will "run off" the page.

Orientation refers to portrait or landscape. Use portrait orientation if you want the reader to hold the page with the short edge at the top; use landscape orientation if you want the reader to hold the page sideways, with the long edge at the top.

The Apply To option works the same way it does for the margin setup. You can apply the settings to the whole document or from the insertion point forward.

Setting the Paper Source

When you choose paper source settings in the Page Setup dialog box (**Alt-U, P**), as shown in the following illustration, your printer will default to that paper source when you print the document.

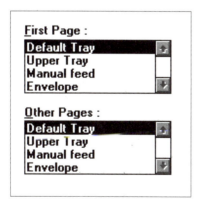

Figure 2.3

If your printer has only one tray, then use the default option of Default Tray. If you have a standard 8 1/2-by-11 tray and another tray that holds a different size, then choose the tray holding the paper on which you want to print. You can also set up a document so that the first page prints from a different tray than the other pages. For example, you can have an envelope print first from its tray, and then the remainder of the document from the tray you choose in the Other Pages box.

The Page Setup Use as Default Option

The Use as Default option lets you use any settings you choose for one document as defaults for any documents based on the template in which you are working.

Word displays this dialog box if you choose this option.

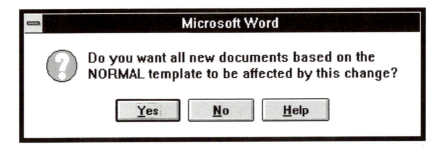

Figure 2.4

Think for a minute before you choose Yes, because all documents you construct in the template style will have *these* default settings. You will have to go back and change the template again to use Word's defaults.

PRINTING

After you have selected the page size and orientation and selected a paper tray, if necessary, you are ready to print a copy of your document. Follow these steps:

1. From the File menu, choose Print (**Alt-F, P**).

    The Print dialog box opens.

2. Chooose OK.

    The current document prints according to the options you have selected.

SECTION BREAKS

You can divide a single document into as many sections as you need. For example, if your document happens to be a book, you can divide each chapter and retain its formatting using the section break. However, a section can be as small as a short paragraph. If you are working in a document that needs to have the same formatting, headers, and footers throughout, you probably do not need to add any section breaks.

How the Section Break Works

A section break contains all the formatting that you add to the section, for example, margins, headers and footers, and page-numbering options. When you add a section break, Word assumes that you will continue using the same section formatting that you have been using. However, when you change the formatting for the new section, the formatting for the previous section remains intact. When you insert the section break, you can force Word to start numbering a section with a specified line number. The following illustration shows two sections divided only by the section break. The section-break line does not print on the page.

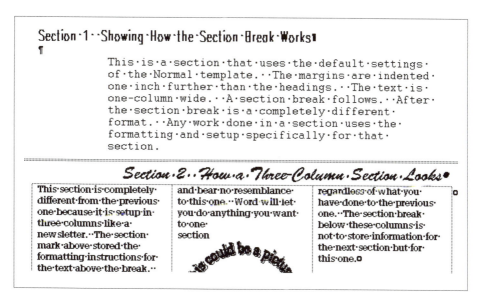

Figure 2.5

Adding a Section Break

To add a section break, position the insertion point where you want to add the break and, from the Insert menu, choose **Break (Alt-I, B)** to display the Break dialog box. Choose the appropriate option in the Section Break box.

The Next Page option creates a new page on which the section will begin.

The Continuous option causes the next section to begin immediately following the previous section. Word does not insert a page break for a continuous option. Use this option if you want sections to have no page break in between.

The Even Page option causes Word to start the section on the next even-numbered page. Therefore, if you are working on an even page when you choose the Even Page option, Word adds an odd page before it starts the new section.

The Odd Page option causes Word to start the section on the next odd-numbered page. Therefore, if you are working on an odd page when you choose the Odd Page option, Word adds an even page before it starts the new section.

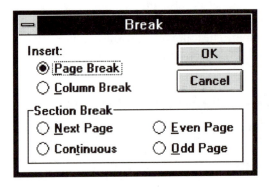

Figure 2.6

PAGE BREAKS

Word inserts page breaks automatically; however, there are a few ways that you can break the pages wherever you choose.

Automatic or "Soft" Page Breaks

Word repaginates in the background to break pages automatically every time you enter a full page of text or graphics. This is a *soft* page break, meaning that no matter how much text or formatting you add or delete, Word adjusts the break as necessary. The soft page breaks are based on the page setup of your document, which was explained in the previous section. The *soft page break* is indicated by a "loose" dotted line (the dots are far apart). The line extends across your screen.

Turning Off Repagination

You can turn off the automatic repagination by choosing **Options** from the Tools menu **(Alt-O, O)**, and turning off **Background Repagination** in the General category. Even if you do turn off this option, Word will still repaginate every time you print, view in page layout or print preview, repaginate (from the Tools menu), or generate an index or table of contents. However, Word will not repaginate while you are typing or editing.

Inserting a "Hard" Page Break

Word lets you insert a page break anywhere you want. This is called the *hard* page break. No matter how Word readjusts page breaks, the *hard page break* never moves. This is particularly useful if you want to keep certain text together. For example, you would not want a page to break so that a heading is the last thing on one page and the text for the heading is on the next.

To insert a page break, position the insertion point where you want to start a page. Then, press **Ctrl-Enter** or press **Alt-I, B** and choose **Page Break**. The hard page break is indicated by a "tight" dotted line. The line extends across your screen.

Using Paragraph Formatting to Break a Page

The Format Paragraph command **(Alt-T, P)** gives you three options for controlling page breaks. They are described in the following sections.

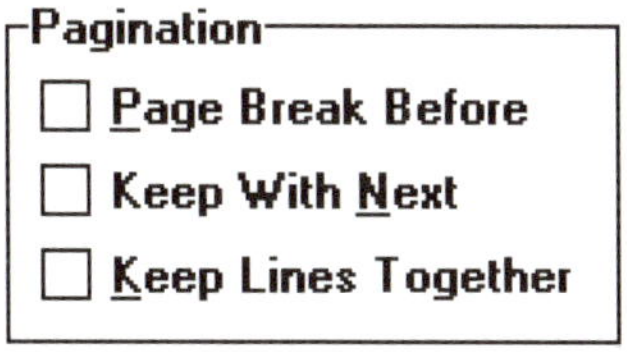

```
┌Pagination─────────────────┐
│  ☐ Page Break Before       │
│  ☐ Keep With Next          │
│  ☐ Keep Lines Together     │
└────────────────────────────┘
```

Figure 2.7

The Page Break Before Option

Word lets you insert a page break before a graphic or text that you would rather have printed at the top of the next page.

To insert a page break before a paragraph or heading, position the insertion point in the paragraph in which you want to start a page. Press **Alt-T, P** or choose **Paragraph** from the Format menu. Then, choose **Page Break Before** in the Pagination box.

The Keep With Next Option

You can keep two paragraphs together on a page and ensure that they are never separated by a page break by using the Keep With Next option. One of the paragraphs may be a heading or a graphic.

To keep two paragraphs together, position the insertion point in the paragraph that you want to keep with the next paragraph. Press **Alt-T, P** or choose **Paragraph** from the Format menu. Then, choose **Keep With Next** in the Pagination box.

The Keep Lines Together Option

There may be times when you want to keep all of a single paragraph together on a page to prevent Word from breaking it with a page break. The Keep Lines Together option will keep all lines in a paragraph together, regardless of its length. If the whole paragraph will not fit on the page where it starts, Word moves it to the beginning of the next page. You can also add text before the paragraph; Word simply moves it down on the page.

NOTE

For related information about pagination, see Chapter 3 "Formatting Characters and Words."

NUMBERING PAGES

Word gives you several methods for numbering pages. You can choose

- the style and placement of page numbers
- whether you want numbers on all pages except the first
- whether to add chapter-page numbers
- whether to add additional text with the page number.

Style and Placement

You can use any font that you use in text for your page numbers, and you have the option of applying them in Arabic or Roman numerals (uppercase and lowercase), and letters (uppercase and lowercase). Also, you can choose whether to have page numbers in the header or footer and where in the header or footer you want them to print.

Numbering All Pages Except the First

Sometimes you may not want to have a page number on the first page of a document. For example, if your first page is a cover or title page, you generally don't need to number it. You can begin numbering with the second page, and you can choose if you want that page to be numbered 1 or 2. See "Creating a Header or Footer" later in this chapter for more information. Follow these steps to add page numbers for all pages except the first to headers or footers:

1. From the Insert menu, choose **Page Numbers (Alt-I, U)**.

   Word displays the Page Numbers dialog box:

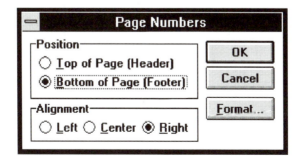

Figure 2.8

2. Choose the position and alignment of page numbers.

3. Choose **Format**.
   Word displays the Page Number Format dialog box:

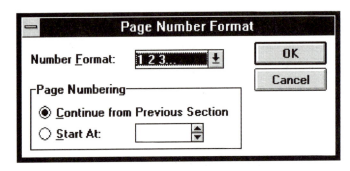

Figure 2.9

4. Choose the Number Format from the drop down list.

5. Choose **OK**.

Word prints page numbers in the format that you chose.

If you want to change the font for page numbers, open the header or footer, select the page number, and choose a font and point size. This changes the font for all page numbers in the section. See Chapter 3,"Formatting Characters and Words," for more information. You can also define your header or footer as a style and add it to a template. See Chapter 6, "Creating a Template," for more information.

Numbering All Pages, Including the First

If you are constructing a document that does not have a cover page or another type of unnumbered page, follow these instructions to have Word number all pages:

1. From the View menu, choose **Header/Footer (Alt-V, H)**.
   Word displays the Header/Footer dialog box.

2. Select **Header** or **Footer**, depending on where you want the page number.

3. Clear the checkbox for **Different First Page** and choose **OK**.
   Word displays the header or footer pane, depending on which you chose.

4. Choose the pound sign.

   Word places a 1 in the first line.

You can format the page number by choosing **Page Numbers** from the Insert menu as described earlier.

Inserting Chapter-Page Numbers

If you are working in a document that has multiple chapters, you can show a chapter-page number, for example, 3-4 for chapter 3, page 4. This method is a little more complicated. It involves adding a field code at the beginning of your chapters. If you want to show chapter- page numbers in the index or table of contents, then you must set up chapter-page numbers in the chapter itself. (See Chapter 7, "Tables of Contents and Indexes," for related information.) Follow these steps to define a field for the chapter-page numbers:

1. From the View menu, choose **Field codes** (**Alt-V, C**).
   Word displays field codes so you can see how to work with them.

2. Position the insertion point at the beginning of the first chapter and press the Insert Field key (**Ctrl-F9**).
   Word inserts the field characters, in which you type the code.

3. Type **seq chapter \h**

   Chapter is the sequence name and **\h** indicates to Word to hide the result of the field to prevent printing it.

4. Press the Update Field key (**F9**) to update the field.

If your chapters are all in one document, then you need to insert a section break at the beginning of each chapter.

N O T E

If you want, you can also add the seq field to headers and footers. You do this if you entered your page numbers directly in the header or footer. Follow these steps:

1. In Normal view, open the header or footer (**Alt-V, H**), depending on which you chose to display page numbers.

2. Position the insertion point where you want the chapter number and press the Insert Field key (**Ctrl-F9**).

   Word inserts the field characters, in which you type the code.

3. Type **seq chapter \c** between the field characters.

4. If you want to format the chapter-page numbers, then select the sequence name (chapter), and format it with the font, point size, and attributes that you want it to have.

5. Press the Update Field key **(F9)** to update the field.

6. Add a hyphen or other separator outside of the field characters and click the **Page Number** button in the upper-left corner of the pane.

   Word adds the page field instead of the page number. The field looks like this: **{seq chapter \c}-{PAGE}**

7. Repeat these steps for each chapter of your document. When you print your document, it will have chapter-page numbers.

HEADERS AND FOOTERS

Adding headers and footers to your document is an easy process, and they can be as simple as just adding a page number, or as elaborate as adding a graphic or logo. Word places header text within the top margin and footer text within the bottom margin.

If you specify a margin in your page setup that is too small for the header or footer you design, Word adjusts the margin to accommodate the design.

Generally, a header or footer is repeated throughout a document with the first page as an exception. However, Word allows you a lot of choices for using them.

Creating a Header or Footer

Word never creates a header or footer automatically. It is up to you to decide whether you need one. One issue to consider is the document size. If someone drops a large, unnumbered document, it can be nightmarish to try to get the pages in the correct order again.

To create a header or footer, make sure you are in Normal view **(Alt-V, N)**. Choose **Header/Footer** from the View menu **(Alt-V, H)**. Word displays the Header/Footer dialog box where you can choose options.

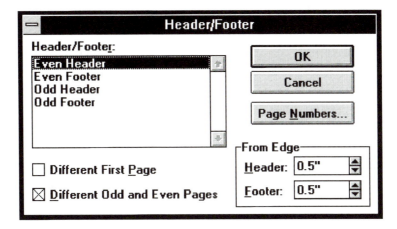

Figure 2.10

The default selection is Header. If you are planning to have the same header or footer for all pages, then select either Header or Footer, depending on which one you need. However, if you want a different header or footer for the first page, for example, a logo, then choose First Header or First Footer and select the Different First Page option. If you want the odd pages to have a different header than the even pages, select that option instead.

If you have two documents open, then Word may not be able to open a header or footer pane. In that case, close all windows except the one to which you want to add the header or footer, and choose the option again.

N O T E

Whether you choose the header or footer options, Word displays the same type of pane at the bottom of your document window, shown in the following figure. The only difference is that the top line of the pane shows whether a header or footer is opened.

Figure 2.11

You type the information that you want to add in the box, and format it the same way you format any other text. See Chapter 3 and Chapter 4 for more information about formatting text. You can also define your headers and footers as styles. Refer to Chapter 5, "Formatting Tutorials," for more information about defining styles.

The three icons at the top-left corner of the pane let you add page numbers, the current date, and the current time. See Chapter 5 "Formatting Tutorials" for more information about using these options.

The Link to Previous button lets you make the header or footer identical to the one in the previous section. If you press the Link to Previous button in the header or footer pane, Word first asks if you want to delete existing headers or footers in the current section and apply the previous one. If you choose Yes, Word makes the header or footer identical to the one in the previous section. If you have not added a header or footer to the previous section, this option will remain dimmed.

By default, Word places the header one-half inch from the edge of the page, however you can enter another measurement or click the up or down arrows to change the default.

The Header/Footer dialog box also lets you choose the type of page number you want, including Arabic, lowercase and uppercase alphabet, and lowercase and uppercase Roman, as shown below. To select the type of page numbering, choose Page Number to display the Page Number Format box.

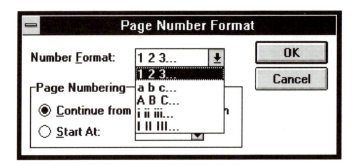

Figure 2.12

The Continue from Previous Section option causes Word to begin numbering the section where the last section left off. For example, if the last page number in section 1 is 54, the first page number of section 2 will be 55. If the last page of the previous section ends with an odd number, Word skips an even page number to leave a blank page, and begins the next section with an odd number. For example, if the last page of section 1 ends with 55, the first page number of section 2 will be 57.

The Start At option allows you to enter a page number on which you want the section to start. You can enter any number, regardless of the sequence of page numbers in other sections. You use this option in conjunction with the page-numbering icon (#) inside the header or footer pane.

You can readjust the position of your headers and footers in Page Layout view, without having to open the separate panes. For more information about Page Layout view, see the section, "Page Views" in Chapter 1.

N O T E

FOOTNOTES

When typing documents on a typewriter or in many other word processing programs, it is difficult to add footnotes. The spacing at the bottom of the page has to be perfect, and if you type one line too many, you must retype the page, delete or move a line, or let the page look very crowded at the bottom.

Word lets you add footnotes in a manner that is similar to the way you add a header or footer. Word opens a pane at the bottom of the workspace where you can add, format, and edit footnote text. You don't have to set options for spacing because Word automatically adjusts the area to accommodate the footnote. There is no line limit, you can make the footnote as long as you want.

Reference Marks

Word places a reference mark in your document so you can see where you added a footnote. The default mark is a number encircled by a faint dotted line, like this:

However, you can customize the footnote mark, using characters that are more meaningful to you. The following procedures include steps for changing the default reference mark.

To add a footnote to a document, follow these steps:

1. Position the insertion point where you want Word to display the reference mark.

2. From the Insert menu, choose **Footnote (Alt-I, N)** Word displays the Footnote dialog box.

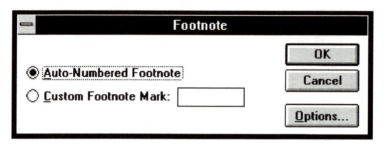

Figure 2.13

3. To have Word number the footnotes automatically, choose **Auto-Numbered Footnote**.

   or

   To choose a reference mark that you prefer, choose **Custom Footnote Mark** and type up to 10 characters.

4. Choose **OK**.

   Word inserts a footnote reference mark at the insertion point and opens the footnote pane.

5. Enter your footnote in the footnote pane, and choose the **Close** button **(Alt-Shift,-C)** to return to the document.

Positioning Footnotes

While the traditional placement of footnotes is at the bottom of a page, Word lets you choose to print them

- at the bottom of the page
- beneath the text anywhere on the page
- at the end of a section or document.

You choose the footnote position by selecting the **Options** button from the Footnote dialog box shown in the previous procedure **(Alt-I, N)**. The options in the dialog box describe where Word places the footnote.

Choosing a Text and Footnote Separator

Word adds a default separator line between the text and the footnote, but you can customize the line to achieve the look and format that you want. You can choose to have

- a customized separator line to which you can add your own format or graphics
- a Continuation notice to show that the footnotes continue to the next page
- a customized separator line for a footnote that continues to the next page.

To change the footnote separator, follow these steps:

1. From the Insert menu, choose Footnote (**Alt-I,N**)

   Word displays the Footnote dialog box, as shown in Figure 2.13.

2. Choose **Options**.

   Word displays the footnote options dialog box as shown in Figure 2.14.

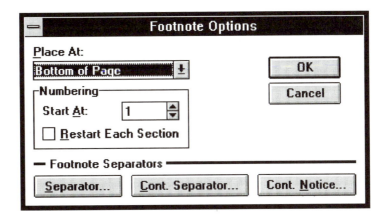

Figure 2.14

3. Choose **Separator** or **Cont. Separator**.

   Word displays the following pane in which you can change the footnote separator or the continuation separator.

Figure 2.15

4. Select the existing separator and type the characters or enter the graphic that you prefer.

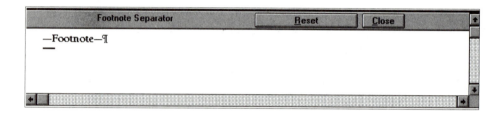

Figure 2.16

or

Choose **Reset (Alt-Shift-R)** to restore the original separator.

5. Choose **Close (Alt-Shift-C)** to close the pane.

When you add footnotes to your document, Word will insert the new separator or characters.

ANNOTATIONS AND REVISION MARKS

When you are working on a document, you may find that you often need to revise it and make notes about the information you add or change. Sometimes, you might want to make reminders to yourself about things you want to change, but you would rather not have them printed. Word gives you the means for annotating the text and adding marks to show where you added, changed, or deleted text or graphics.

Annotating a Document

An annotation has two parts: the annotation mark and the annotation text. The annotation mark is the initials of the author and the number of the annotation. This a very important power feature because if multiple authors work on a document, then you can easily see who added the pieces of material. The annotation is added to the text so you can see it on the screen, but Word formats it as hidden text, and does not print it.

As with footnotes, Word opens a separate pane in which you enter the annotation text. That text does not become part of the document. However, the mark is displayed in the text so you can see what you have annotated.

Follow these steps to annotate your document:

1. Position the insertion point where you want to annotate the text.

2. From the Insert menu, choose **Annotate (Alt-I, A)**.

   Word adds the annotation mark ([ML 1], for example) where you positioned the insertion point, and opens the Annotations pane.

Figure 2.17

You can work in a Word document while the pane is open. You can press F6 or click in the pane in which you want to work.

N O T E

3. Enter the text for the annotation in the pane.

   The following illustration shows that there are two annotations on a page in the document. Each one shows the page number and the initials of the author running Word.

```
Annotations                                    [ Close ]        ▲
  [ML1]This·is·annotation·number·1.¶
  ¶
  [ML2]This·is·annotation·number·2.¶
  ¶
  ___
                                                              ▼
◄ ▐ ░░░░░░░░░░░░░░░░░░░░░░░░░░░░░░░░░░░░░░░░░░░░░░░░░░░░ ►
```

Figure 2.18

4. Choose **Close** to close the pane (**Alt-Shift-C**).

You can edit the annotations by choosing **Annotations** from the View menu **(Alt-V, A)** and entering more text, or selecting existing text and typing over it. You can also copy an annotation and its reference mark into the text if you want. Use the cut and paste methods described in "The Clipboard" in Chapter 1 "Mastering the Word for Windows Environment."

 You can define annotation text and marks as styles that you can apply automatically. See Chapter 6 "Creating a Template" for information about defining styles.

N O T E

Finding Annotations

Word's Go To command makes it easy for you to find annotation marks in your document. Follow these steps to find annotations:

1. From the Edit menu, choose **Go To (Alt-E,G)** or press **(F5)**. Word displays the Go To prompt.

2. Type the letter **a** to go to the next annotation mark, or type the letter **a** and a number to go to a specific mark, or type the letter **a**, the plus sign, and a number that represents the number of annotations you want to move forward—for example, **a+5**. You can also go back a number of annotations by typing the letter **a**, the minus sign, and a number that represents the number of annotations you want to move back, for example **a-3**.

   Word scrolls the text to that annotation mark.

Securing a Document

If you are using Word on a network or in a technical environment, it is quite possible that multiple authors will share responsibility for a document. If that is the case, it is very important that an author does not overwrite another author's text without permission.

Word lets you lock the document so that other authors cannot alter it, but they can add annotations for future updating. Follow these steps to lock the document:

1. From the File menu, choose **Save As (Alt-F, A)** or press **F12**.

    Word displays the Save As dialog box.

2. Choose **File Sharing** and choose **Lock File for Annotations**.

3. To password-protect the file, enter a password of up to 16 characters and choose **OK**.

    The next time anyone tries to open the document, Word prompts for the document password.

Printing Annotations

Although annotations do not show up in the text, you can have Word print them if you set the correct printing options.

Printing the Annotation and the Document

To print annotations along with the document, follow these steps:

1. From the File menu, choose **Print (Alt-F, P)**.

    Word displays the standard Print dialog box.

2. Choose **Options**, and select **Annotations** in the Include with Document box as shown on the following page:

    Word automatically selects the Hidden Text option.

3. Choose **OK** to close the Options dialog box.

4. Choose **OK** to print the document and annotations.

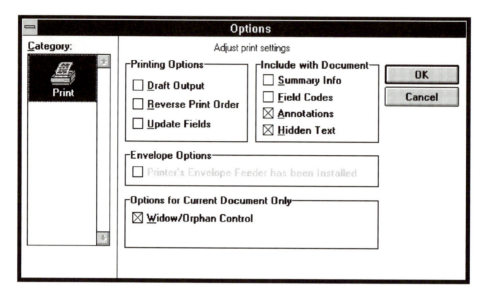

Figure 2.19

Word prints all hidden text (including reference marks) after the document text. Each annotation includes the page number of the reference mark, the author's initials, and the annotation number.

Printing the Annotations without the Document

To print the annotations without the document text, follow these steps:

1. From the File menu, choose **Print (Alt-F,P)**.
    Word displays the standard Print dialog box.

2. Choose **Options**, and select **Annotations** in the Include with Document box.

3. Choose **OK** to close the options dialog box.

4. Choose **OK** to print the annotations.

Word prints the annotations, the page number of the reference mark, the author's initials, and the annotation number.

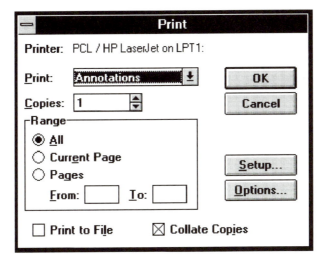

Figure 2.20

REVISION MARKS

Revision marks let you see not only what you changed in the last revision, but how you changed it. Word marks only the paragraphs that you changed, and shows added, deleted, replaced, and moved text. You can choose the character formatting for showing new text, the placement of the revision bars, and whether the bars appear in the text. However, Word marks all deleted text with the strikethrough character formatting.

When you finish revising a document, you can use the Compare Versions command to see the differences in two versions of it. You can also choose to accept or undo the changes when you finish working on a document.

Turning Revision Marking On or Off

Follow these steps to start revision marking.

1. Open a document that you want to edit.

2. From the Tools menu, choose **Revision Marks (Alt-O, K).**
   Word displays the Revision Marks dialog box.

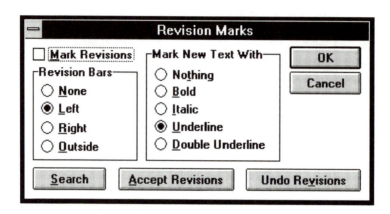

Figure 2.21

3. Select the **Mark Revisions** check box. (If you want to stop marking revisions, clear the check box.)

4. In the **Revision Bars** box, choose where you want the bars to print: no bars, in the left margin, in the right margin, or outside for facing pages. If you choose Outside, Word prints revision marks for left pages in the left margin and for right pages in the right margin.

5. In the **Mark New Text With** box, choose the character formatting you want for added text.

6. Choose **OK**.

Any time you add text, Word displays and prints it in the character format you chose. The following illustration shows a revision mark and some added and deleted text.

¶
~~This·is·an·example·of·deleted·text,·which·Word·marked·with·~~
~~the·strikethrough·formatting.~~··This·is·an·example·of·added·
text.·using·the·underline·option.¶
¶

Figure 2.22

Word displays the letters MRK in the status bar at the bottom of your work area when you use this feature.

Comparing Versions

If you want to see the differences in a document from one version to the next, you can use the Compare Versions command from the Tools menu. This feature lets you choose to have Word mark the changes in the current document compared to a previous version of the same document. When you do this, Word formats the characters added to the previous version with the formatting style you chose. If you did not choose a specific style, Word displays the text with underlining.

To compare versions, follow these steps:

1. From the Tools menu, choose **Compare Versions (Alt-O, V).** Word displays the Compare Versions dialog box.

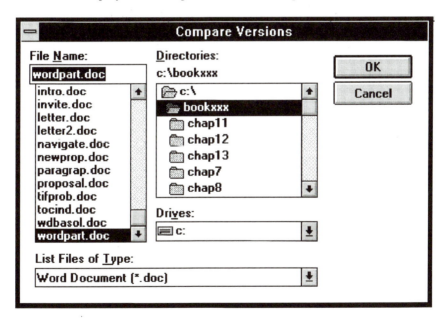

Figure 2.23

2. Type the name the name of the former version of the document into the **File Name** box or select the name of the document, using the **File Name and Directories** lists.

3.   Choose **OK.**

Searching for Revisions

While working in a document, you can search for any revisions you have made. Follow these steps to search for the revision marks.

1.   Open the document (if it is not open already).

2.   From the Tools menu, choose **Revision Marks (Alt-O,K)**

3.   Choose **Search.**

     If you are at the end of the document, Word asks if you want to continue searching from the beginning. Choose **Yes**. Word then finds the first revision mark in the document.

4.   Continue choosing **Search** to review the revisions one at a time. Choose **OK** when you finish.

Accepting and Undoing Revisions

If you choose to mark revisions in a document, you can later accept or undo the changes and remove the marks and revision bars.

Accepting Revisions

To accept all revisions you've made, follow these steps:

1.   Select the text that has revisions you want to keep.

If you do not select specific blocks or sections of text, Word assumes you want to accept revisions for the entire document.

N O T E

2.   From the Tools menu, choose **Revision Marks (Alt-O,K).**

3. Choose **Accept Revisions.**

   If you have not selected text, Word asks if you want to accept all revisions. If you choose **Yes**, Word deletes any text marked for deletion and deletes all revision marks for the document. If you choose **No**, Word displays the Revision Marks dialog box again.

Undoing Revisions

If you do not like the revisions you have made to a document, you can undo them. To undo revisions, follow these steps:

1. Select the text that has revisions you want to undo.

If you do not select specific blocks or sections of text, Word assumes you want to undo revisions for the entire document.

N O T E

2. From the Tools menu, choose **Revision Marks** (**ALT-O,K**).

   Word displays the Revision Marks dialog box.

3. Choose **Undo Revisions**.

   If you have not selected text, Word asks if you want to undo all revisions. If you choose Yes, Word removes all revisions, revision marks, and bars from the document. If you choose No, Word returns to the Revision Marks dialog box.

BOOKMARKS

There may be times when you want to find something in your document quickly. For example, if you insert a reference to another chapter in a book you're writing, you may want to be able to find that reference so you can update it if you change the chapter number or title later.

Word's bookmark function lets you perform something as simple as locating a place or as sophisticated as updating linked text. You can also insert marked text into another document and mark numbers in a calculation and insert the result in your document. (Refer to the documentation provided with your software for more information about using bookmarks for linked text and calculations.)

Additionally, you can create cross-references to other information. Word allows up to 450 bookmarks in any document.

Word does not print the bookmark nor does it display it on the screen. The Bookmark function serves to let you find other text or elements.

Inserting a Bookmark

To insert a bookmark in your document, follow these steps:

1. Position the insertion point where you want to insert a bookmark.

    You have two options:

    ▪ Position the insertion point in the location if you want only to be able to find this location again

    or

    ▪ Select text that you want to mark and be able to find again.

    (You can also press **Ctrl-Shift-F5** to display the Insert Bookmark prompt on the status line where you will insert the bookmark name.)

2. From the Insert menu, choose **Bookmark (Alt-I, M)** to display the Bookmark dialog box.

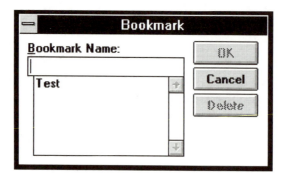

Figure 2.24

3. In the Bookmark Name box, type a name (from 1 to 20 characters) for the bookmark.

If you type a name that you have assigned to another bookmark, Word does not alert you. It removes the original bookmark and gives the name to the area or text you just selected.

WARNING

You can use only numbers, letters, and the underscore character (_) in the bookmark name.

4. Choose **OK**.

N O T E

Finding Your Bookmarks

After you've inserted bookmarks in your document, you can use them to locate the text or areas you need to find.

Follow these steps to locate a bookmark:

1. From the Edit menu, choose **Go To (Alt-E, G)**.
   Word displays the Go To dialog box:

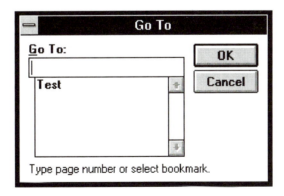

Figure 2.25

2. Type or select the name of the bookmark.

3. Choose **OK**.

    Word scrolls to the area or text that is marked.

    You can also press **F5** to display the Go To prompt in the status bar. Type the bookmark name, and press **Enter**.

If you move text within the document or to another document, (using Cut, Copy, Paste, or Drag and Drop features), you also move the bookmark associated with the text or element.

Putting the Bookmark Feature to Work

Suppose you are building a long document and in most chapters you refer your reader to related information in other chapters. Your reader will have an easier time finding the information if you include a page number. With a lot of other word-processing and desktop publishing packages, the page number reference feature is nonexistent. Since maintaining this construction throughout drafts and revisions could be a nightmare without automation such as Word's, most authors and editors never include that helpful page number in a reference.

Follow these steps to create a cross-reference with a page number:

1. Select the text for which you want to create a page number cross-reference.

2. Insert a bookmark (as described earlier in this section).

3. Position the insertion point where you want Word to display the page number of the referenced text.

4. From the Insert menu, choose **Field (Alt-I,D)**.

    Word displays the Field dialog box shown on the following page.

5. Press **P, P** to select **Page Ref** in the Insert Field Type box.

6. In the Instructions box, select the bookmark name.

7. Choose **Add**.

8. Choose **OK**.

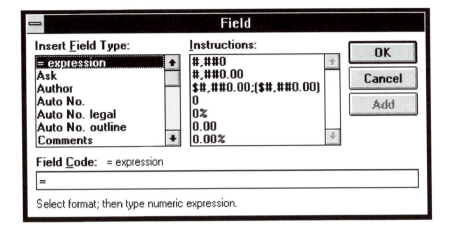

Figure 2.26

Word inserts the PAGEREF field. The result of the field is the page number on which the text marked with the bookmark appears.

Whenever you change the location of marked text, you need to update the cross-reference. To do this, select the PAGEREF field and press the Update Field key (F9).

N O T E

If you want to create a cross-reference to text without page numbers, then repeat steps 1-4 in the previous procedure and then follow these steps:

5. Press **R** to select **Reference** in the Insert Field Type box.

6. In the Instructions box, select the bookmark name.

7. Choose **Add**.

8. Choose **OK**.

   If you change the marked text, press the **Update Field key** (**F9**) to update the cross-reference.

LINKING CHAPTERS IN DIFFERENT DOCUMENTS

It's not always feasible for you to place all chapters of a document in one file. If multiple people are assigned to complete one book, then chances are that some will need to work on different chapters simultaneously. Even if you are the only author of a document, working in and printing a very long document can take its toll on your computer's memory. In that case, you need to attach the files so that you can have correct page numbers when you print.

Word lets you set up your document in smaller pieces so you and your colleagues can work more efficiently. You will still be able to print the master file (which contains all the pieces) as one document, with correct page numbers.

You use Word's INCLUDE field to accomplish this task. The INCLUDE fields are special codes that instruct Word to insert the smaller pieces into the *master document*. The master document contains only a list of INCLUDE fields; you cannot add text to it. However, you can combine the smaller documents in the master document and make editing changes to them, if necessary, before you print. Then before you print, you simply press the Update source key **(Ctrl-Shift, F7)** to copy the changes to the original files.

The editing changes appear in both the master document and the original smaller documents. You only have to make the editing changes once.

Follow these steps to set up a master file:

1. If you have already drafted your document, divide it into smaller documents and save each file with a new name such as Chap1, Chap2, and so on, or if you have not begun drafting, set up a separate file for each of your smaller documents.

 Look for logical divisions in your document, such as sections, parts, or chapters, so it will be less confusing.

N O T E

2. Open a new document, which will be your master document.
3. From the Insert menu, choose **Field (Alt-I, D)**. Word displays the Field dialog box:

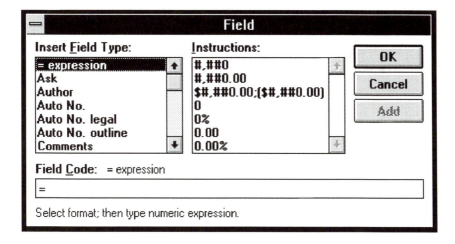

Figure 2.27

4.   In the Insert Field Type box, select **Include**.

5.   In the Field Code box, type the file name for the first of the documents after the word **include**, like this:

Field Code: INCLUDE file-name [place-reference] [switches]

include Chap1.doc

6.   Choose **OK**.

7.   Press **Enter** to begin a new paragraph.

8.   Repeat steps 3 through 7 for each file that you want to include in the master document.

9.   From the File menu, choose Save As **(Alt-F, A)** and type a name in the File name box, for example:

MastBook.doc

10. Choose **OK**.

Word may display the Summary Info dialog box. You can enter any information you like about the document. Choose **OK**.

Ensuring the Correct Setup Before Printing

Before you print the master document, you need to make sure that page numbers, line breaks, and page breaks are correct. Otherwise, the master will print with a lot of problems. It is best to wait until you are almost finished with your multiple-file document to perform these steps. That way, you won't have to do it every time you print.

Follow these steps to ensure correct line breaks and page breaks in your documents:

1. In each document that you include in the master, set the printing options and the starting page and line numbers the way you want.

    This ensures that the page numbers and line breaks on the screen will match the printout of the document.The page breaks in the master will match those in the individual chapters.

2. Perform as many of the following tasks as apply:

Table 2-1

To check whether...	Use this command...
You selected the correct printer.	**Print Setup (Alt-F,R)**
The Hidden Text option is set like you want.	**Print (Alt-F)** Choose **Options** to check the setting for hidden text. Choose **Close** or **Cancel** to close the Print dialog box.
The field codes or results are displayed like you want to print them.	**Field Codes (Alt-V, C)**

3. Print the master document.
    Word applies the correct pagination, line breaks, and page numbers.

SUMMARY

In this chapter, you learned how to set up a Word document's margins and page layout, how to add page and section breaks to your document, and how to use more sophisticated features, such as headers and footers, footnotes, bookmarks, and annotations. The next three chapters will show you how to improve the appearance of a document by formatting it, and how to add columns, tables, and some simple graphic elements to your document.

CHAPTER 3

FORMATTING CHARACTERS AND WORDS

Word's features for formatting characters allow you to

- *change fonts*
- *apply attributes (such as bold, italic, and underline)*
- *change point size*
- *choose letter spacing*
- *insert special symbols*

This chapter shows you a variety of ways to apply and change formats for characters and words (which you can also apply to whole paragraphs if you want).

HOW TO ADD AND CHANGE CHARACTER ATTRIBUTES

The following table shows you how you can quickly change the appearance of characters. Most table entries show multiple ways of changing the characters. What may seem easiest for a die-hard mouse user may seem more cumbersome for someone who prefers the keyboard. You may find that you prefer a variety of ways for applying formats to characters.

Remember that you must select the text you want to format before you can format anything.

N O T E

Table 3-1

To add this formatting...	Do this...
Bold	Choose B from the ribbon. or Press **Alt-T, C** and choose **Bold**. or Press **Ctrl-B**.
Italics	Choose *I* from the ribbon. or Press **Alt-T, C** and choose **Italics**. or Press **Ctrl-I**.
Underline	Choose u from the ribbon. or Press **Alt-T, C** and choose **Underline**. or

Table 3-1 *(continued from previous page)*

To add this formatting...	Do this...
Underline (*Continued*)	Press **Ctrl-U**.
Word Underline	Press **Ctrl-W**. (Word underline does not underline the spaces between words.)
Double Underline	Press **Ctrl-D**. or Press **Alt-T, C** and choose **Double Underline**.
Small Caps	Press **Ctrl-K**. This option displays characters in all capitals, but the ones that would be lowercase are in a smaller point size.
All Caps	Press **Ctrl-A**.
Hidden Text	Press **Alt-T**, **C** and choose Hidden Text. You can see hidden text on the screen, but it does not print, and Word does not leave blank spaces where the hidden text resides. This is particularly useful when you are adding index entries.
Font Change	Click the down arrow beside the font box on the ribbon, and choose a font. or Press **Alt-T, C** and click the down arrow next to the font box, and choose a font.

Table 3-1 (continued from previous page)

To add this formatting...	Do this...
Font Change	or Type the font name in the font box.
Point Size Change	Click the down arrow beside the point size box on the ribbon, and choose a point size. or Type the point size in the point size box.
Superscript and Subscript	Press **Alt-T, C** and choose Superscript or Subscript from the Super/subscript option. Click the arrows in the By box to choose the number of points to raise or drop the text. You generally use superscript and subscript text in mathematical equations. Trademark symbols are usually in superscript format. Refer to Chapter 10, "The Equation Editor", for more information about using this formatting in equations.

CLEARING A FORMAT

You clear a format the same way you add it, but you do not have to use the same method. For example, if you apply the bold format from the ribbon, you can remove it by selecting the text and choosing bold from the ribbon again, pressing **Ctrl-B**, or pressing **Alt-T, C** and clicking beside the Bold option.

USING HYPHENS

Word's special hyphens control paragraph line breaks. You use these when you want to keep hyphenated words from breaking at the end of a line. You can see that these hyphens look different on the screen; however, when you print your document, they look like normal, typed hyphens. The following table explains the differences in the nonbreaking hyphens.

Table 3-2

Use this type of hyphen...	For...
Normal Hyphen (**-**)	Any word that you would normally hyphenate to keep it grammatically correct, such as a compound word, no matter where it falls in the paragraph line.
Optional Hyphen **Ctrl-(-)**	Indicating where you want Word to hyphenate a word that falls at the end of a line.
Nonbreaking Hyphen (**Ctrl-Shift**-(-))	Words that have hyphens you do not want to break at the end of a line. Business letters and most technical documents look better and are easier to read when you use nonbreaking hyphens. Additionally, there are some words, particularly, hyphenated proper nouns (such as Peg Daigle-Riley), that you should not allow Word to break. When you use this hyphen, Word moves the entire word or words if you add or delete text.

Using the Hyphenation Feature

You can choose to have Word hyphenate words in your document and at the correct place in the word. However, most of the time you should reserve hyphenation for documents with narrow columns or for justified text. There is really no need to hyphenate your document more than one time, and usually it's best to wait until you finish constructing it so your line breaks will be logical.

Follow these steps to have Word hyphenate your document:

1. From the Tools menu, choose **Hyphenation** (**Alt-O, H**). Word displays the Hyphenation dialog box:

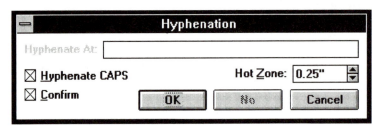

Figure 3.1

2. Choose how you want Word to hyphenate:

Table 3-3

To...	Do this...
Allow hyphenation of capitalized words.	Select **Hyphenate CAPS**.
Choose less ragged margins and more hyphenation.	Decrease the measurement in the **Hot Zone** box, which is the amount of hyphenation you choose. The smaller the measurement, the more words are hyphenated.
Choose more ragged margins and less hyphenation.	Increase the measurement in the **Hot Zone** box.

3. If you want to confirm each hyphenated Word, select the **Confirm** check box.

   This is useful in preventing hyphenation of names.

4. Choose **OK**.

   Word begins hyphenating. If you chose Confirm, then Word displays each hyphenated word and you can choose **Yes**, change the hyphenation point, choose **No** for no hyphenation, or stop hyphenating from that point on.

NONBREAKING SPACES

The functionality of the nonbreaking space is like that of the nonbreaking hyphen. This is often called a "hard space." Use this space when you do not want Word to break a line between two words. Examples for this usage are a person's name—it is generally unacceptable to break a first name from a surname in text. To insert a nonbreaking space, press **Ctrl-Shift-Spacebar**.

CHARACTER SPACING

When you type normal text in Word, it applies default spacing similar to the text you are reading. Many people are comfortable and familiar with this spacing. However, you can change the spacing of the letters to something you find more appropriate or pleasing. Printers call this *kerning*. The amount you choose to kern letters may depend on the type of font you choose. Some fonts look better when you adjust the spacing. The following examples show differences in text with different spacing.

- **Helvetica**   This is the default spacing.
- **Helvetica**   This is condensed spacing.
- **Helvetica**   This is expanded spacing.

Follow these steps to kern text:

1. Select the characters you want to format,

    or

    place the insertion point where you want to enter new text and start the new spacing.

2. From the Format menu, choose **Character** (**Alt-T, C**). Word displays the Character dialog box:

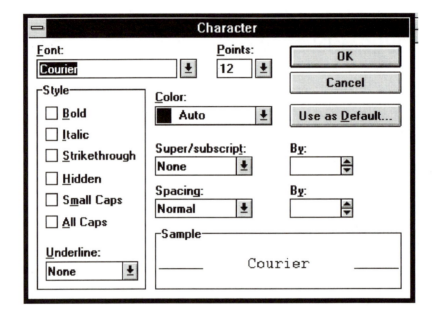

Figure 3.2

3. Under Spacing:

    Choose **Expanded** to *increase* spacing.
    or
    Choose **Condensed** to *decrease* spacing.

4. Type or select a number in the **By** box to change the default spacing.

You can adjust the spacing in quarter-of-a-point increments. For expanding, you can type from 0 to 14. For condensing, you can type from 0 to 1.75.

N O T E

5. Choose **OK**.

In general, save kerning for decorative or special text. Most of us were taught to read with "normal" spacing, which we find more pleasing for regular text.

N O T E

If you decide to change kerned text back to normal text, select the **Normal** option under **Spacing** in the Character dialog box.

SAVING TIME REPEATING AND COPYING FORMATS

Word offers a powerful capability for repeating and copying any formatting. This can save you a lot of time and keystrokes when you are working in a long document or one that requires complex formatting.

Using the Mouse or Keyboard to Repeat Formatting

To repeat a formatting procedure, you must reapply the formatting immediately after you finish. Word "remembers" only the last formatting that you have done.

Follow these steps:

1. After formatting:
   Select the text to which you want to apply the format.
   or
   Place the insertion point where you want to start the new format.

2. From the Edit menu, choose **Repeat Formatting** (**Alt-E, R**) or press **F4**.

Using the Mouse to Copy Formatting

You can copy formatting that you have just applied without copying the text itself. When you do this, you can apply the formatting to another area of the document, or into another open document.

SHORT CUT

Using the Character dialog box (**Alt-T-C**), you can reapply *all* formatting that you have applied to a selection. For example, if you apply bold, italic, and all caps, Word will apply all three to the new selection when you choose to repeat formatting. You cannot do this from the ribbon, since Word "remembers" only the last formatting.

Follow these steps:

1. Select the text to format.

2. Position the insertion point on the character containing the formatting you want to copy.

3. Hold down **Ctrl** and **Shift** while you click the left mouse button.

   Word applies the last formatting you chose, however, the text is not copied to the new selection.

WORKING WITH SPECIAL CHARACTERS

Many documents require special symbols or characters that a keyboard does not provide, but sometimes it's just fun to include some special characters to make a border or use as bullets.

Most fonts come with a set of symbol characters. Word provides symbols for the fonts included with the package. To display the Symbol font, choose **Symbol** from the Insert menu (**Alt-I, S**).

Figure 3.3

The Symbol font includes all of the Greek alphabet plus other characters defined by the American National Standards Institute (ANSI). It's easy to use the Symbol font characters, and you can apply other most other character formatting to them.

Follow these steps to add a symbol or special character:

1. Position the insertion point where you want to insert the special character.
2. From the Insert menu, choose Symbol (**Alt-I, S**). Word displays the Symbols dialog box.
3. In the Symbols From box, select the font that contains the character.
    or
    Type the font name, and then click anywhere in the set of characters to display the font.
4. Select the character. You can:

    ▪ Click the character and choose **OK**.
    ▪ Double-click the character.
    ▪ Select the character with arrow keys and press **Enter**.

    Word inserts the symbol.

Non-ANSI Characters and Symbols

Word lets you insert characters from non-ANSI fonts, but it automatically places the character in a field to protect it in case you change the font of the word or paragraph where you've added the symbol. Also, you cannot delete a character in symbol font using the Backspace key. You have to select it to delete it.

If you want to change the formatting of the character, use the same methods as described for formatting other characters and words. Word will apply any formatting that the symbol font allows.

You can change the size of the character by changing the point size from the ribbon. Some characters are more recognizable in a larger point size, and some print more attractively in a smaller point size. Experiment with printing a few symbols to see which ones look best in certain point sizes.

You cannot change the actual font of the character once you insert it in text. You must select the character and change it from the Symbols dialog box.

N O T E

Special Characters with ANSI Codes

If you need to insert ANSI characters (such as em dashes and en dashes) in text, you can use the numeric keypad to type the actual ANSI code to produce the character. Refer to your Windows documentation for a list of ANSI codes. Follow these steps to insert a code.

Do not use the numbers on the top row of the keyboard to type numeric codes for ANSI characters.

N O T E

1. Position the insertion point where you want to insert a special character.

2. Press **Num Lock** to turn on the Numbers Lock, if it is not already on.

3. Hold down **Alt**, and, using the numeric keypad, type **0** and the ANSI decimal code for the character to insert.

WORKING WITH HIDDEN CHARACTERS

Word gives you the option of hiding or displaying text and special characters while you work. Some examples of text you might want to hide include index entries, table of contents entries, and other field codes. You may need to display the hidden text while you are working, and then hide it when you are ready to print. In fact, you always need to hide table of contents and index entries before you generate those elements of your document. Otherwise, your document will have incorrect page numbering.

Follow these steps to format hidden text:

1. Select the characters you want to format as hidden.
   or
   Position the insertion point where you want to type hidden text.

2. Press **Ctrl-H**.
   or
   From the Format menu, choose **Character** (**Alt-T, C**).

Word displays the Character dialog box.

3. Select the **Hidden** check box and choose **OK**.

The text you selected or the text you type will be in the hidden format. If you choose the Hidden Text option or the All option in the View category of the dialog box (from the Tools menu), Word inserts a dotted underline to indicate hidden text, like this:

This⸱is⸱hidden⸱text.

Hiding and Displaying Hidden Text

Follow these steps to hide or display hidden text:

1. From the Tools menu, choose **Options (Alt-O, O)**.

2. Under Category, select **View**.

3. Under Nonprinting Characters:

    ■ Display hidden text by *selecting* either the **Hidden Text** or **All** check boxes.
    or

    ■ Hide text by *deselecting* both the **Hidden Text** and **All** check boxes.

4. Choose **OK**.

SUMMARY

In this chapter, you learned how to change the appearance of the text in your document by using fonts, adding attributes, kerning, and using special symbols. The next chapter shows you more ways to format and organize your document by aligning text and by adding lists, columns, tables, and borders to your document.

CHAPTER 4

FORMATTING PARAGRAPHS AND OBJECTS

This chapter discusses the following formatting features:

- *paragraph alignment*
- *indentations*
- *tabs*
- *line spacing*
- *lists*
- *tables*
- *borders*
- *columns*

Formatting whole paragraphs in Word is generally no more complicated than formatting a single character. Word makes it very easy to change multiple paragraphs or even whole documents with just a few commands. In many documents, a paragraph is simply a series of sentences separated by a line from other paragraphs. In Word and in this chapter, however, *paragraph* refers to any amount of text and objects, such as graphics, that fall between two paragraph marks.

Like using the character-formatting features, you can format paragraphs using Word's variety of formatting methods, including the commands from the Format menu, the ribbon, the ruler, the Toolbar, and shortcut keys.

Some of the more basic information is covered first, and formatting with desktop publishing features is covered later in the chapter.

PARAGRAPH MARKS

Most of the time, while you are formatting you will probably want to display paragraph marks in your document so you can see exactly where they are. To display the marks, click the Show/Hide Paragraph button on the left end of the Ribbon. You use the same button to display or hide the paragraph and other formatting marks.

ALIGNING PARAGRAPHS

There are four ways to align paragraphs in a document. You can

- Use the Paragraph dialog box.
- Use the ribbon.
- Assign a shortcut key sequence to a paragraph style.
- Define the aligned text as a style and apply the style to any other paragraphs.

See Chapters 5 and 6 for more information about defining styles.

When you align a paragraph, it does not mean that you change the margins—it means that you are placing the paragraph somewhere in relation to the margins.

N O T E

Using the Paragraph Dialog Box

Follow these steps to align paragraphs, using the Paragraph dialog box:

1. Select the paragraphs to align or position the insertion point where you want the alignment to begin.

2. From the Format menu, choose **Paragraph (Alt-T, P)**.

   Word displays the Paragraph dialog box:

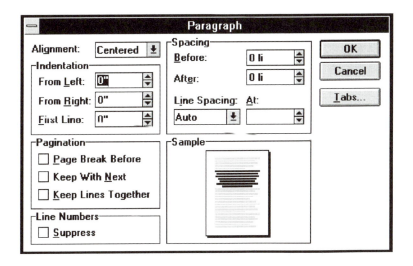

Figure 4.1

3. From the Alignment box, choose one of the following options:

Left: Aligns the paragraph or object with the left margin or paragraph indent. The right edge will be ragged, which means that there is no alignment on the right side.

> The·chart·consists·of·data·markers,·the·value·axis,·the·category·axis,·
> and·the·legend.·In·this·case,·we·have·generated·a·bar·chart.·Graph·will·
> create·a·legend·using·the·heading·for·the·dataseries,·and·the·pattern·
> used·for·the·marker,·so·you·can·identify·which·marker·is·used·with·a·
> particular·dataseries.·Graph·will·then·plot·the·datapoints.·This·chart·
> displays·the·values·in·the·default·datasheet.·¶

Figure 4.2

Information about indenting paragraphs is included later in this chapter.

Centered: Aligns each line of the paragraph between the left and right margins or indents.

> The·chart·consists·of·data·markers,·the·value·axis,·the·category·axis,·
> and·the·legend.·In·this·case,·we·have·generated·a·bar·chart.·Graph·will·
> create·a·legend·using·the·heading·for·the·dataseries,·and·the·pattern·
> used·for·the·marker,·so·you·can·identify·which·marker·is·used·with·a·
> particular·dataseries.·Graph·will·then·plot·the·datapoints.·This·chart·
> displays·the·values·in·the·default·datasheet.·¶

Figure 4.3

Right: Aligns the paragraph or object with the right margin or paragraph indent. The left edge will be ragged, which means that there is no alignment on the left side.

> The·chart·consists·of·data·markers,·the·value·axis,·the·category·axis,·
> and·the·legend.·In·this·case,·we·have·generated·a·bar·chart.·Graph·will·
> create·a·legend·using·the·heading·for·the·dataseries,·and·the·pattern·
> used·for·the·marker,·so·you·can·identify·which·marker·is·used·with·a·
> particular·dataseries.·Graph·will·then·plot·the·datapoints.·This·chart·
> displays·the·values·in·the·default·datasheet.·

Figure 4.4

Justified: Aligns paragraph text so that both the left and right margins have a straight edge, creating blocks. Use this option judiciously because it can create white "rivers" of space in the text, which can make reading difficult.

> The·chart·consists·of·data·markers,·the·value·axis,·the·category·axis,· and·the·legend.·In·this·case,·we·have·generated·a·bar·chart.·Graph·will· create·a·legend·using·the·heading·for·the·dataseries,·and·the·pattern· used·for·the·marker,·so·you·can·identify·which·marker·is·used·with·a· particular·dataseries.·Graph·will·then·plot·the·datapoints.·This·chart· displays·the·values·in·the·default·datasheet.·¶

Figure 4.5

Using the Ribbon

If you have a mouse, using the ribbon makes paragraph alignment much quicker. Follow these steps to align using the Ribbon.

1. Select the paragraphs to align or position the insertion point where you want the alignment to begin.
2. From the ribbon, choose the appropriate alignment button.

For more information about the functions of the ribbon, see Chapter 1, "Mastering the Word for Windows Environment."

N O T E

Using Shortcut Keys

 Word also gives you the option of aligning text using *shortcut keys*. To use shortcut keys, select the paragraphs to align or position the insertion point where you want the alignment to begin and use one of the following key combinations:

Table 4-1

Alignment	Shortcut Keys
Left	Ctrl-L
Center	Ctrl-E
Right	Ctrl-R
Justified	Ctrl-J

INDENTING

Indentations play an important role in giving your document the look you want it to have. Your document will look much more finished if special information, such as quoted material, is indented different from the normal text. The indenting functions are similar to the alignment functions (discussed in the previous section), and you have several methods from which to choose. You can use the Paragraph dialog box, the Toolbar, the ruler, and default tab stops.

Using the Paragraph Dialog Box

Follow these steps to indent paragraphs using the Paragraph dialog box:

1. Select the paragraphs to indent or position the insertion point where you want the indentation to begin.
2. From the Format menu, choose **Paragraph (Alt-T, P)**. Word displays the Paragraph dialog box.
3. Do one or both of these:

    ■   Under **Indentation**, in either the From Left or From Right box, type or select the distance from the left or right margin that you want to indent the paragraphs.

or

- To indent the first line of each paragraph differently from the rest of the paragraph, type or select the distance from the left indent that you want the first line to begin. Remember that entering a negative number moves the first line to the left of the left indentation.

4. Choose **OK**.

    The paragraph now has the indentations you chose.

Using the Ruler

The ruler provides an excellent way for you to see exactly where you set indentations as you work (**Alt-V,R**). You can indent paragraphs without using commands and keystrokes. Before you start, notice the triangular indent markers on the ruler, as shown below. You use these to set indentations.

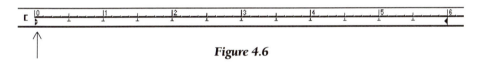

Figure 4.6

The triangle marker on the left is actually two triangles, and you can move them together or separately. To move them together, you click on the bottom one, and simply move it to the left or right as you see fit. This action moves all lines in the paragraph. To move them separately, you hold down **Shift** while you click on the lower triangle and move it to the left or right. This action moves all lines except the first line in the paragraph.

The triangle on the right affects all lines in a paragraph. It does not separate like the marker on the left.

Follow these steps to indent text using the ruler:

1. Select the paragraphs to indent or position the insertion point where you want the indentation to begin.
2. Perform one of the following actions to achieve the indentations you want:

Table 4-2

To Indent...	Do This...
The entire paragraph to a position on the left	Drag the bottom left indentation marker to a point on theRuler where you want the indentation to begin.
All lines in the paragraph, except the first	Hold down **Shift** and drag the bottom part of the left marker on the Ruler where you want the indentation to begin This creates a "hanging" indent, which is described later in this chapter.
The first line of the paragraph	Drag the top part of the left indentation marker.
The entire paragraph to a position on the right	Drag the right indentation marker to a point on the ruler where you want the indentation to begin.

Using the Toolbar to Indent Paragraphs

The Toolbar gives you two indentation choices: Indent and Unindent. Each time you select a paragraph and click the Indent button, Word moves the paragraph to the next tab stop. The Unindent button moves the selected paragraph back one tab stop each time you click.

Follow these steps to indent paragraphs using the Toolbar:

1. Select the paragraphs to indent or position the insertion point where you want the indentation to begin.
2. Click the **Indent** button on the Toolbar.

   To unindent, select the text, and click the **Unindent** button.

Using Shortcut Keys

Follow these steps to indent paragraphs using shortcut keys:

1. Select the paragraphs to indent or position the insertion point where you want the indentation to begin.

2. Press **Ctrl-Shift-F10** to activate the Ruler.

3. Press **Right Arrow** or **Left Arrow** to move the ruler cursor to the point where you want to indent.

4. Press the appropriate key, as shown in the following table:

Table 4-3

For this indentation...	*Press this key...*
Left	L
Right	R
First line	F

5. Press **Enter** to return to the document and apply the changes.

Setting Hanging Indents

A "hanging" indent means that the first line of text is left-aligned and the other lines are indented or "hang" from the first line. Most of the time, you will use hanging indents for formatting lists and bibliographies. You can use the Toolbar, Paragraph dialog box, the ruler, or shortcut keys to create hanging indents. The following examples show hanging indents. The first shows a hanging indent in a bulleted list item. The second shows a bibliographic reference.

> • This is an example of a hanging indent in a bulleted list. All lines after the first one are indented and "hang" indented from the first line.

Figure 4.7

Columbus, Christopher, *How to Get Funding for Sailing Adventures.*
Plume Publications, Genoa. 1493

Figure 4.8

Using the Toolbar to Create Hanging Indents

Word creates the hanging indent automatically when you use the Toolbar to add bulleted and numbered lists. Follow these steps to create a hanging indent using the Toolbar:

1. Select the paragraph to which you want to add bullets or numbering.

2. Click the **Numbered List** button to number the list.

    or

    Click the **Bulleted List** button to give the list bullets.

    Word inserts a number or a bullet in front of the paragraph and adjusts the lines with a hanging indent under the first line.

If you decide to change the bulleted or numbered item back to plain paragraph text, select it, choose **Bullets and Numbering** from the Tools menu (**Alt-O, B**) and choose **Remove**.

Using the Paragraph Dialog Box

This method is for text only, and for when you want to use precise measurements for indenting. Follow these steps to set hanging indents from the Paragraph dialog box:

1. Select the paragraphs to indent or position the insertion point where you want the indentation to begin.

2. From the Format menu, choose Paragraph (**Alt-T, P**).

    Word displays the Paragraph dialog box.

3. In the **From Left** box under **Indentation**, type or select the distance from the left margin that you want to indent all lines except the first.

4. In the **First Line** box under **Indentation**, type or select the negative measurement that you want to indent the first line, as shown in the following example:

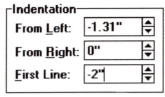

Figure 4.9

Watch the sample box. Word changes the diagram as you change the measurement. If you type a measurement, instead of selecting one, you can click in any other box to see the change in the diagram.

5. Choose **OK**.

Word applies the indentation.

Using the Ruler

Follow these steps to set a hanging indent using the left marker on the ruler:

1. Select the paragraphs to indent or position the insertion point where you want the first line to begin.

2. Hold down **Shift** and, on the ruler, drag the First-Line Indent marker (*bottom* part of the left marker) where you want to begin all lines but the first.

    or

    Drag the First-Line Indent marker left to where you want the first line to begin.

    Word applies the hanging indent.

Using the Shortcut Key

You can set a hanging indent very quickly using the shortcut key sequence. Follow these steps:

1. Select the paragraph(s) to indent.

2. Press **Ctrl-T**.

Word indents all lines except the first to the first default or custom set tab. Each time you press the key sequence, the lines move left to the next tab stop.

To move the lines back, press **Ctrl-G**. Word moves the lines back one tab stop each time you press the key sequence.

Setting Negative Indents

If you have never used a negative indent, it may sound unusual. However, this is an excellent feature to use if you have text, headings, or illustrations that you need to place outside the margin area either on the left or right. The following illustration shows a heading that has negative indents. Notice the position of the heading compared to the zero on the ruler.

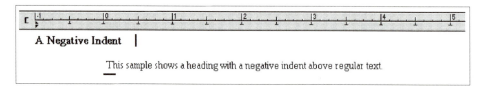

Figure 4.10

Follow these steps to set a negative indentation:

1. Select the paragraphs you want to indent negatively, or position the insertion point at the location where you want the formatting to begin.

2. From the Format menu, choose Paragraph (**Alt-T, P**). Word displays the Paragraph dialog box.

3. Under **Indentation**, type or select a negative number in the **From Left** or **From Right** box, depending on which indentation you need to set.

    Watch the sample box. Word changes the diagram as you change the measurement. If you type a measurement instead of selecting one, you can click in any other box to see the change in the diagram.

4. Choose **OK**.

    Word places the text or object in the margin.

Nesting Paragraphs and Items in Lists

There may be times when you need to nest paragraphs under paragraphs or lists under lists. For example, in paragraph text you would normally nest a paragraph of text quoted from another publication. Follow these steps to nest a paragraph or list:

1. Select the paragraph.
2. Click the Indent button on the Toolbar

   or

   Press **Ctrl-N**.

   Word moves the paragraph to the next tab stop on the right each time you click or press the keys.

TABS

It is easier to set and use tabs in Word than it is on a typewriter. Word provides default tab stops every half-inch; however, you can choose any custom settings you want. Typists generally use the tab stops when aligning text in tables. In Word, you won't need to do that because you can use the table function (described later in this chapter). However, you will need to use tabs in some documents. You can set tabs using the ribbon, the ruler, the Tabs dialog box, or shortcut keys.

Word does not display the tab characters unless you choose to have them displayed. Follow these steps to display the tab characters:

   or
1. From the Tools menu, choose **Options (Alt-O, O)**.

   Word displays the Options dialog box.
2. Under Category, select **View**.
3. Under Nonprinting Characters, select **Tabs**.
4. Choose **OK**.

Word displays the tab characters.

Using the Ribbon and Ruler

The Ribbon provides four buttons you can use to set tab stops. (If the Ribbon is not visible, press **Alt-V, B**). From left to right, the buttons are left-aligned, centered, right-aligned, and decimal.

Follow these steps to set tabs using the Ribbon.

1. Select the paragraphs to which you want to add tab stops.

   or

   Position the insertion point where you want to begin a tab formatting as you type.

2. Set tabs by clicking one of the tab buttons as follows:

Table 4-4

For this alignment...	*Click this tab button...*
Left	Left-Aligned
Centered	Centered
Right	Right-Aligned
Decimal	Decimal aligns decimal points vertically in a list.

3. In the lower half of the ruler, click where you want to place the tab stop.

Word now recognizes this tab stop and others you add for the paragraph in which you are working and for the following paragraphs that you will create.

Using Keys and the Ruler Cursor

You can set tabs using the ruler, without using the mouse because Word provides keys that activate the ruler function. Follow these steps to set tabs using the keyboard and the ruler:

1. Press **Ctrl-Shift-F10** to activate the ruler.
2. Select the paragraphs to which you want to add tab stops.

    or

    Position the insertion point where you want to add tab formatting as you type.
3. Press **Left Arrow** or **Right Arrow** to move the ruler cursor to where you want the tab stop.
4. Set tabs by pressing one of the keys as follows:

Table 4-5

For this alignment...	Press this key...
Left	1
Centered	2
Right	3
Decimal	4

5. Press **Ins** to set the tab stop.
6. Press **Enter** to apply the changes.

Using the Tab Dialog Box

Using the Tab dialog box from the Tab command gives you more flexibility in setting custom tabs. The command also lets you choose whether to use a tab stop leader character like you see in many tables of contents. Also, you can clear all custom tabs and restore the default tabs with just a few keystrokes.

Follow these steps to set tabs using precise measurements in the Tab dialog box:

1. Select the paragraphs to which you want to add tabs.

or

Position the insertion point where you want the tab formatting to begin.

2. From the Format menu, choose **Tabs (Alt-T, T)**.

or

Double-click any tab stop marker on the Ruler

or

Choose **Tabs** from the Paragraph dialog box.

Word displays the Tabs dialog box:

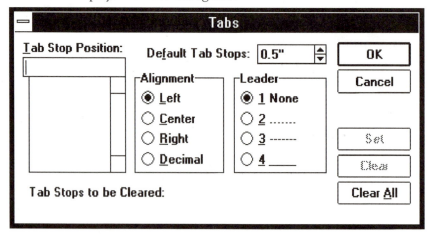

Figure 4.11

3. In the **Tab Stop Position box**, type the precise measurement and abbreviation for the tab spacing. Do not add a space between the two. (For example, type **2pi** for two picas of space.)

Table 4-6

For this measurement...	*Use this abbreviation...*
Centimeters	cm
Inches	in
Lines	li

Table 4-6 (continued from previous page)

For this measurement...	Use this abbreviation...
Picas	pi
Points	pt

4. In the **Alignment** box, select the alignment for the tabs: **Left, Center, Right, or Decimal**.

5. In the **Leader** box, select whether to have leaders and the type: None, periods(.), hyphens(-), or an underscore(_). (Leaders fill the space in the tab.)

6. Choose **Set**.

7. Choose **OK**.

You can set all tab stops using the same procedure.

Changing Your Tab Stops

If you decide you don't like the tab stops you've set, you can change them easily, using this procedure.

1. Display the Tabs dialog box as described earlier.

2. In the Tab Position box, select or type the position of the tab stop you want to change.

3. Select the alignment you want the tabs to have (and a leader if appropriate).

4. Choose **Set**.

You can remove all other formatting, including tab stops, by selecting the text to reformat and pressing **Ctrl-Q**. The formatting reverts to the style the paragraph originally had.

LINE SPACING

The right amount of line spacing is crucial for a printed document. Word, like most desktop publishing packages, uses the point measurement. There are 72 points in an inch. Too many or too few points of spacing between lines makes text difficult to read. Word's default line spacing for normal text is a single space. However, you can change the line spacing to suit your needs. You can choose to have different line spacing in different parts of the document, much in the same way that you use Word's other formatting elements.

Word also automatically adjusts the line spacing for the size and type of font you use. This prevents lines from running together or being too far apart. When you choose fonts and line spacing for a document, it is a good idea ask someone else to read the information to make sure that it is easy to read.

To adjust line spacing, use the Paragraph command (**Alt- T, P**). Word does not provide shortcuts for line spacing in the 2.0 release. If you want, you can press **Enter** to add as many lines of space as you need, but generally, you work more efficiently and improve the quality of your document if you define the line spacing for the task at hand. Also, if you add lines with the **Enter** key and then adjust line spacing for the whole document with the Format command, you may have a lot of extra lines of space.

Making the Adjustments

Follow these steps to adjust line spacing in a document.

1. Select the paragraphs you want to adjust.

2. From the Format menu, choose **Paragraph** (**Alt-T, P**).

3. In the Line Spacing box, select one of the following options.

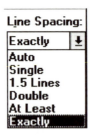

Figure 4.12

Table 4-7

Select this option...	To set...
Auto	Spacing that Word adjusts to accommodate the largest font size or graphic in a line. For example, if you place a graphic or text in a larger font on the same line with text in a small font, Word adjusts the line spacing to accomodate the larger font.
	Tip: If you ever import a graphic, and it looks as though only a line or two has been copied into your document, select the portion of that graphic that you can see and choose the Auto option.
Single	Single-line spacing. Word increases spacing by one line, based on the font type and size you choose.
	This is the same single-spacing that a typewriter uses.
1.5 Lines	One-and-a-half line spacing. Word increases spacing by one and one-half lines, based on the font type and size you choose.
	This is the same one-and-a- half line spacing that a typewriter uses.
Double	Double-line spacing. Word increases spacing by two lines, based on the font type and size you choose.
At Least	This is the same double-line spacing that a typewriter uses.
	The least amount of line spacing that Word can increase to accommodate fonts or graphics.

Table 4-7 (continued from previous page)

Select this option...	To set...
Exactly	Fixed line spacing that Word does not adjust. Use this option judiciously because you may cut off text or any graphics that do not fit.

4. If you choose **At Least** or **Exactly**, then in the **At** box, type or select the amount of space you want between lines, using whole numbers or decimal fractions.

5. Choose **OK**.

Using Before and After Spacing

Defining before and after spacing helps you give your documents a more professional, typeset look. You add space before and after paragraphs, titles, headings, graphics, lists, and tables. Saving before or after spacing in a style can save you a lot of time in formatting.

These are some other benefits of adjusting before and after spacing:

- You can use points or decimal fractions to fine-tune spacing.
- You can make the document more eye-pleasing and easy to read.
- You can move any element to which you have applied the spacing, and the spacing moves with the element.
- The spacing remains consistent no matter what fonts you use.
- When you print the page, Word ignores space before a heading so that the top margin remains intact.

Follow these steps to add space before, after, or both:

1. Select the paragraph(s) to which you want to add space before or after.
2. From the Format menu, choose **Paragraph** (**Alt-T, P**).

Word displays the Paragraph dialog box.

3.   Under Spacing, in the **Before** and **After** boxes, type or select the measurements you want.

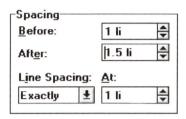

Figure 4.13

4. Choose **OK**.

Word applies the spacing to the paragraphs.

You can change the line spacing in Word's predefined templates if you find it more convenient. See the formatting tutorials in Chapter 5, "Formatting Tutorials" for more information about changing and defining styles.

N   O   T   E

Deciding Where to Add Line Spacing

This table provides guidelines you might use to decide which areas of your document need line-spacing additions or adjustment.

Table 4-8

For this element...	Add space...
Paragraph and body text	Before.
A paragraph, such as quoted text, that needs special separation from other paragraph text	Before and after the special paragraph.

Table 4-8 (*continued from the previous page*)

For this element...	Add space...
Headings	Before and after the heading, but add more space before than after, as a heading needs to be closer to the text it precedes than the text it follows.
Notes, tips, and warnings	Before and after in equal amounts to make sure the information stands out.
Artwork, photographs, tables, and other visuals	Before and after, usually an equal amount.

LISTS

In professional documents, especially technical ones, you will probably need to show a lot of information in the form of lists. Word's powerful feature for bulleted and numbered lists makes it easy to format them. In addition, Word can renumber lists automatically if you add or delete items. This can save you a tremendous amount of time over making the changes manually.

You have two ways to format and work with lists:

- Using the Bullet and Number buttons on the Toolbar.
- Using the Bullets and Numbering dialog box from the Tools command.

Using the Toolbar

The Toolbar provides the quickest way to add bullets or numbers to an existing paragraph. You need only to select a paragraph, and click this button for a numbered item:

or choose this button for a bulleted item:

If you have not selected a paragraph, Word adds a bullet or numbers to an existing paragraph where you left the insertion point. You can add a bullet or number to more than one paragraph at a time by selecting a group of that paragraphs you want to change. Word adds a bullet or number to every paragraph you selected.

When you choose the Numbered List button, Word automatically checks to see if you have formatted the previous paragraph with numbering. If you have, it uses the same numbering style as that paragraph and adds 1 to the number. You can change the bullet and numbering style with the Bullets and Numbering dialog box.

Using the Bullets and Numbering Dialog Box

The Bullets and Numbering dialog box gives you more formatting options than the Toolbar does. You can choose a different size and shape of bullet and six different options for numbering.

Adding and Changing Bullets

Follow these steps to add bullets to paragraphs:

1. Select the paragraph(s) to which you want to add bullets.
2. From the Tools menu, choose **Bullets and Numbering** (**Alt-O, B**).

Word displays the Bullets and Numbering dialog box. The Bullets option is the default and is selected.

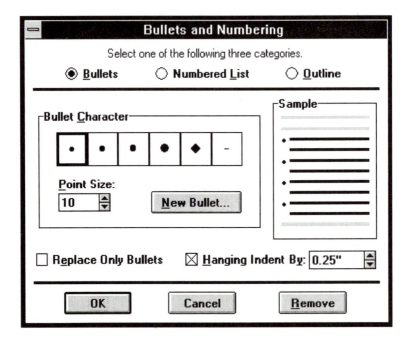

Figure 4.14

3. Choose the options you need, and choose **OK**.

    At this point, you can change the bullet style and size and the hanging indent. See the following table.

Table 4-9

Select this option...	*To...*
Bullet Character	Choose one of Word's predefined bullet styles. The style you choose becomes the default bullet whether you use the Toolbar's Bullet button or the Bullets and Numbering dialog box to add bullets.

Table 4-9 (continued from previous page)

Select this option...	To...
Point Size	Type or select a point size for the bullet. Generally, you should not choose a large bullet for regular text. If you do, the bullet may stand out so much that it distracts a reader from the text. Try a six-or eight-point bullet for regular text. For overheads and documents that use larger point sizes for text, choose a larger bullet.
New Bullet	Define a new bullet style from the Symbols dialog box.You can choose any character in the box. The style you choose becomes the default bullet whether you use the Toolbar's Bullet button or the Bullets and Numbering dialog box to add bullets.
Replace Only Bullets	Change the bullets for paragraphs that already have bullets. This does not add any bullets to selected paragraphs that do not have bullets.
Hanging Indent By	Format the selected paragraphs with hanging indents. The default is 0.25 inch. Word inserts a tab character between the bullets it adds and the text. You do not change any existing formatting by choosing this option.

Adding and Changing Numbers

Follow these steps to add numbers to paragraphs:

1. Select the paragraph(s) to which you want to add numbers.

2. From the Tools menu, choose **Bullets and Numbering** (**Alt-O, B**).

   Word displays the Bullets and Numbering dialog box (See Figure 4.15).

3. Choose **Numbered List.**
   Word displays the numbered list options.

4. Choose the options you need (described in Table 4-10), and choose **OK**.

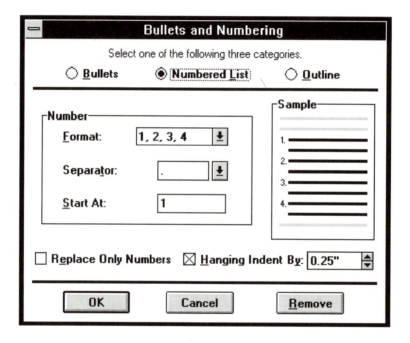

Figure 4.15

Table 4-10

Select this option...	To...
Format	Choose a "numbering" format. The style you choose becomes the default number format whether you use the Toolbar's Numbered List button or the Bullets and Numbering dialog box to add numbers.
Separator	Choose a character to separate the number from the text in the list. You can also choose not to have a separator character.
Start At	Enter a starting number for numbers that Word inserts. The default is 1.
Replace Only Numbers	Change the numbers for paragraphs that already have numbers. This does not add any numbers to selected paragraphs that do not have numbers.
Hanging Indent By	Format the selected paragraphs with hanging indents. The default is 0.25 inch. Word inserts a tab character between the numbers it adds and the text. You do not change any existing formatting by choosing this option.

Adding More Paragraphs to a Numbered List

If you convert a series of paragraphs into a numbered list, and decide to add more items between two of them, you can have Word renumber the list. For example, you might want to add another numbered item between number 3 and number 4. To do this, add the paragraph, and select all the numbered paragraphs again. Then, from the Toolbar or the **Bullets and Numbering** dialog box (**Alt-O, B**), choose to number the items. Word renumbers all the items in the list, placing them in numerical order.

If you add a numbered item to the end of a numbered list, select only that paragraph and number it. Word will give that item the correct number.

Changing Bullets to Numbers and Vice Versa

You can convert a numbered list to a bulleted list and vice versa with just a few keystrokes. You don't have to retype any of the bullets or numbers.

Follow these steps:

1. Select the paragraphs to convert.

2. From the Tools menu, choose Bullets and Numbering (**Alt-O, B**).

3. Select **Bullets** or **Numbered List**, depending on which type you need.

4. Clear the **Replace Only Bullets** or the **Replace Only Numbers** check box if it is selected.

5. Choose **OK**.

    Word asks if you want to convert the list.

6. Choose **Yes**.

Removing Bullets and Numbers

If you decide that you want your paragraphs to have no bullets or numbers after you have added them, you can remove them just as easily as you added them. If you add either, you can remove them immediately by choosing **Undo** from the Edit menu (**Alt-E, U**). However, you must not perform any other mouse or keyboard actions before choosing Undo, since Word can only undo the last action.

Follow these steps to remove bullets or numbers using the Bullets and Numbering dialog box:

1. Select the paragraphs that have the bullets or numbers.

2. From the Tools menu, choose **Bullets and Numbering** (**Alt-O, B**).

3. Select **Bullets** to remove bullets.

   or

   Select **Numbered List** to remove numbers.

4. Clear the **Hanging Indent** By check box if you want to remove hanging indent formatting.

5. Choose **Remove**.

   Word reformats the paragraphs.

FORMATTING TABLES

If you have ever constructed a table using a typewriter or an unsophisticated word processor, you know how frustrating it can be. Setting correct tabs and spacing for each column, not to mention fitting them on the page, has made more than one author reevaluate whether to even include important information in a document.

Word's table feature is so flexible that you can use it for much more than just presenting tabular information. You can use it to construct resumes, business forms, form letters, mailing labels, and even newsletters and brochures. In fact, you can construct almost any text that you need to place in columns using the table feature. You may even want to sit and experiment with the table feature, just playing with it, to see how much you can do.

You have two options for choosing to place information in a table: the Toolbar and the Table menu. Afterward, if you decide you want to present the information in a different format, you can convert the tabular information back to a normal text format with just a couple of clicks or keystrokes.

This section of the chapter covers what you need to know to construct and convert text and tables. However, for more intricate details, see the documentation that was packaged with the software.

Using the Toolbar

The Table button on the Toolbar is the quickest way to set up a table, but it does not give you as many options as the Table menu does. Use the Toolbar for simpler table setup, for example, if you just want Word to use the default table width or if you are just beginning to type tabular information and you need two columns the full width of the page.

Inserting a Table with the Toolbar

Follow these steps to insert an empty table with the Toolbar:

1. Position the insertion point where you want to place the table.

2. Click the Table button on the Toolbar.

3. On the Table button grid, drag the mouse vertically, horizontally, or diagonally to select the number of columns and rows you want the new table to have.

    The shaded areas and the bottom of the grid show the number of rows and columns the table will have.

    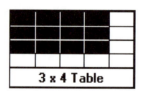

    3 x 4 Table

4. Release the mouse button to insert the table.

Figure 4.16

To display the table gridlines as shown in the previous illustration, press **Alt-A, G.** You can hide the gridlines the same way.

Changing the Column Width   If you want to increase or decrease the column width, drag the mouse cursor slowly over the column divider line. When the cursor changes, hold down the mouse buttons and drag the lines to the position you want.

If you decide that you need more columns or rows you can add them. See "Inserting Rows and Columns" and "Deleting Rows and Columns and Cells" in this section for more information.

Inserting an Empty Table with the Insert Table Command

The Table menu gives you enough options to make almost any kind of table you need. Follow these steps to insert an empty table in your document using the Insert Table command.

1. Position the insertion point where you want to insert a table.

2. From the Table menu, choose Insert Table (**Alt-A, I**).

    Word displays the Insert Table dialog box.

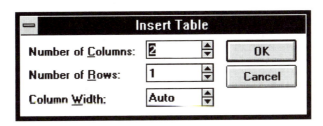

Figure 4.17

3. Type or select the number of columns and rows you want, and select the column width
    or
    Choose **OK** to accept the default settings of two columns, one row and automatic width, which you can change later.

4. If you typed or selected settings, choose **OK**.

    Word inserts the empty table. You can press **Enter** to add lines of space or new paragraphs in a cell or **Tab** to move to the cell in the next column. When you reach the last cell in a row, pressing **Tab** moves the insertion point to the first cell in the next row.

If you define a column that has a cell too long for your page, Word breaks the page before the row containing that cell. It will not break the page in the middle of the cell. Think about this when designing your table so that you do not end up with an awkward document layout. Also, you may want to repeat the headings of long tables on each page, but you must manually copy and paste.

Converting Text to a Table

Suppose you created a table in an earlier version of Microsoft Word for DOS or another word processing package in which you had to construct the table with tabs. You can convert that text to a table format very easily in Word.

Follow these steps to convert text to a table:

1. Select the text or paragraphs you want to convert.

2. From the Table menu, choose convert Text To Table (**Alt-A, T**).

   Word either converts the text to a table with as many columns and rows as are necessary or displays a dialog box that lists different conversion options. If the dialog box is displayed, that means Word cannot determine how to convert the text.

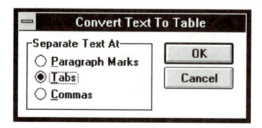

Figure 4.18

If you choose Paragraph Marks, Word inserts one column and as many rows as there are paragraphs. If you choose Tabs or commas, Word converts each paragraph and each line ending in a hard line break to a row of cells.

3. If necessary, in the Convert Text To Table dialog box, select the conversion options you need and choose **OK**.

If you have constructed the text table with irregular tab spacing, or with a combination of tabs and spaces, you may need to go into the original table and use tabs or spacing consistently before you convert. When you are done, check to see if the information is correct in the columns.

If you do not like the results, you can undo the conversion immediately by pressing **Alt-E, U**.

Converting a Table to Text

After you construct a table, you may decide later to present your information as paragraph text or in another format. You can convert the information easily, but if it is a complex table with many elements and special formatting, you will probably have to work with the text some to make it look like you want.

Follow these steps to convert a table to text:

1. Select the rows of the table that you want to convert.

2. From the Table menu, choose Convert Table To Text (**Alt-A, T**).

   Word displays the Convert Table To Text dialog box with its suggested separator selected as the default:

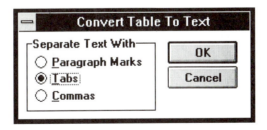

Figure 4.19

3. Select the separator you want.

   or

Choose **OK** to accept Word's suggested separator.

Word converts the table to text.

You should look through the text and see if you need to remove any extra formatting separators.

Inserting a Graphic in a Table

You can insert a graphic in a table cell. For example, if you need to show a table that describes the parts of an object, you can draw them in a drawing application, such as the Draw program or WordArt, and insert them in cells very easily, as the following illustration shows.

Part	Description
Press to Start	This is the start button. Make sure the machine is plugged in before you press the button. To turn off the machine, press the Start button again.

Figure 4.20

Follow these steps to insert a WordArt graphic in a table.

1. Create the table as described.
2. Position the insertion point in the cell in which you want to insert a graphic.
3. Open WordArt from the Insert menu (**Alt-I, O** then choose **MS WordArt** and **OK**).
4. Enter your text and choose a graphic style.
5. Choose **Apply**, then **OK**.

Word inserts the graphic in the cell.

If the graphic does not fit, select the portion you can see, and press **Alt-T,P**. In the line spacing box, select Auto.

For more information about using Draw and WordArt, see Chapter 8, "Microsoft Draw and WordArt."

N O T E

Changing a Table

No matter what dimensions and elements you give tables, you can change them. After you create a table you can

- Move rows, columns, and cells
- Insert rows, columns, and cells
- Delete rows, columns, and cells
- Merge cells to change columns

Inserting Rows, Columns, and Cells

Inserting rows, columns, and cells in a table requires a few more steps than inserting more text in a paragraph or more characters in a word. Pressing Tab creates a new row at the end of the last row in the table, but anywhere else in a table, pressing Tab only moves the insertion point to the next cell. However, it is relatively simple to add more rows, columns, and cells to a table.

Follow these steps to insert new rows between two existing ones, as shown in this example:

Project	Project Lead	Start Date	End Date
Write Functional Spec	Jeff Haas	1/2/92	6/1/92
Write Code	Cindy Adams	3/1/92	12/1/92
Write Documentation	John Kelly	4/1/92	3/1/93

Figure 4.21

1. Select the row below the place where you want to insert a new row

   or

   To add more than one row, select as many rows as the number of rows you want to add, directly below where you want to add them:

Project	Project Lead	Start Date	End Date
Write Functional Spec	Jeff Haas	1/2/92	6/1/92
Write Code	Cindy Adams	3/1/92	12/1/92
Write Documentation	John Kelly	4/1/92	3/1/93

Figure 4.22

2.   From the Table menu, choose Insert Rows (**Alt-A, I**).

Word shifts the selected rows down and adds as many empty rows as are selected.

Project	Project Lead	Start Date	End Date
Write Functional Spec	Jeff Haas	1/2/92	6/1/92
Write Code	Cindy Adams	3/1/92	12/1/92
Write Documentation	John Kelly	4/1/92	3/1/93

Figure 4.23

To insert a row at the end of a table, simply position the insertion point in the last cell in the table and press **Tab**.

Follow these steps to insert a row or column on the far right side of a table:

1.   Point to the right of the table and when the mouse cursor becomes a down arrow, click the right mouse button to select all end-of-row marks.

2.   From the Table menu, choose **Insert Columns (Alt-A, I)**.

If you make the table too wide for the margins, you can decrease the width of the column or reset the margins.

Follow these steps to insert columns between two existing columns in a table:

1. Select the columns to the right of the place where you want to add the new column.

    or

    To add more than one column, select as many columns as the number of columns that you want to add.

    For example, if you have a three-column table and you want to add two more columns between columns 1 and 2, select columns 2 and 3. Always select *to the right* of the point where you want to add columns. To select two columns, select one, then hold down **Shift** while you select the next one.

2. From the Table menu, choose Insert Columns (**Alt-A, I**).

    Word shifts the selected columns right and adds the new ones.

Follow these steps to insert cells in a table:

1. In the existing table, select as many cells as you want to add, and in the configuration in which you want to add them.

    For example, if you want to add two vertically aligned cells, choose two vertically aligned cells.

2. From the Table menu, choose Insert Cells (**Alt-A, I**).

    Word displays the Insert Cells dialog box:

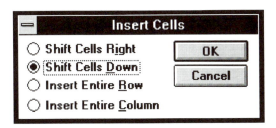

Figure 4.24

Table 4-11

Select this option...	To insert...
Shift Cells Right	Cells and shift the selected ones to the right.
Shift Cells Down	Cells and shift the selected ones down.
Insert Entire Row	A row above the selected cells.
Insert Entire Column	A column to the left of the selected cells.

Deleting Rows, Columns, and Cells

Deleting rows, columns, and cells is just as easy as adding them. One thing to remember, though, is that you cannot use the Delete or Backspace keys to delete any cells in a table—only the text they contain. You have to delete cells from the Table menu.

Follow these steps to delete a row:

1. Select the rows you want to delete.
2. From the Table menu, choose **Delete Rows (Alt-A, D)**

   or

   From the Edit menu, choose **Cut (Alt-E, T)**. You must select the entire row to cut it. Otherwise, you will cut only the text.

Follow these steps to delete columns:

1. Select the columns you want to delete.
2. From the Table menu, choose Delete Columns (**Alt-A, D**).

Follow these steps to delete any number of cells, whether in columns or rows:

1. Select the cells to delete.
2. From the Table menu, choose **Delete Cells (Alt-A, D)**.

Word displays the Delete Cells dialog box:

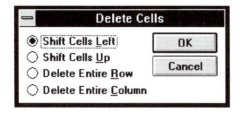

Figure 4.25

3. Select the option to specify how to shift the remaining cells.

4. Choose **OK**.

Moving Rows, Columns, and Cells

You can move a row of cells or move an individual column or cell to another part of a table.

Follow these steps to move a row of cells:

1. Select the row(s) you need to move by

   ■ Choosing Select Row from the Table menu (ALT- A, R)

     or

   ■ Clicking in the selection bar next to the rows you want to select.

2. Drag the selected rows to the position where you want to move them, ensuring that you position the mouse pointer at the *beginning* of the first cell in the destination row.

3. Release the mouse button.

The drag and drop feature works the same in tables as it does in normal text.

N O T E

Follow these steps to move a column or an individual cell:

1. Insert new columns or cells (which are empty) at the point where you want to move the columns or cells.

    Remember to insert as many new columns or cells as you need to accommodate the ones you want to move.

2. Select the columns or cells you want to move, and choose **Copy** from the Edit menu (**Alt-E, C**).

    Word copies the information in the cells to the clipboard.

3. Select the new cells you inserted and choose Paste from the Edit menu (**Alt-E, P**).

4. Select the empty cells from which you moved the text, and choose **Delete Cells** from the Table menu (**ALT-A, D**).

Merging Cells

If you decide that you want to merge two cells to make one column or row, select the cells. Then, from the Table menu, choose **Merge Cells** (**Alt-A, M**). If you change your mind and decide to split the cell, select it, and choose **Split Cells** from the Table menu (**Alt-A, P**).

BORDERS

You can apply a border to text, tables, or graphics, without having to draw lines with hyphen keys or use the drawing features in Word. This is a powerful feature, but very simple to use.

Follow these steps to apply a border to text or graphics:

1. Select the text or graphic to which you want to apply a border.

2. From the Format menu, choose **Border** (**Alt-T, B**).

Word displays the Border Paragraphs dialog box:

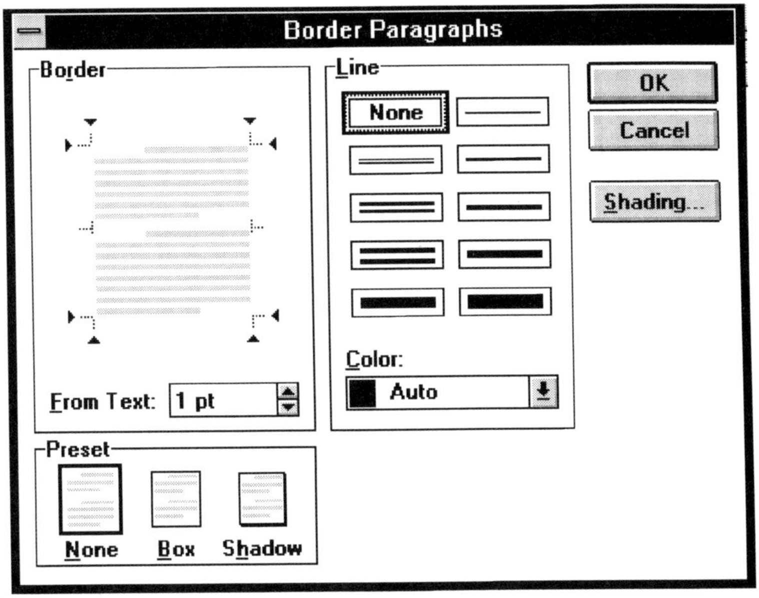

Figure 4.26

The title of this box will be different if you select a graphic.

3. Select the position, line size, line type, preset border type, and color (if applicable).

4. Choose **OK**.

Word applies the border to the text or graphic. You can also apply a border to text and define it as a style.

If you want to shade selected areas, select the **Shading** option from the Border Paragraphs dialog box (Choose **Border** from the Format menu (**Alt-T, B**). Select a percentage of shading from the **Pattern** box (the lower the percentage, the lighter the shading).

See Chapter 5, "Formatting Tutorial" for more information about applying a border.

COLUMNS

You can format a document, a section, or a paragraph in multiple columns. However, you must designate the multiple-column area (no matter how short) as a section by adding a section break. This type of formatting does not require you to use the Table command. (For simple columns, you might prefer setting up a table. See "Formatting Tables" earlier in this chapter.)

The column feature sets up your section like a newspaper layout. To view the layout as you work, you need to use Page View. Normal view displays the text in the correct column width, however, it shows a single column.

Follow these steps to create a multiple-column layout using the mouse:

1. Choose **Page Layout** from the View menu (**Alt-V, P**).

2. Make sure the Toolbar is displayed (**Alt-V, T**).

3. Insert a section break above the area you want to put in columns (**Alt-I, B**).

   Word displays the Section Break dialog box:

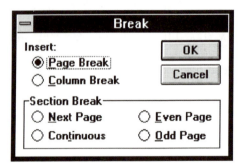

Figure 4.27

4. In the Section Break box, select the section break option you need.

5. Choose **OK**.

   Word inserts the section break.

6. Click in the section.

7. On the Toolbar, click the Text Columns button.

   Word displays the column choices in the sample box.

8. Drag the mouse cursor to the right to select the number of columns you want.

    Word formats the section with the number of columns you choose.

Follow these steps to create a multiple-column layout using the keyboard:

1. Select the text you need to format in columns.

    or

    Position the insertion point where you want to change the number of columns.

2. From the Format menu, choose **Columns** (**Alt-T, O**). Word displays the Columns dialog box:

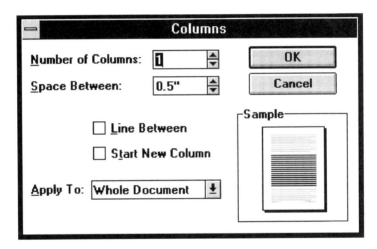

Figure 4.28

3. Type or select the number of columns you want.

4. In the **Apply To** box, select the amount of text you need to format.

5. Choose **OK**.

Word formats the section with the number of columns you choose.

REPLACING FORMATTING

Sometimes you may format a document only to print it and say, "Why on Earth did I format it like THAT?!?" Word lets you find and replace formatting almost as easily as finding and replacing a word. For example, you may decide that the large, bold, font you chose for your headings is overwhelming. Using the Replace command from the Edit menu, (**Alt-E, E**), you can change the formatting for all headings and redefine the heading's style while you're at it. Follow these steps to replace formatting or formatted text:

1. From the Edit menu, choose **Replace (Alt-E, E)**. Word displays the Replace dialog box:

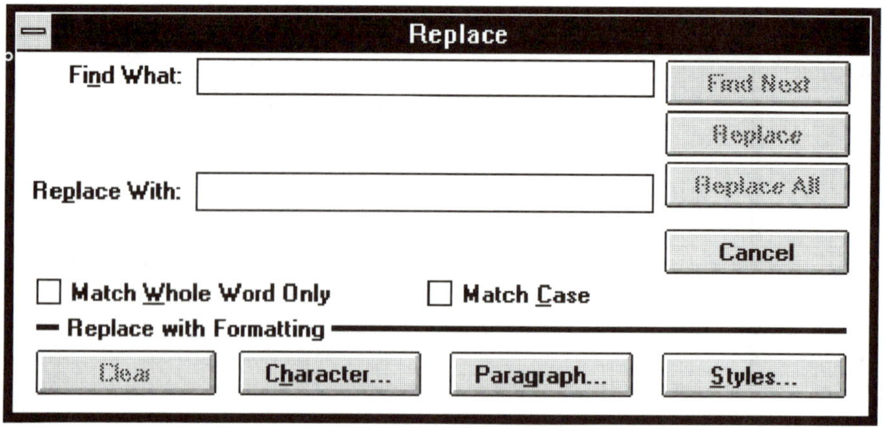

Figure 4.29

2. In the **Find What** box, type the text you want to change.

3. Leave the insertion point in the Find What box, and choose the formats you are looking for by choosing **Character**, **Paragraph**, or **Styles**.

You can choose Clear if you want to remove the formats listed below the Find What box or if you want to start over.

4. In the **Replace With** box, do one of these things:

Table 4-12

To replace...	Do this...
A string of specific text, leaving the formatting intact	Type the replacement characters in the Replace With box. If you see format names listed below the box, choose Clear.
A string of specific text, and its formatting	Type the replacement characters in the Replace With box.
Only formatting of a string of specific text	Delete any text in the Replace With box. Leave the insertion point in the Replace With box and choose Character, Paragraph, and Styles to select new formatting options.

5. Choose **Replace** or **Replace All**.
   Word changes the formatted text or formatting.

6. Select any other options you need at this point. You can find text by typing the specific text in the **Find What** box, deleting any text in the **Replace With** box, and choosing **Find Next**.

SUMMARY

Now that you have seen how to create and format a Word document, the next chapters let you practice what you have learned by providing hands-on tutorials.

CHAPTER 5

LEARNING WITH FORMATTING TUTORIALS

In this chapter, you will learn to use powerful formatting features to:

- *add a header to make your letter look like you printed it on personal stationary*

- *set the margins*

- *drag and drop sentences that are out of place*

- *cut a sentence from its location and paste it in another paragraph*

- *format characters and words*

- *correct some spelling and typographical errors*

- *change a word to a more appropriate one, using the thesaurus*

This tutorial chapter pulls together several of Word's powerful formatting features in one exercise.

Learning how to format text in Word for Windows and how to use its powerful desktop publishing features will help you create professional-quality documents in a short time. You may even find that you can save money that you would normally pay a typesetter to make your documents look good.

Although Word for Windows comes with some preset style sheets, you need to know how to set a format that works best for your specific needs. If you use Word on the job, chances are your department has its own format and style that you will need to create or recreate using Word.

This chapter provides instructions that take you through most of Word's sophisticated formatting capabilities. Because you probably already know how to type on a word processor, we have included text files that you can copy from the disk that was packaged with this book.

- The first file is a simple letter that you can format and improve.
- The second file is a business proposal that needs work. After you load the files, follow the tutorials in this chapter to become more familiar with formatting features:

ABOUT THE TUTORIALS

This first tutorial lets you work on a letter to become familiar with some of Word's text-editing features. If you are a novice user, this is a good place to start so you can quickly become a power user. If you have already become familiar with Word's simpler formatting capabilities, you might want to go on to the next tutorial, where you will use some of the more complex features for a business-related document.

The Letter

Have you ever signed a letter only to realize that you rambled on and did not organize it the way you really wanted? Most of us have probably done that at one time or another.

Making the Letter Better

The first thing you need to do is copy the text file called LETTER.DOC onto your computer in the directory of your choice, and open it in Word for Windows.

```
Al·Stevens¶
123·Oh,·the·Coconut·Grove¶
Cocoa·Beach,·Florida···79495¶
¶
December·14,·1991¶
¶
Dear·Al,¶
¶
It·seems·like·only·yesterday·(and·not·last·spring)·that·you·and·I·were·on·the·phone,·
disagreeing·about·whether·computer·book·authors·should·use·the·names·of·real·
people·in·their·books.··When·I·was·your·editor,·I·wanted·to·change·them·to·names·
I·knew·were·ficticious·in·case·they·didn't·like·it.··And,·I·tried·to·talk·you·out·of·
starting·sentences·with·connectors·like·and·and·but.··But,·now·I'm·on·the·other·
side·of·the·fence,·and·look·what·I've·just·done.¶
¶
The·Oregon·rain·has·set·in,·and·we·know·it·won't·stop·until·July.··Mike·and·I·have·
decided·to·spend·our·rainy·weekends·sharing·with·the·world·what·we·know·about·
how·to·make·great-looking·letters,·forms,·and·documents·with·Word·for·Windows·
2.0.¶
```

Figure 5.1

Follow these steps to enhance and reformat the letter.

1. Move the cursor to the date and select the whole line. Type over the date with the current date.

2. Select the fourth paragraph and the paragraph return after, and release the mouse button.

3. Press and hold down the left mouse button while you move the mouse pointer to the paragraph symbol at the first paragraph.

4. Release the mouse button.

   The fourth paragraph becomes the first paragraph. Don't you think that is a better opening for this letter?

5. Move the mouse cursor to the new fourth paragraph, beginning "Have you performed ." and find the two book titles. Select **Teach Yourself...DOS 5.0**.

6. From the Format menu, choose **Character** (**Alt-T, C**). Go to the check box marked *italic* and select it.

7. Choose **OK**.

8. Select **Teach Yourself...Windows** and repeat Steps 6 and 7.

9. Run Spellchecker (**Alt-O, S**) to scorrect the misspelling of "fictitious."

10. From the File menu, choose **Save** to save the file (**Alt-F, S**).

Now keep the letter file open. There are several steps in the next part of the tutorial that you can use to make great-looking letters.

Making Letter Stationery in the Same File

You can make your letter look like you printed it on stationery by adding a name and address header to your file. This is a very inexpensive way to make business and personal letters look attractive.

Adding a Letter Head

Word does not automatically insert any type of header into your documents . You have to set the header, but it is a simple task. If you have set standard margins for the letter, Word places the header you add in an area that is higher on the page than the work area where you type the body of the text. You have to be in Normal view before you can add a header to the file.

As you create the header, you will be working in another pane and it will look like you are working in another document. However, when you view or print the page, you can see that the header is where it should be.

Follow these steps to add a name and address header to the letter. Later, when you learn about the graphics capabilities in Word, you will see how you can create your own symbol or logo to add to your stationery header.

1. From the View menu, choose **Normal**. (Normal is the default for the default style sheet, so it should be selected already. This step is included to help you get used to the whole process.)

2. From the View menu, choose the **Header/Footer** command.

Word displays the Header/Footer dialog box.

Header/Footer

Header/Footer:
- Header
- Footer

OK

Cancel

Page **N**umbers...

From Edge

Header: 0.5"

Footer: 0.5"

☐ Different First **P**age

☐ **D**ifferent Odd and Even Pages

Figure 5.2

3. Choose the **Odd Header** command and choose **OK**.

   Word opens the header pane.

Because this is a one-page letter, you do not need to worry about odd **and** even headers.

N O T E

4. At the cursor position, type your name and address in the following format:

   Name

   Street Address

   City, State, ZIP

5. Select all three lines.

6. From the Format menu, choose **Paragraph (Alt-T,P)**.

   Word opens the Paragraph dialog box.

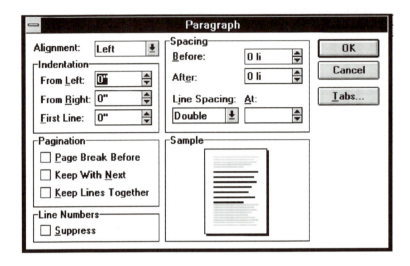

Figure 5.3

7. Click on the down arrow next to the Alignment box to display the alignment options. Choose **Centered** to center the text in the header. Choose **OK** to close the box.

   The text remains selected.

8. While the text is still selected, from the Format menu, choose **Character (Alt-T, C)**.

   The Character dialog box opens as shown in Figure 5.4

9. Click on the down arrow next to the **Font** box to display the list of fonts, and choose **Modern**.

10. Click on the down arrow next to the **Points** box and type **10** over the default of 12.

11. Choose **OK** to close the box.

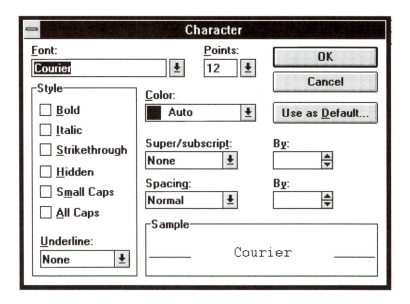

Figure 5.4

You now have a centered name and address header.

Although the header will be separated from the text, you can delineate the header a better way by adding a plain or decorative line under the header.

Keep the header pane open and follow these steps to add the line.

1. Select the last line of the header.

2. From the Format menu, choose **Border** (**Alt-T, B**).

   Word displays the Border Paragraphs dialog box as shown in Figure 5.5.

   The Border Paragraphs box shows a diagram of text on a page. The pointers indicate the horizontal and vertical positions where you can place the borders. The default settings show all pointers, indicating that the entire selected area will have borders.

3. Click on the area at the bottom of the diagram so that only the bottom left and right pointers are still visible, as shown if Figure 5.6.

4. In the Line Box, choose a thin border.

5. Click **OK** to close the Border Paragraphs box.

The letter now has a letterhead. You can now see it in Page Layout view (**Alt-V,P**).

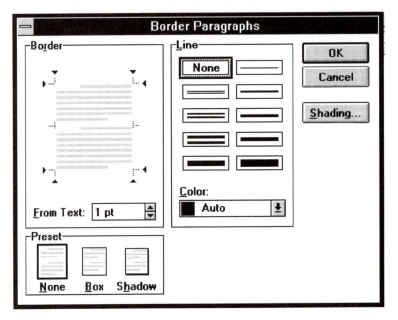

Figure 5.5

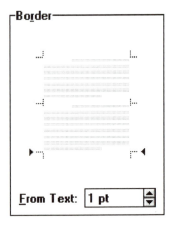

Figure 5.6

If you ever have two windows open, and you want to add a header to one of the documents, you will have to enlarge the current window or close the other window. To enlarge the window, move the cursor to the bottom right corner where you see the empty square. Click the cursor on the square, hold down the mouse button and drag down the cursor to expose more window space.

The Proposal

The proposal tutorial gives you the opportunity to make an unformatted text file into a professional-quality document.

Although Word for Windows comes with a style sheet for a proposal, the style limits you to one specific format. The preset style includes a level-one heading, a level-two heading, and the normal style for the body of your text. That style may suffice for a simple proposal; however, if you are working with a complex hierarchy of information, you will need to use Word's more sophisticated formatting features to produce an impressive proposal.

In this tutorial, you will:

- Create a proposal title page
- Insert page breaks
- Choose fonts for headings
- Use paragraph formatting
- Use the list feature to make a bulleted list of information
- Add footers and page numbers
- Add a header

Additionally, the proposal you will work on contains all of the parts that a professional-quality proposal should contain. So after you print out your work, look at the structure and components of the proposal. This structure makes it easier for busy managers to get the highlights of your report without having to "dig" out the important information. Your managers will be impressed.

Making the Proposal

The first thing you need to do is copy the file called PROPOSAL.DOC from the floppy disk onto your computer's hard disk and open it in Word for Windows, as shown below.

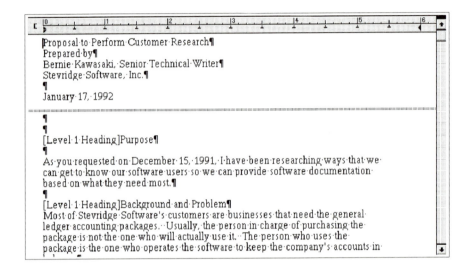

Figure 5.7

The Problems in Bernie's Proposal

When someone asks you for a proposal on the job, its appearance is often as important as the information it contains. The way you put together any business document says a lot about your organization and its communications skills. Many people write in such a manner that they try to get all of the information together first, and then think about the format.

The text for the proposal in the PROPOSAL.DOC file is typical of the first draft of a document. It has the right information thrown in, but it is not easy to read because the hierarchical structure and relevance of the information is not apparent. The headings are all on the same level, the format is unattractive, and the reader must find the most important information buried in paragraphs.

In this exercise, you will gain experience using these powerful formatting features:

- Adding a border
- Setting margins
- Applying left and right headers and footers
- Using the bullets and numbering tool
- Inserting a table

Designing the Title Page

Follow these steps to format the proposal title page.

1. If you have not already done so, copy the file PROPOSAL.DOC from the floppy disk to the directory of your choice and open it in Word for Windows.

   Notice the first five lines. This is information that you generally should place on the front cover of a proposal. In the preset proposal style sheet that comes with Word, this information is placed in the header.

   However, most formal proposals start with a title page that contains the name of the proposal, the author, the company name, and the date. The body of the information starts on the next page, which is page 1.

2. Select the first five lines of the file.

3. From the Format menu, choose **Paragraph (Alt-T, P)**.

4. Click the down arrow next to the Alignment box and choose **Centered**.

5. In the spacing box, click the up arrow next to the Before selection box until you display the number 3 as shown below.

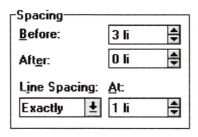

Figure 5.8

SHORT CUT

For this type of alignment, you do not need to assign spacing before and after. If you assigned three spaces before and three after, you would simply have six lines of space between the lines. You will fully use this formatting feature later when you design a style sheet that needs more sophisticated spacing and alignment.

6. Click **OK** to close the box.

    Word centers the text and places the space between the lines. The lines are still selected.

7. From the Format menu, choose **Character (Alt-T, C)** to display the Character box.

8. Click on the down arrow next to the Font box to display the list of fonts and choose **Modern**.

9. Click on the down arrow next to the Points box and choose **14**. Choose **OK** to close the box.

    This gives your title page a more typeset and professional look.

N O T E

Word's Modern font is similar to the popular Helvetica font, which is often used for title pages and headers.

Using the Section Break

Word's section break feature enables you to vary page formatting within a document. This is a powerful feature, and one of the most valuable when you are creating a document in which you need to change headers and footers from section to section. The section break is different from the page break because it allows you to set up certain formatting that the page break does not allow.

Once you set up a section break, all formatting for the section is stored with the section mark. You can treat the section mark the same way you treat any other character — you can cut and paste it, copy it, or delete it. However, if you delete the section mark, you will lose all section formatting.

In the next exercise, you will set up a section break. The cover page of the proposal does not need a header or a footer. However, the remainder of the proposal needs both.

When you create a document, such as a business document that has several sections or chapters, use the section break feature in each section instead of creating each section in a separate file. This makes it easier to work with headers, footers, and page numbering. Unless a document is very long, one file is usually easier to manage than several short ones.

SHORT CUT

1. Position the cursor at the end of the date line, and from the Insert menu, select **Break (Alt-I, B)**.

2. In the Section Break box, choose **Odd Page** and **OK**.

Word inserts the section break. This will cause the first page of the proposal body to be an odd page that starts with 1.

Inserting a section break does not add page numbers to your document. You use this feature in conjunction with the Header/Footer features to start the page numbering.

N O T E

Adding a Running Header

A running header in a document is generally used as a reminder of the highest level topic. In this proposal-formatting exercise, you will add a running header on the even pages that shows that the information is company-confidential, and one on odd pages that shows the proposal title.

Adding an Odd Header

1. From the View menu, choose **Header/Footer** (**Alt-V, H**).

Word displays the Header/Footer dialog box.

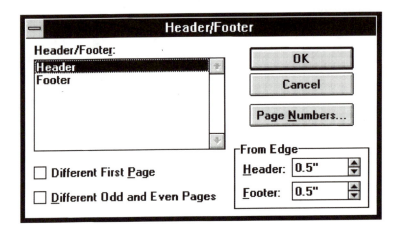

Figure 5.9

 The Different Odd And Even Pages option in the Header/Footer dialog box is selected by default. This option indicates that you want to put different headers and footers on the odd and even pages. If you clear the selection, Word ignores the even header or footer, and uses the odd header or footer for all pages.

N O T E

2. Click **on** Different Odd and Even Pages, Choose Odd Header and choose **OK**.

   Word opens the header for the document and the cursor flashes at the paragraph mark.

3. Type this text in the heading:

   Stevridge Software, Inc.   Company Confidential

4. Select the whole line, and from the Ribbon, click on the Bold button, shown below.

B

Most of the time, you will need to delineate the header from the text on the page. Word's Border feature lets you do this without having to type a line of hyphens. Also, you can use a different font and point size in the header to further distinguish it from the body of the text.

5. Select the line of text, and from the ribbon click on the down arrow next to the Font box, select **Modern**.

6. From the Point Size box on the ribbon, select **10**.

7. Select the line of text you just typed, and from the Format menu, choose **Border** (**Alt-T, B**).

   Word displays the Border Paragraphs dialog box.

8. In the Border box, click the bottom horizontal border area so that the diagram shows only the bottom line pointers. In the Line box, click on the thin double-line border, as shown below, and choose **OK**.

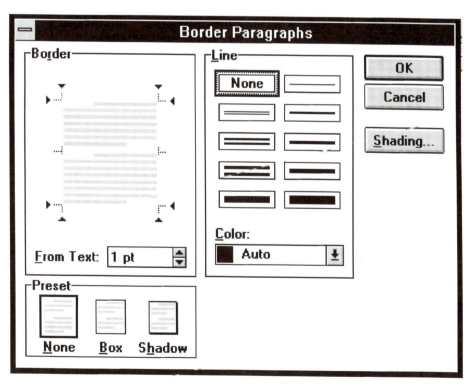

Figure 5.10

You now have an odd header in the proposal document.

The Preset box shows formats for borders that make boxes. By default, None is selected.

N O T E

9. Click **Close** to close the Header box.

If you want to see how the page looks with a header, click the Zoom Whole Page button on the Toolbar.

To return to the normal working page view, click the Zoom 100 Percent button.

Now, save your file and keep it open (**Alt-F, S**).

Adding an Even Header

Add an even header that shows the name of the proposal, the author, and the date. Follow these steps:

1. Open the even header and type this text: **Customer Research Proposal B. Kawasaki January 17, 1992**

2. Apply the same font and border to the even header that you applied to the odd header, and click **Close**. The proposal now has even and odd running headers.

The Link to Previous option in the header or footer pane enables you to duplicate the previous header or footer without retyping any text. If you create a header or footer and choose this option, Word asks if you want to delete the current one and link to the previous one. If you choose Yes, Word will duplicate the header or footer. This is an excellent way to keep your running headers consistent.

SHORT CUT

Adding a Running Footer

When you are creating a business document of any kind, add a footer that at least shows page numbers. (If you drop your document, it can be reassembled more easily if it has page numbers.) Follow these steps to add a running footer.

Make sure the cursor is on the first page of the proposal body—not the on the title page. The title page does not need a page number.

N O T E

1. Make sure your document is in Normal view.

2. Position the insertion point at the first paragraph on the first page of the proposal body.

3. From the View menu, choose **Header/Footer** (**Alt- V, H**).

   Word displays the Header/Footer dialog box with Even Header as the default.

4. Click **off** the **Different Odd and Even Pages** check box to display only Header and Footer in the dialog box as shown below.

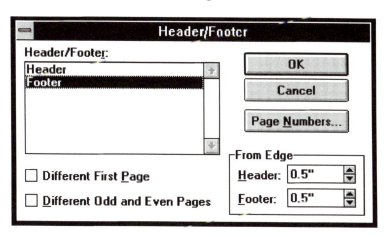

Figure 5.11

5.   Choose **OK**.

Word opens the Odd Footer pane. Notice the three icons at the top left corner of the pane.

The pound sign button on the left is for adding page numbers; the button in the middle is for adding the current date automatically; the button on the right is for adding the current time. You have already put the date in your header, and the time is not important in this instance. Click the pound sign to insert a page number.

In a two-sided document with facing pages, the odd right page number should be flush right with the margin, and the even left page number flush left with the margin. However, because this proposal is short and you probably want to distribute single-sided copies, all page numbers here should be flush right.

6.   Tab the page number until it is flush right. Headers and footers should have the same font. Select the page number and apply the Modern font in bold at 10 points (all from the ribbon). Using the same methods for applying borders as you used in the headers, apply a border above the page number. The footer pane now looks like this:

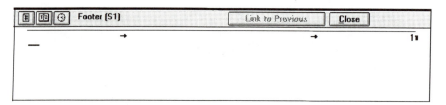

Figure 5.12

Showing Different Levels of Headings

Word's ability to use fonts and its character attributes, such as bold, italic, and underline, make it easy to distinguish headings from body text. In any document where you need to show a hierarchical structure of information, it is important to use different characteristics for each heading level. Unless all of your information is on the same level (quite unlikely in a business document), never use the same font and point size for all heading levels.

In this exercise, you can select fonts and point sizes for the three levels of headings. To make the headings in the provided text easier for you to find, they are labeled as levels 1, 2, or 3. Follow these steps to format the headings. You only need to apply the options to the first of each of the level headings. In the exercise following this one, you will define those headings as styles, and apply them to the other headings the easy way.

1. Select the first level-1 heading, **Purpose**.

2. From the ribbon, click the down arrow beside the Font box to display the list of fonts, and select **Modern**. (The font where the insertion point is positioned will be highlighted in the box.)

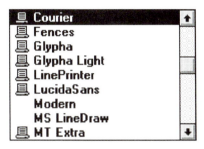

Figure 5.13

Word applies the Modern font to the heading and the heading remains selected. Do not deselect it.

3. From the ribbon, click the down arrow beside the Point size box to display the list of point sizes available for the Modern font. Choose **15**.

Word places the font in the 15-point size, and the heading remains selected. Do not deselect it.

4. From the ribbon, click the **Bold** option to make the heading bold.

The first level-1 heading is now 15-point, bold Modern, and it will stand out from the body of the text and from the other levels of headings. Ignore the other level-1 headings. You will change those later when you define this proposal as a style sheet.

5. Select the first level-2 heading, **Mailing Questionnaires**, and using the same steps as for the level-1 heading, apply the **Modern** font.

6. Change the point size to **13**, and make the heading bold, using the Bold button from the ribbon.

7. Select the first level-3 heading, **Questionnaire Strong Points**, and using the same steps as for the level-1 heading, apply the **Modern** font.

8. Change the point size to 11, and make the heading bold, using the Bold button from the Ribbon.

Your document now has clear delineation for the different levels of headings. Don't worry about the other headings right now. The exercise in the next chapter helps you to use Word's powerful style definition feature. You will apply the styles you have just made to the other headings and build a complete style sheet that you can use any time you want to build a similar document.

Margins and Indetations for the Document

Most business documents are created for 8 ¹/2-by 11-inch paper. Word's default for margins works just fine for this and most other documents. However, you might want your body text to have different indentations and than your overall document. Your documents can be easier to read if the text is indented further than the headings. This makes text more attractive and easier to read.

Word offers six options from the Paragraph command for adjusting line-spacing. Understanding how to use the paragraph indentations and line-spacing features will help you to create documents that are more visually pleasing. It is also important that you understand how to adjust line spacing for use with other formatting elements, such as font sizes.

In the following exercise, you will change the paragraph indentations and adjust the line spacing only for the first paragraph of regular text. In the next chapter, you will define that body text indentation as a style, then convert the other body text very easily by applying the style.

Follow these steps to indent the text.

1. Select the first paragraph under the heading **Purpose**.

2. From the Format menu, choose **Paragraph** (**Alt-T, P**) to display the Paragraph dialog box.

   The Alignment box shows Left as the default. This is the correct alignment.

3. In the Indentation box, change the From Left option to **.75** as shown below.

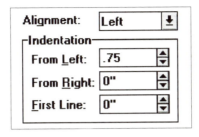

Figure 5.14

Word indents the text ³/4-inch from the margin.

You can use the up and down arrows to display ¹/10-inch increments. However, you must enter any other increments from the keyboard.

N O T E

4. In the Spacing box, change the **After** option to **1**. This causes Word to add a line of space after each paragraph return. You will not need to press the Enter key twice after you finish a paragraph to have an extra space between paragraphs.

Leave the other paragraphs as they are for now. When you define this indented text as a style in the next chapter, you can then change all the other body text.

Using Bulleted Lists

A list is the best way to show similar items in business and technical writing because the information is easier to find. Busy professionals often do not have the time to "dig" for information that is buried in paragraphs.

In this exercise, you will make some of the information into bulleted and numbered lists.

N O T E

Use numbered lists to show order, for example, the steps in a task or procedure. Use bulleted lists to show items that are not dependent on each other or not in sequence.

Follow these steps to make a bulleted list.

1. Move the cursor to the second (one-line) paragraph under the heading **Questionnaire Strong Points**.

2. Select that line and the two paragraphs under it.

3. From the Toolbar, choose the Bulleted List option.

Word adds bullets with hanging indents to the listed information.

You can set options that change the shape and size of the bullets in the Bullets and Numbering dialog box. Choose **Bullets and Numbering** from the Tools menu (**Alt- O, B**) to display that dialog box, shown below.

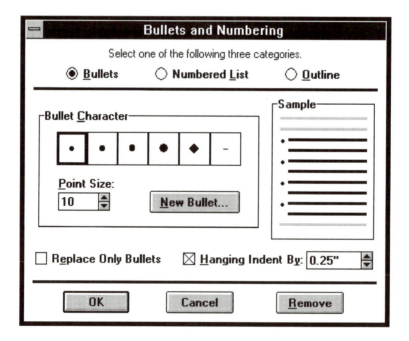

Figure 5.15

In this dialog box, you can choose any of the bullets shown as your default bullet. If you do not choose a bullet style before you make a bulleted list, Word applies the 10-point round bullet. You can change the point size of any of the bullets and you can define other bullets by pressing the New Bullet option and choosing a symbol. For a formal proposal or other business document, however, it is best to use a simple bullet.

Always choose a bullet style and size that does not "jump off the page" at you. Large bullets distract the reader from the information at hand. In general, a 10-point round bullet works just fine. In any case, don't use a symbol that will cause someone to stop and ask, "What is *that* thing? Don't they have anything better to do than draw little pictures?"

N O T E

Bulleted information looks best if you use the hanging indent. Without it, the information is no easier to read than if it were in a regular paragraph. Always indent the information to align with the text on the first line following the bullet. You can change the hanging indent in the Bullets and Numbering dialog box by clicking on the up or down arrow next to the Hanging Indent By box, or by entering a measurement in the box.

Continue this exercise, by making the short paragraphs under these headings into bulleted lists:

- Telephone Survey Strong Points
- Telephone Survey Wcak Points
- Visiting Customer Site Strong Points
- Visiting Customer Site Weak Points.

Using a Numbered List

As mentioned earlier, use numbered lists to show the order in which events should happen or to make a point about a number of things that need to be done. Word's Numbered List feature is powerful in that it can renumber a list automatically. This is very important because a numbering mistake in a numbered list is very noticeable.

Follow these steps to make a numbered list.

1. Scroll to the last heading in the proposal, **Breakdown of Tasks and Expenses**.

2. Select the second, third, and fourth paragraphs, and from the Toolbar, choose the Numbered List button.

Word converts the information into a numbered list.

Converting List Types

You can easily convert a bulleted list to a numbered list or vice versa. To convert a list, select all of the information in one of the bulleted lists on which you just worked. Then, select the Numbered List option from the Toolbar or from the Tools menu select **Bullets and Numbering (Alt-O, B)**. You can choose the Numbered List option to make changes to the list.

If you ever need to add an item to a numbered list, let Word perform the renumbering. Simply add the item, select all items, and apply the numbered list feature again.

SHORT CUT

Tabs and Line Spacing in Lists

While Word automatically converts bullets to numbers and vice versa, it is up to you to decide whether you want to use the same text alignment for the list. You might want to indent the list a bit, rather than have the bullets and numbers flush left with the text. In this proposal, indent only the first bullet in the first list. In the next chapter, you will define this as a style and apply the style to all other bullets. Follow these steps:

1. Scroll to the first bulleted item under **Questionnaire Strong Points** and select the whole line.

2. From the Format menu, select **Paragraph (Alt-T, P)** to display the Paragraph dialog box.

3. In the **From Left** box under Indentation, click on the up arrow until you display **0.75**". In the Pagination box, click **Keep Lines Together**. (This keeps Word from inserting a page break that would put part of a bulleted item on one page and part on another.)

4. Choose **OK**.

   Don't worry about the other bullets or lists for now. When you define the indented bulleted list as a style in the next chapter, you can change all of them very quickly.

5. Save the file and close it.

CHAPTER 6

CREATING A TEMPLATE

In this chapter, you will

- *define the styles in the proposal that you worked on in Chapter 5*

- *create a new template that contains all those styles*

Do you ever feel like you're spinning your wheels by entering the same information to your documents over and over? Creating and using a template can help you cut down tremendously on the time you spend repeating the same actions.

By creating a template, you can store the format of a document so you can use it whenever you need to produce the same type of document. Additionally, Word enables you to choose which commands, Toolbar buttons, and key combinations you want to make available when you work with a template.

CREATING A TEMPLATE

Word for Windows is packaged with some preset templates. However, it is important that you know how to create your own templates so you can become a more independent power user. Once you master the task of creating your own formats and style sheets, you become a *desktop publisher* instead of a *word processor.*

When you save the template, you can recall it again to create a similar document. If you decide later that you want to add or delete styles, you can make the changes easily and update your template. Your templates are not set in concrete. Word enables you to change them whenever you like.

There are three ways that you can create a template in Word:

■ Convert an existing document to a template.

■ Modify an existing template.

■ Create a new document from the File menu and select the Template option under New.

The first exercise in this chapter helps you to master the more powerful of the three methods. You can use the text you worked on in Chapter 5 to define styles for

■ headers and footers

■ all levels of headings

■ paragraph indentations

■ line spacing for the body text and lists.

ADDING A NEW TEMPLATE TO THE TEMPLATE LIST

The default template is Normal, so you need to define a new template for this proposal type. Otherwise, you would have to change or add styles to the Normal template; this is not a good idea because you might want to use the existing Normal template for another document sometime.

After you create the new template, Word adds it to the list of templates in the new dialog box.

To complete this exercise, you need to copy PROPOSAL.DOC from the floppy disk (packaged with this book) to your hard disk.

Follow these steps to save PROPOSAL.DOC as a template.

1. From the File menu, choose **Open** (**Alt-F, O**).

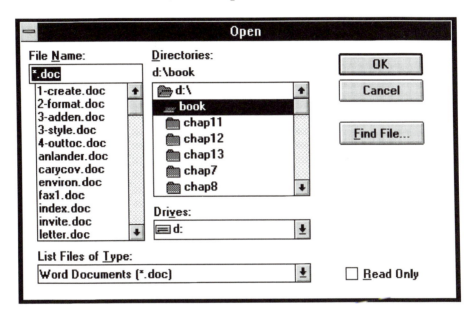

Figure 6.1

2. In the File Name box, type **PROPOSAL.DOC**.

3. Choose **OK**.

   You have saved the document; now you will save it again and convert it to a template.

4. From the File menu, choose **Save As** (**Alt-F, A**).

5. In the File Name box, type **NewProp**.

6. Select **Document Template** under the Save File As Type box, and choose **OK**.

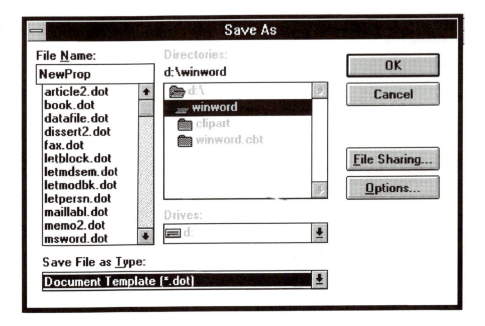

Figure 6.2

Word displays the new template name, **NewProp**, along with the other preset template names in this list. Now you are ready to convert the styles in the proposal.

CONVERTING YOUR PROPOSAL

In this exercise, you will define your proposal's title page as a *style*. By doing this, you will eliminate more than a dozen manual formatting steps.

1. Select all information on the title page.
2. From the Format menu, choose **Style** (**Alt-T, Y**).

   Word displays the Style dialog box, which shows all formatting you applied in the Description box.
3. Type **Title Page** in the Style Name box, as follows.

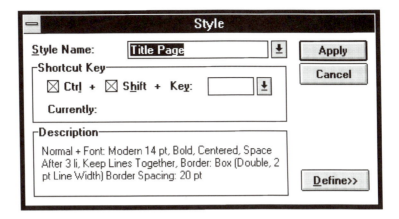

Figure 6.3

4. Choose **Define**.

   Word expands the Style dialog box, which gives you more formatting options as shown in Figure 6.4.

5. Select **Add to Template** and choose **Apply**.

Word adds the Title Page style to the NewProp template.

While you're in the Style dialog box, you can define a shortcut key that, when pressed, will apply the style to selected text. You can do this for all styles that you define. However, it is important to remember that by doing this, you can accidentally overwrite another shortcut key sequence. Choose a key sequence that you know you won't need to use for anything else. Always write down the shortcut keys when you define them, since multiple shortcuts may be difficult to remember.

N O T E

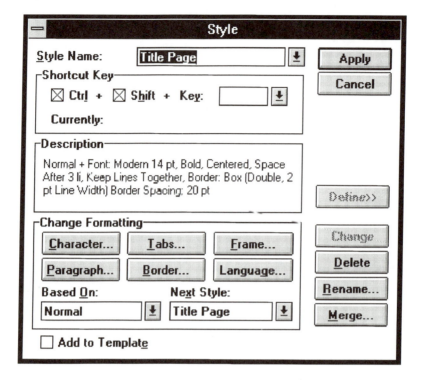

Figure 6.4

Defining Heading Styles

In Chapter 2, you applied some styles to one of each of the heading levels. In this exercise, you will define the three levels of headings in your document as styles in your template. Again, you will save many keystrokes in future documents by performing this task.

1. Scroll to the first heading in the document, which is *Purpose,* and select the entire line.

2. From the Format menu, choose **Style** (**Alt-T, Y**).

   Word displays the Style dialog box. The Description box shows all formatting that you applied to the heading earlier, as shown in Figure 6.5.

3. Enter the name, **Head 1**, in the Style Name box as shown in Figure 6.5 and choose **Define**.

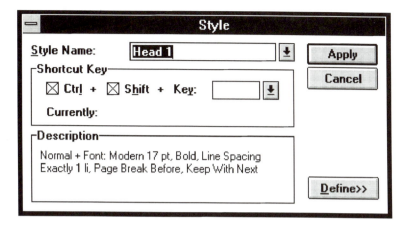

Figure 6.5

Word expands the Style dialog box, which includes the Change Formatting box.

Figure 6.6

The Based On box in the Change Formatting box is where you can base one or more new styles on another existing style. For example, if you give Head 1 a certain font and spacing, you can base other headings on Head 1, and they will inherit any format changes. If you redefine the base style, then all styles based on the base style will be automatically redefined as well. You don't have to define a base style, however. There may be times when you want to change some styles, but not the ones on which they are based.

Because you added the formatting to the heading earlier, you do not need to add any additional formatting. If you choose to add any other formatting, Word will update the Description box.

N O T E

4. Choose **Add to Template** to add the style to the template.

5. Scroll to the next Level 1 heading, labeled **Background and Problem**, and select the whole line. (Ignore the words **Level 1 Heading**. You can delete those later.)

6. Click the down arrow beside the style box and select **Head 1**.

7. Using the same procedure you used in Steps 1 through 6, define your level-two and level-three headings. Choose **NewProp** if you want to see the styles in the **NewProp** template.

Defining the Body Style

Earlier, you selected the first paragraph under **Purpose**, and indented it three-fourths of an inch to further separate the headings and text, and adjusted the line spacing. Now you can define that paragraph as the base style for all other body text by following these steps:

1. Select the first (indented) paragraph under **Purpose**.

2. From the Format menu, choose **Style (Alt-T, Y)** type **base text** in the Style Name box and press define.

3. From the format menu, select **Style (Alt-T Y)**

   Word displays the extended Style dialog box.

   This is the style you will use for all paragraph body text in the proposal. As you continue these exercises, you will base other styles, such as bulleted lists, on this style.

4. Click Add to Template and choose **Apply**.

Defining Running Header and Footer Styles

Defining a style for a running header and footer is as simple as defining styles in the body of the text.

When you define a header or footer style Word does *not* place the text in a header or footer automatically. You must still open the header or footer to apply the style.

N O T E

Follow these steps to define your footer style:

1. From the View menu, choose **Header/Footer** (**Alt-V, H**).
2. Select **Odd Footer** and choose **OK**.

    Word opens the odd footer, which displays the text you typed earlier.
3. Select the line of text in the footer and, from the Format menu, choose **Styles**.
4. In the Style Name box, type **Odd Footer** and define the style using the same steps you used earlier to define the heading and body styles.
5. After you define the style, close the footer pane.

Basing Another Style on the Base Text Style

Consistency is one of the most important aspects of any professional document because it indicates your attention to detail in your work. Word helps you to keep your documents in a consistent style.

In this exercise, you will define the bulleted items as a style and base it on the style you created in the last exercise.

Defining the Indented Bullets as a Style

Although Word defines a bullet style, you may very well want to use different spacing for the tabs, a different bullet style, such as a dingbat, or even different line spacing and indentation.

After you apply bullets to text, you can redefine them just like the other text you've been working with.

1. Select a bulleted item under the summary heading.
2. Indent the item to align with the base text (.75").
3. Define it as a style called body bullet, using the same steps as for the other styles.

PUTTING STYLES TO WORK

In the exercises you have performed, you have been working mostly on business documents. However, Word for Windows is well-suited for an incredible number of other kinds of documents. For the remainder of this chapter, you will learn about some other kinds of formatting for a variety of documents. In addition, we have included some written communication tips to help you when you use Word for Windows for personal use and for business.

WHERE TO START?

One could start almost anywhere when talking about defining styles and templates, but considering that many of us are hoping at this printing to recover from a recession, let's work about that all-important resume. Word's capabilities help you to construct the best possible resume, without having to pay a professional typesetter.

Styles for Your Resume

Everyone needs to keep their resumes up-to-date. You never know when that "once-in-a-lifetime" opportunity will occur. Even if you are happily married to your job, you should still take take a couple of hours to construct your resume. If anything does happen, you've got a place to start. After you finish the resume, use the formatting you've learned about to construct a letter of interest on your own personal letterhead stationery.

Getting Started

Start at the beginning. In this exercise, you will put your name, address, and phone number in the header, and define two heading styles, and a body style. Sound too simple? Well, your resume should be simple. For most professions, managers are looking for simple but complete resumes that point out your skills. However, your resume also points out certain organizational and written communication skills that are just as important as any other. Too often, resumes are "trashed" because the applicant either tried too hard or not hard enough to submit the right kind of resume. The resume template is included on the disk; however you might want to try defining it yourself and making some changes as you go.

Follow these steps to build a resume template.

1. From the File menu, choose **New** (**Alt-F, N, N**).

   Word displays the New dialog box, which shows defaults of the Normal template and document.

2. Choose **OK**.

   Word opens a document named **Document2**.

3. Save the document with a name you choose. Use the .DOT extension.

4. From the View menu, choose **Header/Footer** (**Alt- V, H**).

   Word opens the **Header** pane.

5. In the header pane, type your name, address, and phone number on separate lines.

6. Select all four lines and, from the ribbon, apply the **Modern** font and point size you like. Choose **B** for bold, and center the text.

7. Select the last line, and from the Format menu, choose **Border** (**Alt-F, B**) and apply the border and line options as shown below, and choose **OK**.

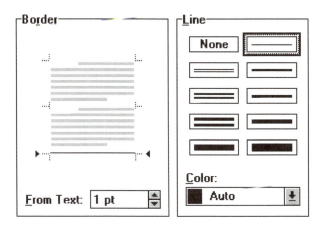

Figure 6.7

8. Close the Header box.

   Remember, you will not see the header when you work in Normal view, but you can see how it looks in Page Layout view.

9. At the insertion point, which is still on line one of the document, type **Career Summary**.

10. Select the line of text, from the Format menu (**Alt-T, P**), choose **Character** and give it the attributes shown below.

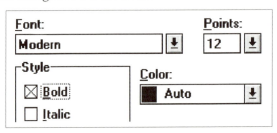

Figure 6.8

11. Select the line again, from the Format menu, choose **Paragraph** (**Alt-T, P**) and apply the styles illustrated in Figure 6.9.

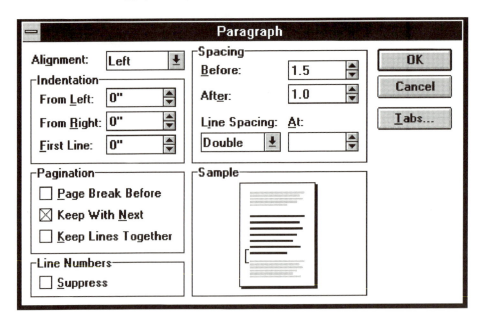

Figure 6.9

12. Define this line as a style, called Heading 1.

If you know that your resume will be only one page, then choosing Keep With Next is not important, since this feature prevents a page break between the heading and text. However, if your resume will be two pages, then select this formatting. (Oh, you heard a resume should never be more than one page? Well, that depends on how long you've been working. Some resume developers allow one page for every 10 years of service.)

N O T E

13. Using the same principles you have been applying in these exercises, choose a level-2 heading for the names of companies where you worked, your titles, and the dates you were employed.

14. Type three lines of text below Career Summary (use the summary of your own career).

15. Select the text and format it with a font and point size that you like from the ribbon. Then, choose from the Format menu **Paragraph** (**Alt-T, P**), and apply the formatting shown in Figure 6.10.

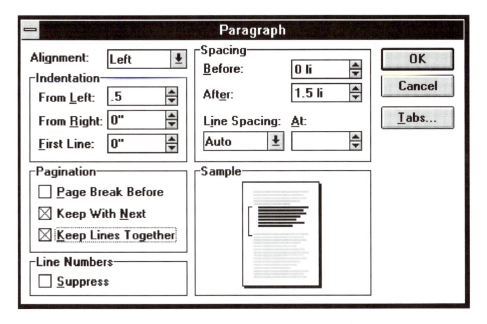

Figure 6.10

Now continue to choose and refine formatting for your resume. Keep it simple. Never use more than two fonts and two or three character formats. No one will be impressed by your knowledge of how many styles you can apply to your resume.

When you finish, define the styles and save the file as a template.

SUMMARY

Chapters 5 and 6 have used hands-on exercises to let you practice formatting documents and shown you how to use your existing documents to create document templates, a powerful time-saving feature that makes you work easier. The following chapters explain some of the more advanced features of Word.

CHAPTER 7

GENERATING TABLES
OF CONTENTS AND INDEXES

This chapter describes how to:

- *automatically generate tables of contents*

- *generate other types of lists, such as figure lists*

- *format a table of contents*

- *Word to create and format an index*

Tables of contents and indexes are often the most valuable tools you can give your reader. After all, to use information in any document, you have to be able to find it. Word provides the means for you to build very simple or very complex tables of contents and indexes. Even if you split your document into multiple files, you can link the files and still compile these components of your document with ease.

TABLES OF CONTENTS

There are two ways to build tables of contents and other lists:

- generating with headings
- generating with fields

Generating with headings is very simple. Generating with fields requires some thought and work on your part, but Word gives you a great alternative to the old way of compiling the table of contents manually, which leaves room for many errors if you change text or pagination later.

Using either method, there are two main steps that you need to follow:

1. Choose the items you want to appear in the table and apply a style or insert a table of contents field.
2. Generate the table of contents.

Generating with Headings

Generating the table of contents with headings is the simpler of the two methods. To generate a table of contents using headings, you must have applied a heading style to each heading type that you want to include in the document and table of contents. (This also applies to any subheading or caption you want to include.) Word lets you decide how many levels you want to include, and you can use this feature to generate several types of tables. For example, you can include lists such as figures, tables, or photographs in addition to the table of contents.

The following procedure provides the steps for generating a table of contents using headings. If you have not applied heading styles to your document, see Chapters 5 or 6 for information.

1. Make sure you have applied the correct heading styles to all headings in your document.
2. Position the insertion point where you want to include the table of contents in your document (generally, after your title page and before the first chapter or section).
3. Hide any text formatted as hidden by choosing the Show/Hide Paragraph button on the Ribbon.

or

From the Tools menu, choose **Options** (**Alt-O, O**) and then **View**. Then clear the **All** and **Hidden Text** check boxes in the Nonprinting Characters box to ensure correct page numbers.

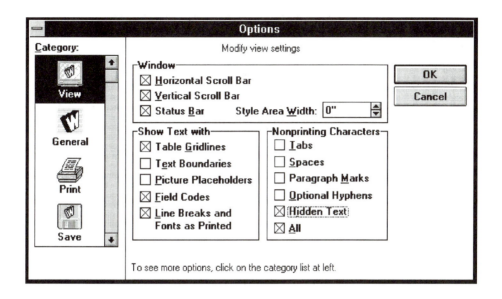

Figure 7.1

4. Display field results (if any) by choosing the **Field Codes** command from the View menu (**Alt-V, C**).

5. From the Insert menu, choose **Table of Contents** (**Alt-I, C**).

   Word displays the Table of Contents dialog box:

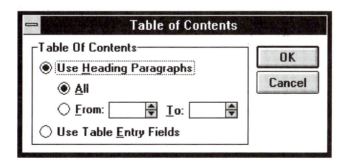

Figure 7.2

6. Enter the number of levels you want to enter, and choose **OK**.

or

If you want to include all levels, select **All** and choose **OK**.

You can halt the process at any time by pressing **Esc**.

N O T E

When Word finishes compiling the table of contents, you can view it where you inserted it.

If you have many levels of headings in your document, you might want to include only headings 1 through 3 or 4 in your table of contents. If you include many levels, for example, 5 or 6, your table of contents may be very long and unattractive. Generally, your reader will get a clear picture of the contents with a few levels.

N O T E

Generating with Fields

Generally, you use fields to generate a table of contents when you have defined your own heading styles or if you want to create a table other than the table of contents. For example, you may want to include a list of figures or a list of graphics, such as tables, illustrations, or photographs. To generate this list, however, you must first insert the fields in the text. You can do this while you are developing your document, or afterward when you are ready to generate your table.

Before You Start

There are two things you need to understand before you begin building a table of contents with field codes.

▪   A *field* is a set of codes that instructs Word to insert information into a document automatically. When you use fields to build a table of contents, you insert codes or "switches" in the items you want to include.

- A *switch* is a code that you insert in a field. When you insert the switch, you tell Word exactly how you want the table of contents or list to be constructed and how you want it to look.

The following table gives descriptions for the switches you will see in the procedures for building tables of contents with fields.

Table 7-1

Switch	*Description*
\o	Creates a table of contents from outline headings with levels within the range you specify. For example, **\o 1-3** means to include heading levels 1 through 3 in the table.
\f	Creates a table from the list identifier you insert to show the type of table to build. For example, **\f i** means you want to create a list of illustrations. (You choose the list identifier, as long as you are consistent in using it.) This chapter includes a list of suggested list identifiers.
\l	Indicates the specific level of the entry you want to include. For example, **tc "Types of Tools" \f f \l 3** means that you want "Types of Tools" to be a level-3 entry in a table of figures.
\h	Tells Word to hide the results of a field. You will not see it on the screen or in print unless you display hidden text.
\d	Indicates that you want Word to use a separator other than the default hyphen between chapter-page numbers. For example, **{toc \s chapter \d ": "** means that Word will print the chapter-page numbers in the table like this: **1:2** (for chapter 1, page 2).

Table 7-1*(continued from previous page)*

Switch	Description
\r	Begins a sequence number in a table with th number you specify. For example, **\r 1** mean that the list or table will begin with 1 as the first item.

The Types of Fields You Use

In the procedures that follow, you will see two types of fields: **tc** and **TOC**.

The **tc** field specifies each item that you want to appear in the table of contents and indicates its location so that Word assigns a page number to each heading. You insert this kind of field by choosing **Field** from the Insert menu, and selecting tc from the list or by typing **tc** followed by the text you want to include in the field code box. You must surround the text with double quotation marks.

The **TOC** field is inserted when you choose Table of Contents from the Insert menu. This field actually causes Word to compile the outline headings or tc fields as a table of contents at the point where you insert the field.

The Update Field Key

When you press the Update Field key (**F9**) in the TOC field, Word updates the table of contents. If you do not press this key when you add entries to update the table of contents, then Word does not recognize the addition.

Creating a Table of Contents Using Fields

Follow these steps to insert fields and create a table of contents.

1. If hidden text is not displayed on the ribbon, click the Show\Hide Paragraph button to make hidden text visible.

   or

   From the Tools menu, choose **Options (Alt-O, O)**.

In the View category, select the **Hidden Text** check box, and choose **OK**.

2. Position the insertion point immediately following the text you want to include in the table of contents.

3. Press the Insert Field key (**Ctrl-F9**).

   Word inserts the brackets in which you enter the text.

4. Type the letters **tc**, a **space**, and then the text you want to insert as the table entry surrounded by double quotes, for example, **tc "Generating with Fields"**.

5. Repeat Steps 2 through 4 for each entry you want to include in the table of contents.

6. Position the insertion point where you want to insert the table of contents in your document.

7. Clear any hidden text by choosing the Show/Hide Paragraph button on the ribbon.

   or

   From the Tools menu, choose **Options** (**Alt-O, O**) and then **View**. Then clear the **All** and **Hidden Text** check boxes in the **Nonprinting Characters** box and click **OK**.

8. Display field results (if any) by choosing the **Field Codes** command from the View menu (**Alt-V, C**). (If they are already displayed, you don't need to do this.)

9. From the Insert menu, choose **Table of Contents** (**Alt-I, C**).

   Word displays the Table of Contents dialog box.

10. Select **Use Table Entry Fields**.

11. Choose **OK**.

You can halt the process at any time by pressing **Esc**. When Word finishes compiling the table of contents, you can view it.

Inserting Fields to Build a Table of Contents

You can insert table of contents entries by pressing the Insert Field key (**Ctrl-F9**) and typing **toc** and **\f** to let Word know that you are using fields instead of headings. While you have the insertion point in the TOC field, press the Update Field key (**F9**).

If you are working in an outline, you build a table of contents using field codes with the levels 1 through 3 outline headings. To do this, press the Insert Field key (**Ctrl-F9**). Then, type **toc \o** and the level in the TOC field like this:

toc \o 1-3

Press **F9** to update the field.

When you generate the table of contents, Word compiles it based on these levels in the fields.

If you compile the table of contents with the Insert Field key, be sure you clear the display of field codes and hidden text before you press F9. Otherwise, your pagination may not be correct.

N O T E

Creating Sublevels with Fields

If you choose to use fields for designating table of contents entries, you can assign the levels that you want to headings, rather than have Word automatically assign the levels. When you use the heading styles to create the table of contents, Word looks for the level 1 headings and places the level 2 under the level 1. Then it places the level 3 under the level 2 and so on. If you want to use this feature, you indicate the level of the heading by adding a number from 1 to 8 in the table of contents field. Follow these steps to create a table of contents using fields.

1. On the ribbon, click the Show\Hide Paragraph button to show hidden text.

   or

   From the Tools menu, choose **Options (Alt-O, O)**.

   In the View category, select the **Hidden Text** check box, and choose **OK**.

2. Position the insertion point immediately following the text you want to include in the table of contents.

3. Press the Insert Field key (**Ctrl-F9**).

   Word inserts the brackets in which you enter the text.

4. Type the letters **tc**, a space, the text you want to insert as the table entry surrounded by double quotes, **\l** (a backslash and letter l), and a **number** from 1 to 8 , like this:

   tc "Generating with Fields" \l 3

You then generate the table of contents by following steps 5 through 11 in the procedure under "Creating a Table of Contents Using Fields" earlier in this chapter.

When you generate the table of contents, Word assigns the appropriate sublevel based on the number in the field.

Generating Other Tables and Lists

This is a particularly powerful feature. Some packages allow you to generate a table of contents, but if you want to generate other lists, you're on your own. In long documents, it is very time-consuming to type every list you want your reader to have as reference.

You can generate other kinds of tables, including lists of figures, photographs, or any other items you want to include. However, there are a few more steps involved. You have to create list identifiers so that Word will know which items to include in the table when you generate it. Read the following section to learn about list identifiers.

Always generate all tables and lists before you generate the final table of contents. That way, your table of contents can include other lists and tables as entries.

N O T E

Using List Identifiers in Fields

A *list identifier* is a set of characters that you include in the fields that Word uses to generate a table. Generally, you use the list identifier when you want to generate a table that includes more than just headers in the text.

Follow these steps to add list identifiers to fields.

1. On the ribbon, click the Show\Hide Paragraph button to show hidden text.

   or

   From the Tools menu, choose **Options (Alt-O, O)**.

   In the View category, select the **Hidden Text** check box, and choose **OK**.

2. Position the insertion point immediately following the text you want to include in the table of contents.

3. Press the Insert Field key (**Ctrl-F9**). Word inserts the brackets in which you enter the text.

4. Type the letters **tc**, a space, the text you want to insert as the table entry surrounded by double quotes, a space, \f, a space, and a list identifier. This is an example:

   tc "Generating with Fields" \f f

   In this example, the last **f** is a suggested list identifier for figures. See the following section in this chapter for more information about suggested characters.

5. Clear any text formatted as hidden by choosing the Show/Hide Paragraph button on the ribbon.

   or

   From the Tools menu, choose **Options** (**Alt-O, O**) and then **View**. Then clear the **All** and **Hidden Text** check boxes in the **Nonprinting Characters** box.

6. Insert a toc field at the place where you will generate the table of contents. Include the /f plus the list identifier you used in step 4, like this: {toc \f f}.

7. Position the insertion point in the toc field.

8. Clear hidden text and field codes.

9. With the insertion point in the toc field, press the Update Field key (f9).

Suggested Characters for List Identifiers

Word allows you to use any character you want as a list identifier. However, because creating a table is a complex task, it will be easier if you use an identifier that is meaningful for the type of table you create. You can use only one character, and using a letter probably the most logical choice.

N O T E Although you use the Table of Contents command to generate tables and lists other than the actual table of contents, you can name the table or list anything you want. When Word generates the table, it does not name it. You simply add the heading, such as **List of Figures**, on a line above where you want to insert the list or table.

The following table suggests list identifiers for different types of tables you might generate. The important thing to remember is that **you must not mix the identifiers**. If you do, you may end up with an item in a list in which it does not belong.

Table 7-2

For this list type...	Use this list identifier...
Authorities	A
Appendixes	E
Charts/Graphs	G
Contents	C
Drawings	D
Figures	F
Illustrations	I
Lists	L
Notes	N
Photos/Pictures	P
Tables	T
Tips	S
Warnings	W

Occasionally, you may have an item that you want to include in more than one list. In that case, you need to create a table of contents field for each list in which you want the item to appear. For example, if you want an illustration number to appear in a table of figures and in the table of contents, you need to put both of the following fields after the text that will be in the two lists:

{tc \f \i}

{tc \f \f}

Although it may seem a little complicated, you can save yourself hours of time and trouble in a long and complex document by using the table of contents fields to generate lists and tables.

SHOWING CHAPTER AND PAGE NUMBERS IN A TABLE OF CONTENTS

Word offers chapter-page numbering, which is often one of the deciding factors managers use for choosing Word for use in a corporate environment. Authors who write documents with multiple chapters, such as most technical documentation, require the feature if they do not want to number pages sequentially. See **Chapter 2, "Setting Up a Word Document"** for more information about numbering pages in chapters.

If you have set up your document so that each chapter has a chapter-page number, such as 1-1 for Chapter 1 and 2-1 for Chapter 2, then it is very important that your table of contents or any other table shows this numbering scheme.

Follow these steps to generate your table of contents if you have set up chapter-page numbers in your document.

1. Insert entries for your table of contents in your document. Use header styles, or fields, as described earlier in this chapter.

2. For each chapter, position the insertion point at the end of the chapter.

3. From the Insert menu, choose **Break (Alt-I, B)**.

4. Under **Section Break**, choose any options you want (if you haven't already).

5. Choose **OK**.

6. For each chapter, from the Insert menu, choose **Page Numbers (Alt-I, U)**.

Word displays the Page Numbers dialog box.

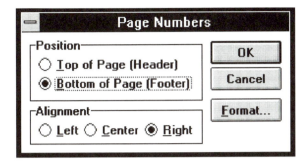

Figure 7.3

7. Select **Format**, then select **Start At** and type or select the number **1**. (Word enters **1** as the default starting page number.)

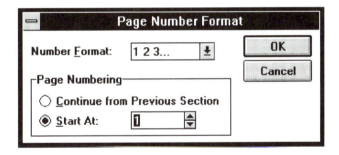

Figure 7.4

8. Choose **OK** twice to close both dialog boxes.

   If you have inserted headers, footers, or both in your document, Word asks if you want to replace the existing header or footer with page numbers. Choose **No**.

9. Position the insertion point at the beginning of the first chapter, and press the Insert Field key (**Ctrl-F9**).

   Word inserts the field characters.

10. In the field, type **seq**, a space, a **sequence name**, a space, and **\h** like this:

    {seq chapter \h}

    (Typing **\h** hides the result of the field.)

11. With the insertion point in the field, press the Update Field key (**F9**).

Whenever you press F9 to update the SEQ field, Word no longer displays the field on the screen. If you want to see the SEQ codes, choose Field Codes from the View menu (Alt-V, C) at any time.

N O T E

12. Repeat steps 9 through 11 for each chapter of your document.

    or

    Copy the field and insert it at the beginning of each chapter.

13. Position the insertion point where you want to insert the table of contents (usually before the first chapter), and press the Insert field key (**Ctrl-F9**).

14. Do one of the following:

    Type **toc \s** *SequenceName*, for example, **toc \s chapter**, if you created entries using heading styles.

    or

    Type **toc \f \s** *SequenceName*, for example, **toc \f \s chapter**, if you created entries using fields.

15. Position the insertion point at the table of contents field.

16. Clear any hidden text by choosing the Show/Hide Paragraph button on the ribbon.

    or

    From the Tools menu, choose **Options** (**Alt-O, O**) and then **View**. Then clear the **All** and **Hidden Text** check boxes in the **Nonprinting Characters box**.

17. Display field results (if any) by choosing the **Field Codes** command from the View menu (**Alt-V, C**).

18. With the insertion point in the table of contents field, press the Update Field key (**F9**).

Now, when you generate the table of contents (or an index), you will see the chapter and page number for each entry.

Changing the Default Separator

Word uses the hyphen as the default separator between the chapter and page number, for example 2-1. However you can change the separator to a character that you choose. To change the separator, add a **\d** switch to the table of contents field, followed by the character(s) you choose and enclose the character in double quotation marks. Use the following example as a guide:

{toc \s chapter \d ".".}

Creating a List of Figures with Consecutive Numbers

Have you ever had to go back in your document and add more information and illustrations? If you haven't, then congratulations. You are a rare find. If you have, then you probably know how frustrating it can be to renumber the items and then redo the tables and lists.

Keeping the caption numbers consecutive usually means you have to renumber all figures by hand, one at a time, from where you added a figure to the end of the chapter or document. Word makes it easy for you to apply automatic numbering to your figures, so you don't have to worry about it. The program renumbers all captions in sequence each time you update or change one.

Follow these steps to apply automatic numbering to captions for any items you want to number consecutively:

1. From the View menu, choose **Field Codes** (**Alt-V, C**).

    Word displays all field codes in the document.

2. Position the insertion point in **each** caption you want to number, press the Insert Field key (**Ctrl-F9**), and type **seq SequenceName**.

    For example, If you wanted the caption for your first figure to be

    Figure 1. Mike and Vicky's All-Purpose Widget Splicer, you would enter:

    Figure {seq figure}. Mike and Vicky's All-Purpose Widget Splicer.

    The field looks like this:

    Figure 1. Mike and Vicky's All-Purpose Widget Splicer.

3. For each field, position the insertion point in the field, and press the Update Field key (**F9**).

   Now, Word will update the caption numbers automatically throughout your chapter.

You can have Word add these captions in a table of contents that will give you a list of figures. To do this, you apply heading styles to the captions. Make sure you use a heading style that you are *not* using anywhere else in the document. Then, when you generate the table of contents, make sure you enter the same number in both the From and To boxes in the Table of Contents dialog box.

You can also compile a list of figures using the fields. Read the following section to learn how.

Using Fields to Create a List of Figures

This is the procedure to use if you do not want Word to increment each figure number by 1. You would probably use this procedure if you have several chapters in one Word document, and you want figure captions to have numbering you choose.

After you apply the automatic numbering to captions using fields, you can generate your list of figures. In this instance, you would *not* need to define and apply a heading style to the captions (as was explained in the previous section). However, you can apply a style to your figure captions if you want.

In this procedure, you add the **\r** switch to begin the sequence with a number that you specify; for example, adding **\r 1** causes the figure captions to begin with the number 1. Afterward, you maintain the proper sequencing by applying the **\c** switch. The **\c** switch does not increment the value.

Follow these steps to number captions in sequence and create a list of figures using fields:

1. From the View menu, choose **Field Codes (Alt-V, C)**.

   Word displays all field codes in the document.

2. Position the insertion point in **each** caption you want to number, press the Insert Field key (**Ctrl-F9**), and type **seq SequenceName**.

   For example, If you wanted the caption for your first figure to be **Figure 1. Mike and Vicky's All-Purpose Widget Splicer for Windows**, you would insert the following field:

Figure {seq figure \r 1}. Mike and Vicky's All-Purpose Widget Splicer for Windows. {tc "Figure {seq figure \c}. Mike and Vicky's All-Purpose Widget Splicer for Windows" \f f}

Remember to use the field code feature for each field; do not add the brackets manually.

N O T E

3. For *each* field in the sequence of fields, position the insertion point in the field, and press the Update Field key (**F9**).

4. Use fields to create table of contents entries, as explained in "Generating with Fields" earlier in this chapter.

5. In the first field where you want to begin numbering the captions, add a sequence field that contains the **\r** switch.

In the following example, the figure caption is in a table of contents field with a sequence field added. The figure will be the first in a List of Figures. The table of contents will be generated using fields, not headings.

You can update fields automatically by selecting Update Fields in the options dialog box from the Print dialog box. (**Alt-F, P**, **Alt-O,U**).

SHORT CUT

{tc "Figure {seq figure \r 1}. Mike and Vicky's All-Purpose Widget Splicer for Windows." \f f}

The first caption now looks similar to:

Figure {seq figure}. Mike and Vicky's All-Purpose Widget Splicer for Windows.{tc "Figure {seq figure \r 1}. Mike and Vicky's All-Purpose Widget Splicer for Windows." \f f}

6. Go to the second figure (and then all figures that follow), and add the **\c** switch to maintain correct numbering for the remainder of the figures.

The **c** switch prevents the SEQ field from incrementing by 1 each time you update. (This is most useful if you want to number figures by chapter and figure number, covered further after this procedure.)

The second figure caption field should now look like this:

Figure {seq figure}. Mike and Vicky's All-Purpose Widget Splicer for Windows. {tc "Figure {seq figure \c}. Mike and Vicky's All-Purpose Widget Splicer for Windows." \f f}

7. Select the entire document (**Ctrl-5 on the keypad**), and press the Update Field key (**F9**).

8. Position the insertion point where you want to place the List of Figures, and press the **Insert Field** key (**Ctrl-F9**).

9. Type **toc \f** and the list indicator. If your list indicator is **f**, for example, your table of contents field code looks like this:

    {toc \f f}

10. Hide any text formatted as hidden by choosing the Show/Hide Paragraph button on the ribbon.

    or

    From the Tools menu, choose **Options** (**Alt-O, O**) and then **View**. Then clear the **All** and **Hidden Text** check boxes in the **Nonprinting Characters** box.

11. Display field results by choosing the **Field Codes** command from the View menu (**Alt-V, C**).

12. Position the insertion point in the table of contents field, and press the Update Field key (**F9**).

    Word generates the list.

List with Chapter-Figure Numbers

If you use chapter-page numbers in your document, then you need to show the chapter-figure numbering construction in your lists and tables also. Follow these steps to create figure captions with chapter-figure numbers.

1. Apply section breaks (**Alt-I, B**) to each section in the document.

2. Start the page numbering at 1 in each section by choosing **Page Numbers** from the Insert menu (**Alt-I, U**), choosing the **Format** button, and typing **1** in the **Start At** box.

3. Insert a SEQ field containing an identifier, for example, **{seq chapter}**, for each section.

The entry for the *first* figure caption should look like this:

Figure {seq chapter \c}-{seq figure \r 1}. A Personal Computer Monitor {tc "Figure {seq chapter \c}-{seq figure \c}. A Personal Computer Monitor." \f f}

Use the following caption for figures that follow Figure 1. Notice that the **\r1** option is the difference between the first and the following figure captions.

Figure {seq chapter \c}-{seq figure}. A Personal Computer Monitor {tc "Figure {seq chapter \c}-{seq figure \c}. A Personal Computer Monitor." \f f}

When you create the list of figures for your document with chapter-page numbers, use this TOC field:

{toc \f f \s chapter}

Updating Your Table of Contents

You can generate a table of contents any time you want while working in a Word document. If you add information to your document after you generate the table of contents, you can run it again, and Word will replace the current table of contents with the updated version. Even if you add some text without a new heading, generate the table of contents again to ensure correct page numbering.

Follow the instructions earlier in this chapter for generating with heading styles or field codes to update the table of contents. When Word asks if you want to replace the existing table of contents, choose **Yes** to replace or **No** to cancel.

Changing the Look of the Table of Contents

Word formats the table of contents automatically, and uses the built-in style for up to eight levels, no matter what style you apply to the text in your document. However, you can change the way the table looks two ways:

- Redefining the standard style
- Reformatting after compiling

The standard table of contents looks like this:

Tables of Contents and Indexes....................1
    Generating with Headings....................1
    Generating with Fields....................4
        Inserting Fields to Build a Table of Contents....................5
    Creating Sublevels with Fields....................6
    Generating Other Tables and Lists....................8
        Using List Identifiers in Fields....................8
        Suggested Characters for List Identifiers....................10
Showing Chapter and Page Numbers in a Table of Contents....................11
        Changing the Default Separator....................15
    Creating a List of Figures with Consecutive Numbers....................15

Figure 7.5

This style is based on the Normal paragraph styles with

- a 0.5 indent on the right
- a left-aligned tab at 5.75 inches
- dot leaders
- a right-aligned tab at 6.0 inches

Redefining the Standard Style

The best way to change the table of contents formatting is to redefine the styles, because if you merely apply a new format to the table of contents after you generate it, Word will throw out the new formatting when you compile it again. (However, if you want to apply formatting directly to the compiled table of contents, simply select the text and apply styles using the paragraph and character formatting from the Format menu or from the ribbon.)

You redefine Word's standard table of contents style by using the same formatting you use to define other styles. To redefine the table of contents style, follow these steps.

1. Build and generate your table of contents or other table as described earlier in this chapter.

2. Apply and define the character and paragraph formatting to the table, using commands and options from the Format menu.

   See Chapter 6 for more information about defining styles.

3. From the File menu, choose **Save All**.

Now, each time you generate a table of contents or other table that you define, Word applies that style to it.

INDEXES

Word's indexing feature makes it easy for you to compile a simple main-entry index or a complex one with multiple levels of entries. When creating an index, you need to have a draft of your document, although it does not have to be complete. Some authors add index entries as they develop the draft. The choice is yours, but many authors prefer to have the document nearly complete before starting. That way, they don't have to remember how they listed an entry in yesterday's version.

Single-Level Entries

An index with single-level entries shows only main entries from the text, with no indented subentries. This type is the simplest index to build. For many documents, however, the single-level index will not be enough, and you will need to include a multiple-entry index.

Multiple-Level Entries

A multiple-level index is probably more useful in any long document. This type of index is a little more complicated to build in Word and requires more thought. You will need to plan what to index, and you will probably have to make some notes as you add entries.

Inserting Index Entries

Before you generate the index in Word, you need to insert the entries in the text. You have two options for inserting the entries:

- selecting text (words or phrases) in the document
- typing the entries next to the text you want to index

You can have a maximum of 64 characters in any index entry.

If you choose to type entries to index near the text rather than select the text itself for an entry, make sure you type the entry next to the topic to index. Otherwise, the typed entry may fall on the next page, and the page numbers will not be correct in the index.

N O T E

Follow these steps to insert entries in the text:

1. Select the text in the document that you want to appear as an index entry.

   or

   Position the insertion point where you want to type the index entry.

2. From the Insert menu, choose Index Entry (**Alt-I, E**).

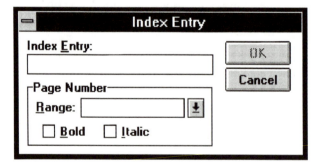

Figure 7.6

Word displays the Index Entry dialog box. If you chose to make existing text an entry, the selected text appears in the Index Entry box, like this:

Index Entry:

Indexing a document

If you did not select text, the Index Entry box is clear.

3. In the **Index Entry** box, type an entry or edit the existing entry.

4. If you want, you can choose to have the page number, bold, italic, or both.

5. If you want to show a range of pages for an entry, enter or select a bookmark name. See "Indicating a Range of Pages" following this procedure for more information.

6. Choose **OK**.

   Word will include the entry in the index when the index is generated.

Indicating a Range of Pages

If a subject in your document is discussed over a range of pages, you can show that range in the index. For example, a topic may appear on pages 3 through 5. Follow these steps to show the range.

1. Select the text you want to cover in the index entry.

2. From the Insert menu, choose **Bookmark** (**Alt-I, M**).

   Word displays the Bookmark dialog box.

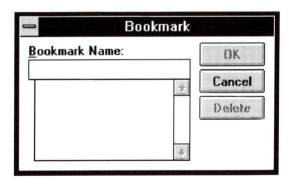

Figure 7.7

3. Enter a name for the bookmark. The name must start with a letter and can be a maximum of 20 characters. Do not enter spaces in the name.

4. Choose **OK**.

5. From the Insert menu, choose **Index Entry** (**Alt-I, E**).

6. Type the index entry.

    or

    Accept the entry in the Index Entry box.

7. In the **Range** box under Page Number, type or select the name of the bookmark.

8. Choose **OK**.

Creating Subentries

To create subentries, you have to type text instead of selecting it. Any entry can have to up seven subentries, but two or three is most common and most readable, especially if you choose to have a multiple-column index.

Follow these steps to create index subentries.

1. Position the insertion point where you want to type the index entry.

2. From the Insert menu, choose **Index Entry** (**Alt-I, E**).

    Word displays the Index Entry dialog box.

3. Type the main entry, followed by a colon. Then type each subentry, each separated by a colon like this:

    Cats:Short-Haired:Devon Rex

4. Choose **OK**.

Each time you add different subentries to a main entry, you must enter the main entry again. For example, to have index entries that look like the following:

Cats

> Long-Haired 5
>> Himalayan 7
>> Norwegian Forest 9
>> Persian 4
> Poorly Behaved 16
>> Bastet Stevens-Lottridge 17
>> Xanadu Stevens-Lottridge 19
> Short-Haired 11
>> Devon Rex 13
>> Siamese 14

You need to type each of these entries beside the text where they appear in the document:

Cats:Long-Haired:Himalayan
Cats:Long-Haired:Norwegian Forest
Cats:Long-Haired:Persian
Cats:Poorly Behaved:Bastet Stevens-Lottridge
Cats:Poorly Behaved:Xanadu Stevens-Lottridge
Cats:Short-Haired:Devon Rex
Cats:Short-Haired:Siamese

To have a main entry with no page numbers, do not type an index entry for the main entry, but do include the main entry with any subentries. In the examples above, Word "sees" the main entry with subentries, and automatically places the main entry on a line with no page number.

N O T E

Following an Entry with Text Instead of a Page Number

Sometimes you may need to cross-reference an entry with "See reference" or "See also reference" instead of a page number.

Follow these steps to add text after an entry.

1. Select the text you want to index.

   or

   Position the insertion point where you want to create the entry.

2. From the Insert menu, choose **Field** (**Alt-I, D**).

   Word displays the Field dialog box.

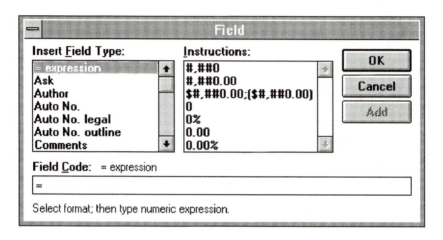

Figure 7.8

3. In the Insert Field Type box, select **Index Entry**.

   Word applies the field name **xe** automatically to the Field Code box, like this:

   Field Code: XE text [switches]

xe

4. In the Field Code box, after xe, type the following things in this order:

   ■ the index entry in double quotation marks

   ■ the switch \t, with a space before and after

   ■ the text to include in double quotation marks

For example, to have this entry in the index:

Felines, see Cats

Make the field code look like this:

{xe "Felines" \t "see Cats"}

5. Choose **OK**.

In a lot of indexes, the "see" references appear in italic type. To do this, add the **\i** switch after the last double quotation mark like this:

{xe "Felines" \t "see Cats" \i}

Showing Chapter-Page Numbers in an Index

If you set up your document so that you have chapter- page numbers, then you need to show those page numbers in the index. This procedure incorporates use of the SEQ field, which you also use to show chapter-page numbers in the table of contents (described earlier in this chapter).

Follow these steps to show chapter-page numbers in the index:

1. Insert index entries where you want them your document.

2. Go to each chapter, position the insertion point at the end of the chapter, and from the Insert menu, choose **Break** (**Alt-I, B**).

    Word displays the Break dialog box:

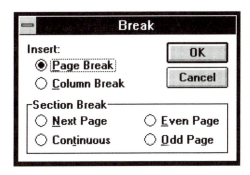

Figure 7.9

3. Under Section Break, choose the option you want, and choose **OK**.
4. From the Insert menu,

   a. Choose **Page Numbers (Alt-I, U)**.

   b. Choose **Format**.

   c. Select **Start At**.

   d. type **1**.

5. Choose **OK** twice to close both boxes.

   If you have added headers and footers in your document, Word asks if you want to replace the existing header or footer with page numbers. Choose **No**.

6. Position the insertion point at the beginning of the first chapter and press the Insert Field key (**Ctrl-F9**).

7. Between the field characters ({}),type **seq** followed by a space, a sequence name, another space and the **\h** switch like this:

   seq chapter \h

   The \h switch hides the result of the field. Word does not display it in the document text.

8. With the insertion point in the field, press the Update Field key (**F9**).

   Word hides the SEQ field, and you no longer see it on the screen. If you want to view the SEQ fields, choose Field Codes from the View menu.

9. Repeat steps 6 through 8 for each chapter.

   or

   Copy the field and insert it at the beginning of each chapter.

10. Position the insertion point at the end of the text in the document and press the Insert Field key (**Ctrl-F9**).

11. Between the field characters, type **index** followed by a space, the **\s** switch, another space, and the sequence name like this:

    index \s chapter

12. Position the insertion point inside the index field.

13. To ensure accurate page numbers, make sure the field codes are not displayed.

    Click the Show\Hide Paragraph button on the ribbon.

or

From the Tools menu, choose **Options** (**Alt-O, O**) and then **View**. Then clear the **All** and **Hidden Text** check boxes in the Nonprinting Characters box.

14. With the insertion point in the Index field, press the Update Field key (**F9**).

    When you generate the index, all index entries will have the chapter and page number.

Generating the Index

Follow these steps to generate an index so you can include it in your document.

1. Insert all index entries.

2. Clear hidden text and field codes.

3. From the insert menu, choose **Index** (**Alt-I, I**).

4. Select a format:

   If you want to display subentries below the main entry, select the Normal Index option button.

5. If you want a blank line or letter separationg alphabetic sections of your index, in the Heading Separator box, choose Blank Line or Letter.

6. Choose **OK**.

You can cancel the index generation any time by pressing ESC.

Changing the Index Format

As with the table of contents, Word formats the index automatically when you generate it. However, you can change the formatting to make it look like you want.

You redefine Word's standard index style the same way you change the table of contents style. To redefine the index style, follow these steps.

1. Build and generate your index.

2. Apply and define the character and paragraph formatting to the index, using commands and options from the Format menu.

See Chapter 6 for more information about defining styles.

3. From the File menu, choose **Save All**.

Now, each time you generate an index, Word applies that style to it.

SUMMARY

In this chapter, you have learned how to make your Word documents more valuable to your readers by generating and adding tables of contents, lists of figures and tables, and indexes. In the chapters that follow, you will learn how to add graphic elements, such as graphs and drawings, to your documents.

USING MICROSOFT DRAW AND WORDART

D raw is a graphical drawing program that only runs inside of Word. With Draw, you can create diagrams and pictures to enhance your text documents. This chapter explains how you can use Draw to:

- *create many common geometric shapes*

- *fill those shapes with patterns*

- *rotate, flip, or resize those drawings*

- *import picture files created by other applications into your Word document, and edit the converted pictures*

OVERVIEW OF MICROSOFT DRAW

Draw is an **embedded application**. You can invoke Draw only within Word, and you can put the drawings you create with Draw only into a Word document. Draw is not as advanced as some of the more sophisticated drawing packages, but chances are you'll find it more than adequate for most of your basic needs.

As an embedded application, Draw also provides you with a nice feature: you can double-click a drawing in your Word documents, which invokes Draw on the drawing, allowing you to edit and change graphic images in your Word documents quite easily. When you finish updating the drawing, you can have Word automatically update the drawing in the document.

Draw does not create a separate graphics file for your drawing. All output from Draw is stored in your main document. This means that you cannot save a drawing as file, the drawing must be saved in a Word document. If you want to create a drawing for use in many documents, you should create a document that consists only of that drawing, then you can insert that document in another document whenever you want to include the image.

Other File Formats

You can import other files into Draw. The formats supported depend on the file filters that you have installed, so if you're not sure if your file format is supported, see if you can successfully import the file into Draw. Remember, even if you can import the file, and edit it, you can save it only as a Word document. You cannot save the file back out in its original format. Think of this process as a "one way street"—you can import a file into Draw, edit the file, and save the drawing in your Word document, but you cannot save the edited results back into your original picture file.

STARTING THE DRAW PROGRAM

You must be running Word and have a document open to use the Draw program. There are two ways to invoke Draw from Word.

1. Open a document.
2. From the Insert menu, choose **Object** (**Alt-I, O**).

   Word displays the Object dialog box.

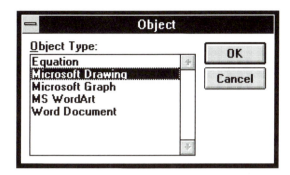

Figure 8.1

3. Select **Microsoft Drawing** and choose **OK**.

The other way to open the program is to double-click on an existing Draw graphic.

Word displays the Microsoft Draw work area, with the name of document in which you are working displayed across the top.(If you clicked on an existing Draw graphic, you will see the graphic in the work area.)

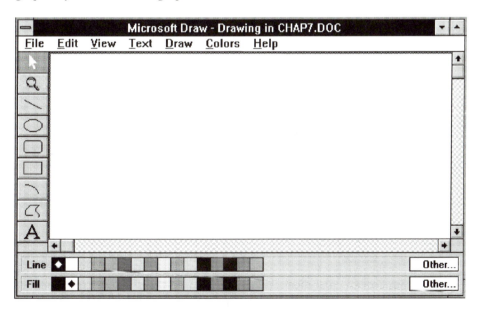

Figure 8.2

Now you can create or work on the graphic you need.

The Drawing Tools and How to Use Them

The vertical line of buttons to the left of the drawing window (as follows) are the tools you use to draw and "paint" objects. Like the different brushes and tools an artist might use, each Draw tool has a unique purpose.

Figure 8.3

To use any drawing tool, you must click on it. The Arrow Tool is the default. Each of the drawing tools is described as follows:

Arrow Tool

Use the Arrow Tool to select items, to drag the selection box, and to move objects.

Zoom Tool

Use the Zoom Tool to enlarge and reduce the view of the graphic. This tool does not enlarge or reduce the graphic itself, only the view.

Follow these steps to zoom in and enlarge the view:

1. Click the object you want to enlarge.
2. From the View menu, choose a view size option of up to 800%.

   The Draw program displays the object and centers it.

   or

1. Select the Zoom Tool.
2. Position the magnifying glass over the object you want to enlarge, and click the mouse button.

   Each time you click the mouse button, the view of the object increases in size. If you started with a Full Size, the first click increases the view to 200%, the second click increases to 400%, and the third to 800%, which is the maximum enlargement.

Follow these instructions to zoom out or reduce the view:

From the View menu, choose a view size. (The minimum is 25%.)

or

1. Select the Zoom Tool.
2. Position the magnifying glass on the drawing, hold down **Shift**, and click the mouse button.

   Each time you click the mouse button, the view of the object decreases in size. If you started with a Full Size, the first click decreases the view to 75%, the second click decreases to 50%, and the third to 25%, which is the maximum reduction.

To return to the Full Size view, choose **Full Size** from the **View** menu (**Alt-V, F**).

Line Tool

Use the Line Tool to draw a straight line in any direction. Follow these steps to draw a simple line:

1. Select the Line Tool.

   The mouse pointer becomes a crosshair.

2. Position the pointer where you want to start the line.

3. Hold down the mouse button and drag the pointer to where you want the line to stop.

If you want to constrain the line to a straight vertical, horizontal, or 45-degree angle, hold down **Shift** while you drag.

N O T E

4. Release the mouse button.

   If you need to delete the line, select it (click it anywhere) and press **Del**. This action deletes only the selected line in a drawing. All unselected lines remain.

Ellipse/Circle Tool

Use the Ellipse/Circle Tool to draw an ellipse or a circle. Follow these steps:

1. Select the Ellipse/Circle Tool.

   The mouse pointer becomes a crosshair.

2. To draw an ellipse:

   ■ Position the pointer where you want to start.

   ■ Hold down the mouse button and drag diagonally in any direction.

3. To draw a circle:

   ■ Position the pointer where you want to start.

   ■ Hold down **Shift** while you hold down the mouse button and drag diagonally in any direction.

Holding down **Shift** is what causes the circle to have the same height and width.

N O T E

Rounded Rectangle/Square Tool

Use the Rounded Rectangle/Square Tool to draw a rectangle or a square with rounded corners. Follow these steps to draw a rounded rectangle or a square:

1. Select the Rounded Rectangle/Square Tool.

    The mouse pointer becomes a crosshair.

2. To draw a rectangle with rounded corners:

    ■ Position the pointer where you want to start.

    ■ Hold down the mouse button and drag diagonally in any direction.

3. To draw a square:

    ■ Position the pointer where you want to start.

    ■ Hold down **Shift** while you hold down the mouse button and drag diagonally in any direction.

Holding down **Shift** is what causes the square to have the same height and width.

N O T E

Rectangle/Square Tool

Use the Rectangle/Square Tool to draw a rectangle or a square. Follow these steps to draw a rectangle or a square:

1. Select the Rectangle/Square Tool.

    The mouse pointer becomes a crosshair.

2. To draw a rectangle:

    ■ Position the pointer where you want to start.

    ■ Hold down the mouse button and drag diagonally in any direction.

3. To draw a square:

    1. Position the pointer where you want to start.

    2. Hold down **Shift** while you hold down the mouse button and drag diagonally in any direction.

Holding down Shift is what causes the square to have the same height and width.

N O T E

Arc Tool

Use the Arc Tool to draw an arc, a pie wedge (a "filled" arc), a circular arc or a circular pie wedge. All arcs and pie wedges are 90 degrees at first. You can edit them later to make them less than 90 degrees. Follow these steps to draw an arc or pie wedge:

1. Select the Arc Tool.

2. To draw an arc, make sure the Filled option from the Draw menu is *not* selected.

   or

   To draw a pie wedge, select the **Filled** option from the Draw menu.

3. Position the pointer where you want to begin one end of the arc.

4. Hold down the mouse button and drag to where you want to end the arc.

5. Release the mouse button.

When you draw an ellipse, you can determine the quadrant by the direction you drag. The distance you drag the pointer determines the size of the arc.

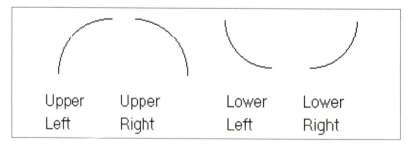

Figure 8.4

It's easy to make an arc into a pie wedge and vice versa. Follow these steps:

1. Select the arc or pie wedge.

2. To change an arc to a pie wedge, choose **Filled** from the Draw menu (**Alt-D, F**).

    or

    To change a pie wedge to an arc, choose **Filled** from the Draw menu, and remove the check mark.

Freeform Tool

Use the Freeform Tool to draw freehand-style objects, polygons (such as pentagons or octagons), or a combination of the two styles. Draw allows you to draw straight and "curved" lines in the same graphic. However, the curved lines are really a lot of short, straight, connected lines that appear to make a curve. Follow these steps to draw a freeform object:

1. Select the Freeform Tool.

    The mouse pointer becomes a crosshair, and then a small pencil icon when you click the left mouse button.

2. Begin drawing.

It's a little difficult sometimes to draw a straight line with the freeform tool. If you don't have a very steady hand, you might want to draw your straight lines with the Line tool, and then select the Freeform tool to draw the curved lines. If you prefer to use the Freeform tool for all of your drawing, however, then use the Show Guides option from the Draw menu (**Alt-D, W**) to help you draw a straighter line.

N O T E

When you finish your drawing and point to another tool, it looks as though you are still drawing a line, even though you don't want to. However, when you click another tool, the unwanted line disappears.

Text Tool

Use the Text Tool to add text to your drawing. A single line can contain a maximum of 255 characters, and is called a *text object*. Any character formatting that you apply affects the entire line, not just one word. If you want to add text with different formatting, you have to create another text object for that text. Follow these steps to use the Text tool:

1. Select the Text tool.

   The mouse pointer becomes an I-beam cursor.

2. Position the cursor where you want to begin the text object, and start entering the text.

N O T E When you press **Enter**, you start a new line, which means that you are creating a new text object. You can move these lines independently of each other, or you can group them to move them together. See "Grouping and Ungrouping Objects" later in this chapter for more information. You can change text formatting from the Text menu. See "Text Menu" later in this chapter for more information about changing text formatting.

Line and Fill Color Palettes

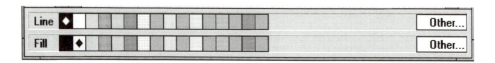

The Line and Fill Color Palettes are below the Draw tools. If you do not see the palettes when you open Draw, choose Show Palette from the Color menu (**Alt-C, P**) Use the Line Color Palette to choose a color for a line, frame, text, the pattern foreground, and the foreground color in a bitmap. Use the Fill Color Palette to choose a color that you want to fill a pattern background and the background color in a bitmap.

You can add color to an object before or after you draw it. When you choose a color, Draw marks it with either a diamond shape or a check mark. The diamond shape indicates the default (preselected) color, which Draw uses until you choose another color. The check mark shows which color you are using currently. If you have selected two or more objects, you will see check marks only in the colors that all the objects share. See "Edit Menu" later in this chapter for more information about selecting more than one object.

Follow these steps to choose a color *before* you begin drawing an object:

1. Select the Arrow tool to ensure that you have not selected any objects in the drawing area. You should not see any selection handles on any of the objects.

2. Point to a color you want on either palette depending on the object (as described in the first paragraph in this topic), and click the mouse button.

   Draw adds a diamond to the color you choose indicating that color is now the selected color.

After you draw an object, follow these steps to choose a color:

1. Select the individual object or group of objects you want to color.

   The colors you are now using have check marks on them. If you have selected several individual objects or a group, you will see check marks on only the colors that all the objects share.

2. Point to a color on either palette depending on the object (as described in the first paragraph in this topic), and click the mouse button.

   The object you selected changes immediately to the selected color, and Draw marks the color with a check mark.

The following table shows how Draw changes color depending on what you select:

Table 8-1

If you...	*Then Draw...*
Select several objects and choose a color from the Line Color palette.	Changes the frame color of only those objects that have frames.
Select objects that have *no* frames and choose a color from the Line Color palette.	Adds frames to all of the objects.
Choose a color from the Fill Color palette.	Changes the fill color of only those objects that are filled.
Choose a color from the Fill Color palette and none of the objects are filled.	Adds fill color to all of them.

EDITING AN EXISTING DRAWING

If you need to make changes to an existing drawing in your document, double-click a picture or object in your document. Word opens the Draw program over your drawing, and you can edit it like you want.

Any changes you make to an imported graphic will be updated only in your Word document—the original picture file will not be updated.

N O T E

MICROSOFT DRAW COMMANDS AND TOOLS

This section explains the different menu options within Draw and the kinds of tasks you can perform with them.

The Menu Bar

This section discusses the different options available in the menu bar. The menu bar appears along the top portion of your Draw window, and contains these menus:

- File
- Edit
- View
- Text
- Draw
- Colors
- Help

File Menu

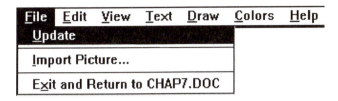

You can use the File menu to:

- Insert your drawing into your Word document (Update)

- Import a drawing prepared by an application other than Microsoft draw (Import Picture...)

- Return to your Word document without inserting your drawing (Exit and Return to <File Name>)

You must save your drawings created in Draw in a Word document, because you cannot save them as stand-alone files.

Updating Your Document   After you finish a drawing, you can add it to the document in which you were working. To update your document and insert your drawing, select Update from the File menu (**Alt-F, U**). Word inserts the drawing in your document at the current cursor position (the location of the insertion point where you opened the Draw program.)

Importing a Drawing   Word lets you import a picture directly from another application without having to use the Clipboard to copy and paste it. However, the picture must come from a bitmapped file (.BMP) or a Windows metafile (.WMF).

   To insert a picture file created by another application, choose Import Picture from the File menu (**Alt-F, I**). Word inserts the picture at the last position of the insertion point in the Word document. Fortunately, Word makes any necessary adjustments to imported pictures automatically. For example, if the drawing is too large to fit on your document page, Word scales the drawing to fit in the area. The program gives you a message to let you know about the scaling Also, if Word cannot match a feature exactly, it substitutes the closest matching feature it can find.

Unfortunately, you may not like some of the other automatic changes, which are these:

■ If the picture was created in an application that had the brush pattern feature, and that feature was used in the drawing, Word changes the brush pattern to solid black. (Only device-independent bitmaps *used as brush patterns* are imported without this change.)

■ Bitmaps become opaque.

■ Hatched patterns become opaque.

Follow these steps to import a picture:

1. From the File menu, choose **Import Picture** (**Alt-F, I**).

   Word displays the Import Picture dialog box:

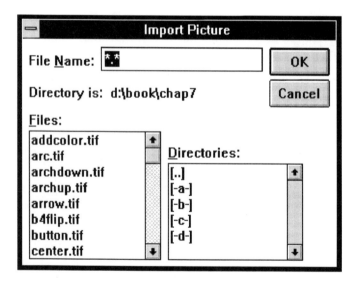

Figure 8.5

2. In the **File Name** box, enter the drive, directory, and file name.

   or

   Select the name of the picture from the **Files** list.

3. Choose **OK** to import the picture.

Returning to the Application   If you simply want to return to your Word document without inserting your drawing, select Exit from the File menu (**Alt-F, X**). If you have not saved your drawing, neither Word nor Draw will save it.

Edit Menu

The Edit menu lets you modify your drawing or undo the effect of the most recent command. Not only can you manipulate objects the same way as text, you can place them "in front" or "in back" of other objects.

Edit	View	Text	Draw
Undo		Ctrl+Z	
Cut		Ctrl+X	
Copy		Ctrl+C	
Paste		Ctrl+V	
Clear		Del	
Select All		Ctrl+A	
Bring to Front		Ctrl+=	
Send to Back		Ctrl+-	
Edit Object		Ctrl+E	

Figure 8.6

Some Basic Editing Concepts   Before you master the editing commands, you need to understand two basic concepts in Microsoft Draw: the Clipboard and selection of objects.

The Clipboard   Whenever you copy something, Draw places it on the Clipboard, which is a temporary holding location for graphics or text. The Cut and Copy commands from the Edit menu take any objects you have selected and move or copy them to the Clipboard. Once you store an object in the Clipboard, you retrieve it by using the Paste command. Objects remain in the Clipboard *only* until you save something else to the Clipboard. Then they are deleted. Remember that only the last item you copied is retrievable for pasting. However, you can *paste* an item from the Clipboard over and over before you *copy* something else to the Clipboard.

While you are in the Draw Program, you *cannot* use the Cut, Copy, and Paste commands from the Word ribbon; however, you can use these shortcut keys:

- Cut (**Alt-E, T**)
- Copy (**Alt-E, C**)
- Paste (**Alt-E, P**)

Selecting One or More Objects   Most of the edit commands expect you to have selected objects prior to invoking the command. For example, invoking a Copy command doesn't make any sense when you don't have anything to copy. You can select objects using one of several methods:

Follow these steps to select a single object:

1. Select the Arrow tool.

2. Position the pointer inside the object you want to select, then click the mouse button.

   or

   Draw a selection rectangle around the object by positioning the pointer outside of any object, holding down the mouse button , and dragging the pointer to create a rectangle that encloses the object.

   When you release the mouse button, the object inside the selection rectangle is selected.

Follow these steps to select multiple objects:

1. Select the Arrow tool.

2. Position the pointer inside the object you want to select, then hold down **Shift** while clicking on each object.

   or

   Draw a selection rectangle around the objects by positioning the pointer outside of any object, holding down the mouse button, and dragging the pointer to create a rectangle that encloses the objects you want to select. When you release the mouse button, any objects inside the selection rectangle are selected.

Figure 8.7 shows three circle objects, with none of the objects selected.

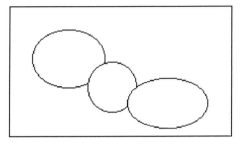

Figure 8.7

Now, suppose you want to select the ellipse. Select the Arrow tool, position the pointer inside the ellipse, and click the mouse button. You'll see *selection handles* appear around the object (the small black boxes). These handles show that the object has been selected, as shown in the following illustration.

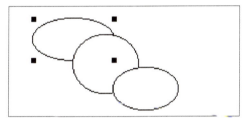

Figure 8.8

Next, suppose you also want to select the middle circle. Position the pointer inside the middle circle, hold down **Shift**, and click. The selection handles for the middle circle appear, and the selection handles for the first circle remain.

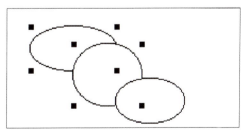

Figure 8.9

Undoing Your Last Change   The **Undo** command (**Alt-E, U**) reverses your most recent action. For example, if you select an object, and then delete it by accident, choose the Undo option to restore your object.

It's *very* important to note that the Undo feature can reverse only your most recent change — for example, if you accidentally delete an object, then edit something using another option, you *cannot* choose Undo twice to restore the deleted object.

N O T E

Cutting Objects to the Clipboard   The Cut command removes all *selected* objects from the drawing and puts them in the Clipboard. Follow these steps to cut an object to the Clipboard:

1. Click the Arrow tool.
2. Select the objects you want to cut by clicking on them. If you want to select multiple objects, hold down **Shift** while you click each object.
3. From the Edit menu, choose **Cut** (**Alt-E, T**).

   All objects that you selected disappear.

Be sure you click **Edit** from the Microsoft **Draw** menu. Choosing Edit from the Word menu closes the Draw program.

N O T E

Word places the objects on the Clipboard. You can retrieve them and paste them in another area by positioning the insertion point where you want the objects and selecting Paste from the Edit menu. Word may not place the objects exactly in the spot you want; however, you can move them. See "Pasting Objects from the Clipboard to the Document" later in this chapter for information about moving the graphic.

Copying Objects to the Clipboard   The Copy command places a copy of all the selected items on the Clipboard, without deleting them from the document.

Follow these steps to copy an object to the Clipboard:

1. Click the Arrow tool.

2. Select the objects you want to copy by clicking them. If you want to select multiple objects, hold down **Shift** while you click each object.

3. From the Edit menu, select Copy (**Alt-E, C**).

Draw places all selected objects on the Clipboard. You can retrieve them and paste them in another area by positioning the insertion point at the location you want and selecting Paste from the Edit menu.

Draw may not place the objects exactly in the spot you want; however, you can move them. See the following section in this chapter for information about moving the graphic.

Pasting Objects from the Clipboard to the Document   Once you cut or copy an object to the Clipboard, you can paste the object into any location in your drawing. Select **Paste** or hold down **Ctrl** while pressing **V**. Draw inserts the object into your drawing. The object may not be placed exactly where you want it to be (you cannot select the precise location in a drawing where a graphic object is pasted).

If you want to move the object, follow these steps:

1. Place the cursor inside the object.

2. Hold down the left mouse button.

   A ghost image replaces the object (the object is outlined with dashed lines).

3. While holding down the mouse button, drag the ghost image to where you want the object to be and release the mouse button.

You can also resize the graphic after you place it in the document. While you have the graphic selected, move the mouse pointer slowly over one of the corner selection handles until the handle becomes an arrow on both ends. Then, move the pointer to push in or pull out on a handle to resize it. Remember, though, that sometimes the graphic loses detail if you size it too small. Also, a graphic may need more detail if you size it too large.

Deleting the Selected Objects   Once you select an object, you can choose to delete it, instead of cutting it or copying it to the Clipboard. When you delete an object, Word does not copy it to the Clipboard, and you cannot restore it with the Paste command. Follow these steps to delete an object:

1. Select the object.

2. From the Edit menu, choose **Clear** (**Alt-E, E**).

or

Press **Del**.

Draw deletes all the selected objects.

If you want to restore the object, you can choose **Undo** from the Edit menu (**Alt-E, U**). Note that Undo only reverses your most recent editing operation, so you must *not* have done any other editing operations between deleting the object and restoring it with Undo.

Selecting All Objects in the Drawing   You may want to select all the objects in a drawing. This may be useful when you want to delete or move everything or resize the drawing. There are two ways to select all objects:

1.   Choose Select All from the Edit menu (**Alt-E, A**).

   or

2.   Hold down **Shift** while you click each item to select it.

Putting Selected Objects in Front of or Behind All Other Objects   You may find that you want to move an object in front of or behind other objects. Use the **Bring to Front** (**Alt-E, F**) or **Send to Back** (**Alt-E, B**) commands to do so. These commands move the selected object or objects in front of or behind all the other objects in the drawing.

In this picture, the circle is "in front" of the square (the circle obscures part of the square):

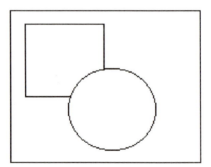

Figure 8.10

By selecting the circle and then choosing the Edit command Send to Back, the square obscures the circle as shown in Figure 8.11.

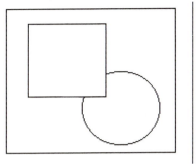

Figure 8.11

Editing a Text Object   The last option in the Edit menu is Edit Object. Use this command to edit text that you have inserted into the drawing.

Follow these steps to edit text in your drawing:

1. Select the text you want to edit.

    Draw changes the option to Edit Text.

2. Place the cursor inside the text area, and add, delete, or change the text as you want.

View Menu

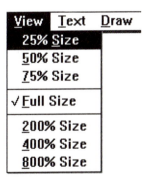

Use the View menu whenever you want to change the amount and size of your drawing that is currently on the screen. Choosing 25%, 50%, or 75% "shrinks" your drawing, making more of it visible in the window. Choosing 200%, 400%, and 800% enlarges your drawing, allowing you to see more detail. Think of this as changing how "close" you are to the drawing, since selecting a different view does not affect the drawing itself, only how you look at it. The way the drawing appears in the document is unaffected by the view.

You can also use the Zoom tool to change the view of the drawing. See "Zoom Tool" earlier in this chapter for more information.

Text Menu

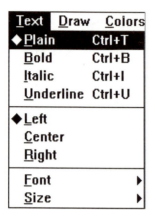

The Text menu allows you to control the characteristics of the text you insert into the drawing, in terms of the font, size, character formatting, and placement.

Changing Text Style   There are four main types of text styles in the Draw program:

- Plain
- Bold
- Italic
- Underline

Note that you can have more than one style for a piece of text just like you can in a Word document. For example, you can give text both italic and bold attributes.

Follow these steps to change the text style:

1. Select the text to change.

2. From the **Text** menu, choose the appropriate text style(s):

    - **Plain (Alt-T, P)**
    - **Bold (Alt-T, B)**
    - **Italic (Alt-T, I)**
    - **Underline (Alt-T, U)**

If you want to combine text styles, select the text and click the style you want to add. Each time you select one character format, Draw closes the menu. You must open it again to add each type of formatting. A check mark appears next to the styles that are active for the text you have selected.

Aligning Text   You can align text with respect to the insertion point location in one of three ways:

- Left
- Center
- Right

Table 8-2

If you select...	Then Draw...
Left	Aligns the leftmost portion of the text you type with the initial starting point you chose (|text).
Center	Centers the text around the starting Point (te|xt).
Right	Aligns the rightmost portion of the text with the starting point (text|).

Choosing Left, Center, or Right determines how the next text you enter will be processed. The active mode is indicated by a diamond next to the option. In the following menu, the left alignment mode is selected:

```
 Text   Draw   Colors
◆Plain        Ctrl+T
 Bold         Ctrl+B
 Italic       Ctrl+I
 Underline    Ctrl+U
─────────────────────
◆Left
 Center
 Right
─────────────────────
 Font              ▶
 Size              ▶
```

Figure 8.12

Changing Fonts   You can change the font that you use when creating a text object. Choose **Font** from the Edit menu (**Alt-T, F**), and select the font and size you want to use. Any new text you enter appears in this font. You can also change the font of existing text. Click on the text object to select it, then choose the new font you wish to use.

The fonts in the Font list show all the fonts that you have installed to use with Word.

N   O   T   E

Changing Text Size   From the Text menu, choose **Size** (**Alt-T, S**) to make the text size you want to create, and select the point size from the menu that pops up:

> **8**
> 10
> ◆12
> 14
> 18
> 24
> 36
> 40
> 48
> 56
> 72
> 96
> <u>O</u>ther...

Figure 8.13

You can also change the size of existing text by clicking on the text to select it, then choosing Size, and selecting the size you want.

Draw Menu

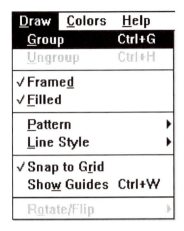

The Draw menu lets you choose the characteristics of the text and graphics you draw. You can group and ungroup objects, select borders and contents of objects, select pattern and line styles, and choose alignment with a grid to ensure that objects in your drawings are aligned properly.

Grouping and Ungrouping Objects   When you create a drawing that contains a wide variety of objects, you may find at times that you want to do the same thing, at the same time, to a number of objects in the drawing. For example, you may want to move a group of objects from one section of the drawing to another. *Grouping* provides a means for you to do this.

Follow these steps to group objects together:

1. Select the objects.

   ■ Draw a selection rectangle around them by chhosing the Arrow tool, clicking outside the objects, and holding and dragging the diagonally.

     or

   ■ Hold down **Shift** while clicking on each of the objects.

2. From the Draw menu, select **Group** (**Alt-D, G**).

   Word replaces the selection handles for each object with a set of selection handles for the entire group.

At this point, you can move, delete, copy, or resize the selected object(s). From then on, when you click on any object in the group, you select all the objects in the group. You can also undo the effects of grouping objects by *ungrouping* them.

Follow these steps to ungroup objects:

1. Select the group.

2. From the Draw menu, select **Ungroup** (**Alt-D, U**).

(If Ungroup is not available, then the object you have selected is not group, and you cannot ungroup it.)

Now, you can select each element in the group individually.

Outlining (Framing) an Object   The frame of an object refers to the outline around it. You can either choose to show the frame for an object or not. However, be aware that if the object you are drawing has a background the same color as the screen background, the object will be invisible. The only way you will be able to find it is to click on the area you think it is in or select the area with a selection rectangle, and see if the selection handles appear.

To switch between framed and unframed versions of an object, choose Framed from the Draw menu (**Alt-D, D**). A diamond symbol next to Framed indicates that the frame for the object will be drawn; no diamond symbol indicates that no frame will be drawn. Note the setting for frame also determines whether frames will be created for new objects. A frame is useful in setting off a graphic from text or in making a small graphic stand out more.

This is an example of an graphic with a frame around it:

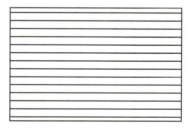

Figure 8.14

This is an example of a graphic with no frame around it:

Figure 8.15

Filling an Object with a Pattern or Color   You can fill an object with a pattern, like the following picture, which is a circle filled with squares:

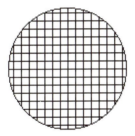

Figure 8.16

To fill an object with a pattern, select the object, then choose **Pattern** from the Draw menu (**Alt-D, P**). Draw displays the pattern chart:

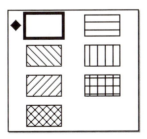

Figure 8.17

If you want to fill an object with a color instead, click on the object, then choose Filled—a diamond indicates that the Filled option is active. Choose the color with which you want to fill the object from the Fill color bar at the bottom of the pane.

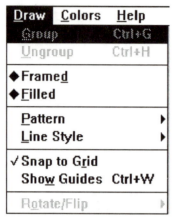

Figure 8.18

Setting the Line Style for the Frame   You can select the type of line to be drawn as the frame for the selected objects. Choose **Line Style** from the Draw menu (**Alt-D,L**), and select the line style and thickness in points that you want to use to frame the current object. Note that the line style you choose remains in effect until you change it to some other style through the Line Style menu. If you just want to outline a graphic, choose a thin line. Many times, heavy lines detract from the graphic itself.

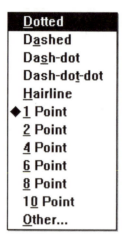

Figure 8.19

Aligning the Objects with a Grid   You can choose to have Draw align graphics with an invisible grid. When you choose the **Snap to Grid** option (**Alt-D, R**), Draw forces you to start and stop any graphics on one of the invisible grid points. Choosing this option makes it easy for you to create drawings that line up correctly.

Rotating and Flipping the Object   You can select an object in Draw and either rotate or flip it, by choosing the appropriate **Rotate** or **Flip** option from the Draw menu:

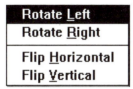

Figure 8.20

The action of each of the options is best illustrated by a picture. Note that these options only apply to graphics objects. You cannot rotate or flip text.

This is the original graphic:

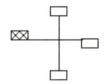

Figure 8.21

This is the graphic after flipping it vertically:

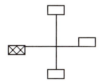

Figure 8.22

This is the graphic after flipping it horizontally.

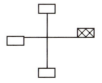

Figure 8.23

This is the graphic after rotating it to the right:

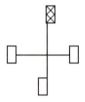

Figure 8.24

This is the graphic after rotating it to the left:

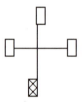

Figure 8.25

Colors Menu

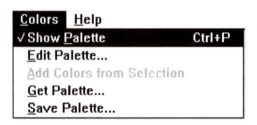

The Colors menu lets you choose to show the palettes, edit the colors on the palette, add colors from a selected object, open the palette, and save it. The default option is Show Palette. If you want to hide the pallete, choose the Show Palette option to remove the check mark.

Modifying the Color Palette   The colors available to you while drawing are visible at the bottom of your drawing window as shown in the following figure.

Figure 8.26

You can chose to either display this color bar, or remove it by clicking **Show Palette** from the Colors menu (**Alt-C, P**). A check mark next to Show Palette indicates that the line and fill color bars will be displayed, if no check mark is present, the color bars will not be displayed.

Adding an Object's Colors to the Color Palette   Each palette has up to 100 colors, and the two are identical. You can add colors to the color bars two ways. The first is very simple: select an object, then select **Add Colors** from Selection (**Alt-C, A**), which copies any new colors from the selection to the color choices.

The second method requires a little more work, but you can determine exactly the elements of the color you add. As you work in the following procedure, don't be too concerned with how much you know about color and color definitions. Use your judgment to choose a color you like. You may find that you enjoy "playing" with this powerful feature to choose colors for your drawing. Follow these steps:

1.   From the Colors menu, choose **Edit Palette** (**Alt-C, E**).

    Draw displays the Edit Palette dialog box.

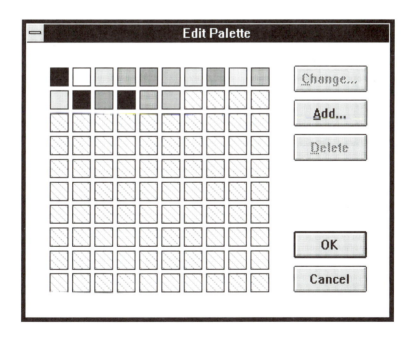

Figure 8.27

2. Select a color that you want to add, and choose **Add**.

    or

    Double-click an empty color square.

    Draw displays the Add Color dialog box.

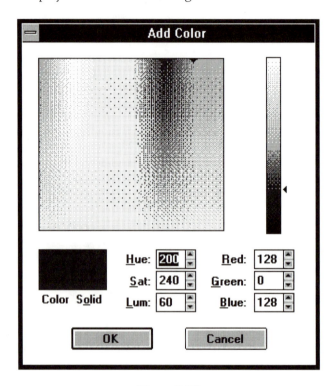

Figure 8.28

The Add Color dialog box shows the Color Matrix, a shade bar, and the currently selected color. You can choose the hue, saturation, and luminosity as described in Table 8-2.

Table 8-3

Use this option...	To set the...
Hue	Pure color You can enter 0 to 239.
Sat (Saturation)	Degree of difference from gray. You can enter 0 to 240.
Lum (Luminosity)	Closeness to black or white. You can enter 0 to 240.
Red, Green, and Blue	Primary colors of your monitor. If you change the settings of any of these colors, you will see that you also change the current color in the Color box, and in the postitions of the arrow pointers in the Shade Bar and Color Matrix.

The following table explains the purpose of the colored areas in the dialog box:

Table 8-4

This area of the Add Color dialog box...	Shows...
Color Matrix (largest area)	All available pigments.
Color	The currently selected color, which is determined by all the settings in the box.
Solid	The pure color that the color you selected mostly closely matches.
Shade Bar	All shades of the currently selected pigment.

3. Use one of the following methods to replace the current color with the color you need to add to the palette:

    ■ Click on a color in the Solid side to display the same color in the Color side.

    ■ Click on a color in the Color Matrix.

    ■ Drag the diamond pointer through the Color Matrix to display each color as it passes over.

    ■ Click on a shade in the Shade Bar.

    ■ Drag the pointer up and down the Shade Bar to display the shading gradations.

    ■ Change the Hue, Saturation, and Luminosity values.

    ■ Change the Red, Green, and Blue values.

4. Choose **OK** to transfer the new color to the Edit Pattern dialog box.

    Draw displays the Edit Palette dialog box again.

5. Choose **OK** to add the new color to the palette.

Saving and Restoring Palettes   You can also save your palette for future use. When you save a document where you have added a drawing, the palette is automatically saved with the drawing. However, if you want to save the palette as another file, you can. That way, if you want to use the palette for other drawings, you will have access to it. Follow these steps to save a palette.

1. From the Colors menu, choose **Save Palette** (**Alt-C, S**).

    Draw displays the Save Palette dialog box:

Figure 8.29

2. Select the directory where you want to save your palette from the **Directories** list.

3. In the box below **Save Palette As**, enter a name for the palette.

4. Choose **OK**.

   Draw saves the palette as the file you entered.

Later, if want to retrieve the file to use the palette in another drawing, follow these steps:

1. From the Colors menu, choose **Get Palette** (**Alt-C, G**).

   Word displays the Get Palette dialog box:

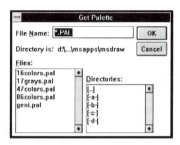

Figure 8.30

2. Select the directory that contains the palette you want to retrieve from the **Directories** list.

3. Select the name of the palette you want to use from the **Files** list.

4. Choose **OK**.

   Draw opens the file.

Help Menu

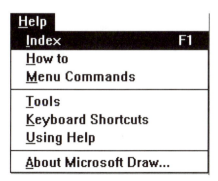

The Help menu is similar to the Help menus in other Windows products. It provides brief procedural and reference information and "help on help."

WORDART

The WordArt feature is powerful, but simple and fun to use. This is a feature of Word itself rather than part of the Draw application. You might consider using this feature to design a logo or add a simple graphic or icon to any type of document. Word gives you 19 fonts, nine angles or styles, and options for placement, shadowing, and stretching text vertically. The following examples show the types of graphics you can create with WordArt:

This is the Button style:

Figure 8.31

This is the Arch Up style:

Figure 8.32

This is the Arch Down style:

Figure 8.33

This is the Upside Down style:

Figure 8.34

This is the Slant Up (Less) style:

Figure 8.35

This is the Slant Up (More) style:

Figure 8.36

This is the Slant Down (Less) style:

Figure 8.37

This is the Slant Down (More) style:

Figure 8.38

This is the Plain style:

Plain Jane

Figure 8.39

Inserting a WordArt Object

Follow these steps to insert a WordArt object in your document.

1. Position the insertion point where you want to add the object.
2. From the Insert menu, choose **Object (Alt-I, O)**.

Word displays the Object dialog box:

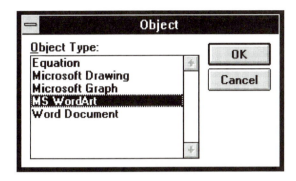

Figure 8.40

3. Choose **MS WordArt** and choose **OK**.

   Word displays the WordArt work area:

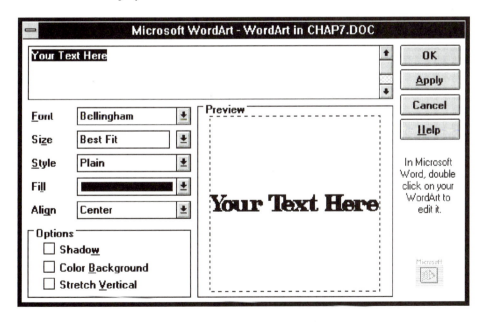

Figure 8.41

4. Type the text you want to use, then choose any options for font, size, style, fill (if necessary), and options in the **Options** box.

Word shows the art changes in the Preview window as you design the drawing.

5. Choose **Apply** and **OK** to close the dialog box.

Word returns to the document in which you were working and places the object where you left the insertion point.

SUMMARY

As you can see, the Draw program and WordArt give you many options for creating and adding drawings in your document. You don't have to be an artist or graphic designer to make your own impressive designs. If you followed the formatting tutorials in earlier chapters, go back now and open the letter you created. In the heading, you might experiment with WordArt to add a personal logo to make a letterhead. First open the document, then the heading. Play with it for a while to see what you can do.

CHAPTER 9

USING MICROSOFT GRAPH

This chapter discusses the following topics:

- *invoking graph*

- *the data sheet*

- *the chart*

- *trying different chart formats*

- *manipulating data*

- *the menu bar*

Microsoft Graph enables you to take numerical data, such as a line of numbers or data from a spreadsheet, and display it graphically in your Word document. With Graph, you can create bar, column, line, pie, and many other kinds of charts. Like Microsoft Draw, Graph saves charts (and data used to create the chart) as embedded objects—meaning that you can double-click a Graph chart in your drawing and change the characteristics of the chart, such as the font, data used to create the chart, or type of chart (from bar chart to pie chart, for example).

You can run Microsoft Graph only within Word. Since Graph stores charts and data as embedded objects in your Word document, Graph does not create a chart that you can use outside of Word.

Although you can edit data that you import from another application, such as a Lotus 1-2-3 file, those changes are only made to the *copy* of the data Graph has stored in your document. Your original source of information—your Lotus 1-2-3 file—will not **N O T E** be updated.

OVERVIEW

There are two windows within the Graph application: the *chart* window and the *datafile* window. The chart window contains the picture that Chart creates of your data. The datafile window contains the data to be charted. You use Graph by creating a datafile, then instructing Graph as to how you want the datafile to be charted. You can create this datafile manually or by importing data from another application, such as Lotus 1-2-3. Once you create the datafile, you can apply a variety of different charting formats to it and add any text you want to the chart.

When you use Graph, you will be switching back and forth between the chart and the data sheet. Graph takes data from the data sheet and uses it to generate the chart. You can control what data is used from the data sheet and you can also control how it is graphed.

When you invoke Graph from within a Word application, Graph brings up a default chart and datafile windows. You may find this annoying. This chapter discusses how to change the chart and datafile to something else. However, you can't prevent Graph from displaying a chart and datafile—you can only change which chart and datafile is used by default.

Invoking Graph

You can only invoke Graph from within Word.

Follow these steps to invoke Graph:

1. From Word's Insert menu, choose **Object** (**Alt-I, O**).

2. Select **Microsoft Graph** from the list in the Object dialog box.

   Any chart you create will be inserted in your document at the current insertion point.

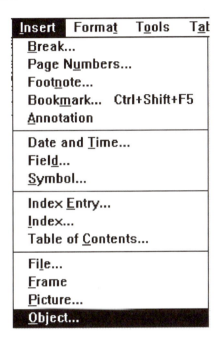

Figure 9.1

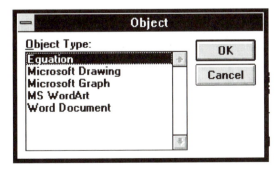

Figure 9.2

The Data sheet

The following illustration shows the default data sheet:

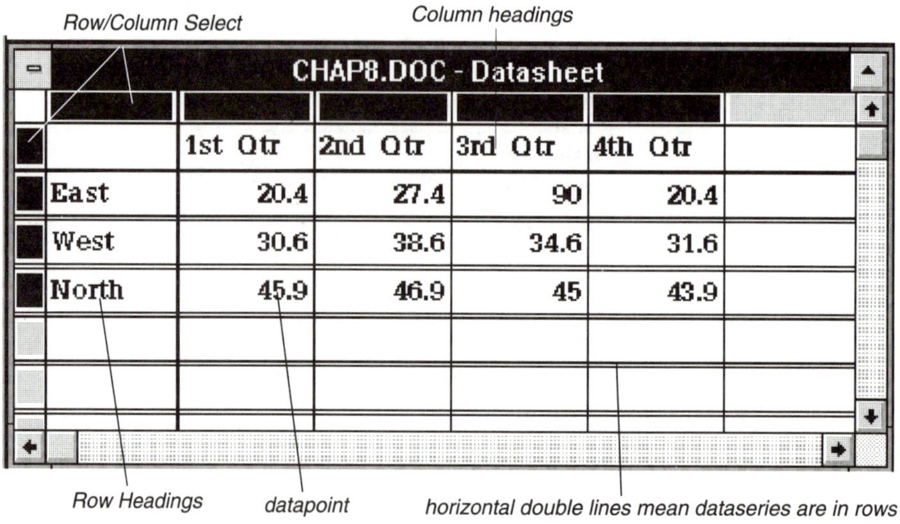

Row/Column Select   Column headings

	1st Qtr	2nd Qtr	3rd Qtr	4th Qtr	
East	20.4	27.4	90	20.4	
West	30.6	38.6	34.6	31.6	
North	45.9	46.9	45	43.9	

CHAP8.DOC - Datasheet

Row Headings   datapoint   horizontal double lines mean dataseries are in rows

Figure 9.3

Each box in the data sheet is referred to as a *cell*. Each cell that contains data is called a *datapoint*. The datapoints are organized in groups called *dataseries*. In our example above, the dataseries are organized in rows (which you can tell by the direction of the double lines), with the dataseries named by the row headings East, West, and North. In this example, the labels at the top of the graph identify what time the datapoint occurred. Using these headings and labels, you can determine the East region had a result of 20.4 in the first quarter.

You can select a cell simply by clicking it. You can select a row or column by clicking the row or column on the left or top side of the data sheet. You can also format datapoints in the data sheet to tell Graph how you want negative numbers displayed, for example. Formatting will be discussed in the "Format" section, later in this chapter, under the main heading "Microsoft Graph Commands."

The Chart

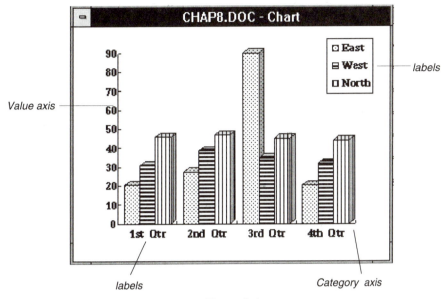

Figure 9.4

The chart consists of data markers, the value axis, the category axis, and the legend. In this case, a bar chart was generated. Graph will create a legend using the heading for the dataseries and the pattern used for the marker, so you can identify which marker is used with a particular dataseries. Graph will then plot the datapoints. This chart displays the values in the default data sheet.

An example will show you how to use the chart. In the example data sheet, East had a value of 20.4 for the first quarter. Looking at the legend in the chart, you see that the pattern for East is small dots. Looking at the labels at the chart, you can see that the data marker for East in the first quarter is lined up with 20 on the value axis.

GRAPH BASICS

Unlike the other Word tools and applications you've seen earlier, Graph comes with a built-in default data sheet and chart, so you will not need the program disk to use this tutorial.

Trying Different Chart Formats

As a first step, try changing the default chart to some different formats. To prepare for this exercise:

1. Have Word running, and a new, empty file open.

2. From the Insert menu, choose **Object** (**Alt-I, O**).

3. Select **Microsoft Graph** from the list in the dialog box.

4. Choose **OK**.

Graph is invoked, and your display should be similar to this:

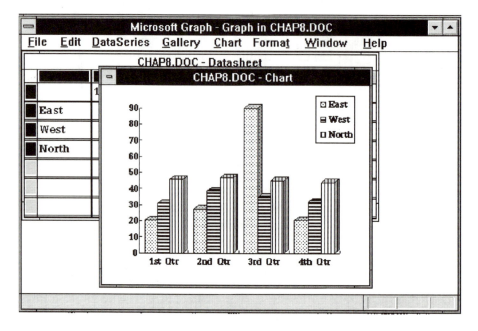

Figure 9.5

Two windows are open; one is the chart and the other is the data sheet. The first exercise shows you how to change the chart formats from one type to another.

Line Chart

The default chart type is the column chart. Another chart type is the line chart. To change to the line chart format:

1. Click the chart window to make it active.

2. From the Gallery menu, choose **Line** (**Alt-G, L**).

3. Select chart number **5**.

4. Choose **OK**.

You should see the chart window change to the format pictured below:

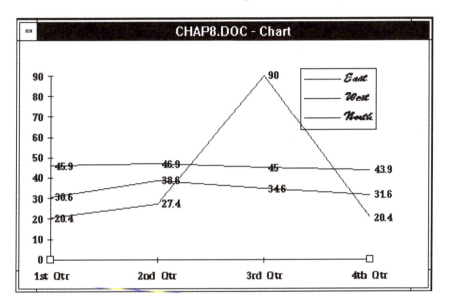

Figure 9.6

Note that this represents exactly the same data, but in a different way. The line format makes trends obvious—note how the big jump for East in the third quarter is highlighted.

Pie Chart

Next, try the pie chart format.

1. From the Gallery menu, choose **Pie** (**Alt-G, P**).

2. Choose chart number **6**.

3. Choose **OK**.

You should see the chart change to the format pictured below:

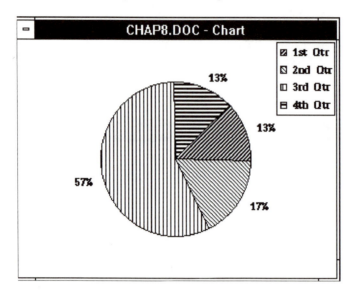

Figure 9.7

The pie chart gives you a good idea how data items in a dataseries contribute to the total. The pie chart also only uses data from one series in the data sheet—because we didn't specify one, Graph used the data from the first series. This was the data for East. If the data for East was dollars earned each quarter, the pie format highlights that the third quarter contributed over half of the earnings.

3D Charts

Graph also has an extensive array of 3D charts. 3D charts can make the process of comparing data among many dataseries easier. In this example, you will generate a 3D column chart.

1. From the Gallery menu, choose **3D column (Alt-G, O)**.
2. Choose chart number **6**.

    You should see the chart change to something similar to the one pictured below:

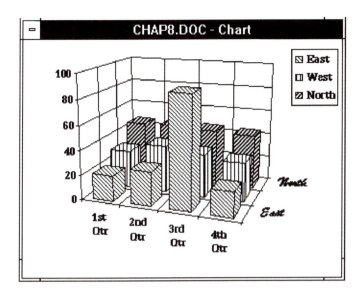

Figure 9.8

The 3D chart lets you see both the trends in individual dataseries and how the dataseries are related to each other. It is immediately obvious from the chart that the third quarter for East stands out from the rest of the data. The 3D format also has a more pleasing appearance than the 2D effect.

Manipulating Data in the Data Sheet

Now that you've got an introduction to using the different chart formats, turn your attention to the data sheet. You can select only certain portions of the data sheet to plot, and control how data is displayed in the data sheet.

Selecting Portions of the Data Sheet to Plot

1. Click the label "East" in the data sheet.
2. From the DataSeries menu, choose **Exclude Row/Column** (**Alt-D, E**).
3. Click **Row** in the dialog box that pops up and click **OK**.
4. Click the label **North** in the data sheet.
5. From the DataSeries menu, choose **Exclude Row/Column** (**Alt-D, E**).
6. Click **Row** in the dialog box that pops up, and click **OK**.

You should now have only the West row appearing in bold. Now you can create a pie chart for the data in the West dataseries:

1. Click the chart window to make it active.

2. From the Gallery menu, choose **Pie** (**Alt-G, P**).

3. Choose any chart type you want.

    You should now see a pie chart with the data for West.

Formatting Cells in the Data Sheet

You can also choose to format the cells in the data sheet. For example, suppose the data in the default data sheet represented dollar amounts. You might want to have the data preceded with a dollar sign, but you could not simply enter a dollar sign in front of the data, as the dollar sign isn't a valid character to include in the field. You will change the formatting of the data sheet to include the dollar sign for all the cells:

1. Click the data sheet to make it active.

2. Select all the cells in the data sheet by placing the cursor in the upper-left-hand data cell (20.40), pressing the left mouse button, and holding the left mouse button down while you drag the cursor down to the bottom right-most cell that has data in it (43.90).

3. From the Format menu, choose **Number** (**Alt-T, N**).

4. Select the option **$#,##0.00; ($#,##0.00)** and choose **OK**.

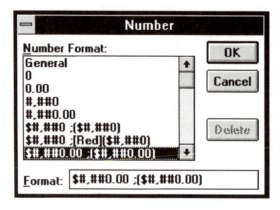

Figure 9.9

You should now see the data sheet change to have dollar signs in front of all the data cells you selected.

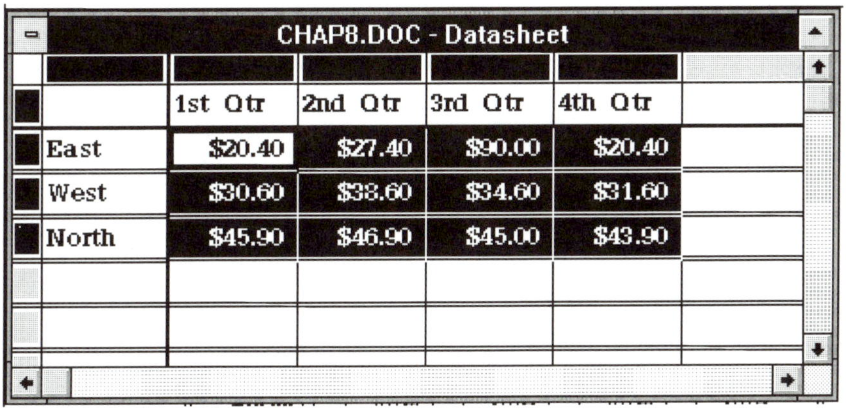

CHAP8.DOC - Datasheet					
	1st Qtr	**2nd Qtr**	**3rd Qtr**	**4th Qtr**	
East	$20.40	$27.40	$90.00	$20.40	
West	$30.60	$38.60	$34.60	$31.60	
North	$45.90	$46.90	$45.00	$43.90	

Figure 9.10

MICROSOFT GRAPH COMMANDS

This section shows each of the menu items in the Graph menu and explains each of the options within the menus and when each should be applied. To help you get started, the following quick-reference table shows you how to jump ahead to a particular section.

Table 9-1

If you need to...	Then refer to the section for...
Import data from a file or other application	File menu
See what the current version of the chart looks like in the document	File menu

Table 9-1 *(continued from previous page)*

If you need to...	Then refer to the section for...
Change the default data and graph file	File menu
Exit Draw	File menu
Copy, delete, or insert items in the datafile	Edit menu
Choose rows or columns of data to be graphed	DataSeries menu
Choose the type of chart (pie, line, bar, etc.)	Gallery menu
Edit the chart (add labels, arrows, legends, axes)	Chart menu
Change patterns (fill bars in the chart with dots, for example)	Format menu
Change the font	Format menu
Change the legend	Format menu
Change the column width	Format menu
Switch between chart and overlay	Format menu
Switch between 2-D and 3-D views	Format menu
Change the color palette	Format menu
Switch between the chart and data display	Window menu
Change the size of the chart or data window	Window menu
Help	Help menu

The Menu Bar

The Menu bar appears along the top of the Graph window. All the Graph commands are accessible from here.

Figure 9.11

This section discusses each of the menu commands, and the options available within each command. If the menu command has a number of different options, the options are summarized in a quick reference table.

File

Use the File menu whenever you want to import data from another application, place the chart in your Word document, or exit and return to Word.

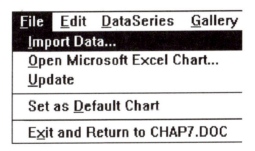

Figure 9.12

Importing Data from Another Application Whenever you want to import data from another application, use the **Import Data...** command from the File menu (**Alt-F, I**). Graph converts data from other applications, such as Lotus 1-2-3, based on the file extension (Quattro Pro users: note that you need to save your spreadsheets in the 1-2-3 format, if you want to import the spreadsheet into Draw). Data will be imported starting at the current cell you have selected in the data file. You can also import data from a plain ASCII text file, with the data separated by commas, or tabs, like the following:

```
1, 2, 4, 8, 16, 32, 64
```

You can also choose a certain range of cells to import if you are importing a spreadsheet.

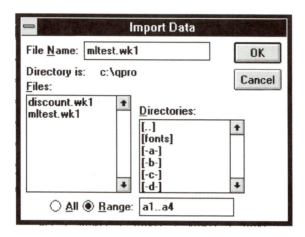

Figure 9.13

In the bottom of the Import Data dialog box, select **Range** (**Alt-R**), then type the range name of the range of cells you want to import in the box to the right.

Opening a Microsoft Excel Spreadsheet   To import data from a Microsoft Excel spreadsheet, choose **Open Microsoft Excel Spreadsheet** from the File menu (**Alt-F, O**). Graph displays a dialog box that enables you to select the Excel spreadsheet that you want to import.

Updating the Document   If you want to see how your changes will look in your document, choose **Update** from the File menu (**Alt-F, U**). This updates your drawing in the document, but leaves you in Graph. Use this command when you are making changes to a chart, but are not ready to exit Graph.

When you are finished with the document, choose **Exit** from the File menu (**Alt-F, X**). This closes Graph, then pops up a dialog box, asking if you want to update the graph in the document.

Selecting a Default Data Sheet   You may find that you want to bring up a different spreadsheet than the default sheet that Graph uses. The Set as Default sheet enables you to do this. First, you must have the chart and data in use by Graph—you cannot select a file and tell Graph to use that file as a default directly. Once you have the chart and data that you want to use as a default, choose **Set as Default** from the File menu (**Alt-F, D**). Graph displays this chart and data as the default from this point on, unless you go back and change the default.

Returning to the Main Document   Once you are satisfied with the document, choose **Exit and Return** to save the chart and data and return to your main document. Graph asks you if you want to update the drawing in your document before exiting.

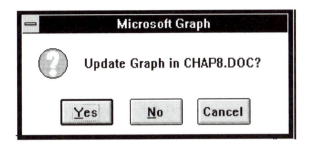

Figure 9.14

Table 9-2

If you want to ...	*Then choose...*
Update the chart in the document, and save any changes to the data file.	Yes
Exit Draw without updating the chart and losing any changes made to the data file.	No

File Quick Reference   Use this table as a quick guide to using the File menu.

Table 9-3

If you want to...	*Then choose...*	*Using this quick key...*
Import data from a file or other application.	Import Data	**ALT-F, I**
Import data from an Excel application.	Open Microsoft Excel Chart...	**ALT-F, O**
Update the chart in the main document without leaving Graph.	Update	**Alt-F, U**

Table 9-3 (continued from previous page)

If you want to...	Then choose...	This quick key...
Change the default for the current chart and data.	Set as Default Chart	**Alt-F, D**
Exit Graph, save chart and data, and update document.	Exit and Return to, then choose Yes for the Update Graph dialog box	**ALT-F, X, Y**
Exit Graph, without saving chart and data and without updating document.	Exit and Return to, then choose No for the Update Graph dialog box	**ALT-F, X, N**

Edit

Use the Edit menu whenever you want to edit data contained within your datasheet or cut or copy items within your chart. Using the Edit menu options, you can copy rows or columns of data in the datasheet, and insert and delete columns and rows.

Edit	DataSeries	Gallery
Undo Font		Ctrl+Z
Cut		Ctrl+X
Copy		Ctrl+C
Paste		Ctrl+V
Clear...		Del
Select All		Ctrl+A
Delete Row/Col...		Ctrl+-
Insert Row/Col...		Ctrl++

Figure 9.15

The Undo command may differ from the previous example. The Undo command is dependent on the last action you took—if you made changes to a font, then you would see an Undo Font command, shown above.

N O T E

Undoing the Last Edit Operation   The Undo command reverses the last operation you performed. Note that you can undo only the previous command; you cannot undo commands that occurred earlier than the last command. For example, if you accidentally deleted some data from your chart, you would need to choose Undo as your next step, to recover the data. If you deleted the data then performed another action, such as changing some text, you would be able to undo only the text change. You would not be able to undo again and restore the data you deleted, since that action occurred two steps back. In this case, you might simply want to exit Graph without updating the chart, so you could start over.

To undo the last action taken, choose **Undo** from the Edit menu (**Alt-E, U**). If you want to undo *all* the actions you've taken on the current chart and datasheet, you can Exit Graph from the File menu (**Alt-F, X**) and answer **No** to the dialog box that asks you if you want to update the document. *You will lose any changes* you made to the chart or datasheet in this session with Graph.

Cutting or Copying Objects to the Clipboard, then Inserting the Objects in a New Location   You can copy or delete items in your chart or datasheet using the commands from the Edit menu. For example you can copy data in one or more cells to other cells in the datasheet. You can select an item in the chart, such as the legend, and delete it.

Like other Word applications, Graph divides the Cut and Paste and Copy and Paste operations into two steps—first you **cut** or **copy** the selected item from the data sheet or chart, then you **paste** it into the location you want in your main document.

Table 9-4

If you want to...	Use...
Move an item in a chart or datasheet from one location to another	Cut
Copy an item in a chart or datasheet	Copy

Follow these steps to cut selected items:

1. Select the objects you want to cut.
2. From the Edit menu, choose **Cut** (**Alt-E, T**).

The items are now removed from the datasheet or chart and are stored in the Clipboard. You can now use the **Paste** command to insert the items where you want.

Follow these steps to copy selected items:

1. Select the objects you want to copy:

2. From the Edit menu, choose **Cut** (**Alt-E, C**).

   A copy of the selected items is placed in the Clipboard. You can now use the **Paste** command to insert the objects where you want.

Follow these steps to paste selected items:

1. Place the insertion point where you want the objects to appear. If you want to replace one or more items with the items you are about to paste, select all the items you want to replace.

   (Graph replaces them during the paste operation)

2. From the Edit menu, choose **Paste**. (**Alt-E, P**)

   Graph copies the object to the selected area of the datasheet or chart.

Graph uses the Clipboard to temporarily store the objects—meaning that you can actually paste the data cells into another Draw datasheet that you may have open in another window.

N O T E

Deleting the Selected Objects   As you might expect, you can simply choose to delete an object or objects, instead of using the **Cut** command to put the objects in the Clipboard. You can use the delete operation to remove:

■ data from the datasheet

■ formatting information from the data sheet

■ items from the chart

The procedure is essentially the same as that for the Cut command:

To delete objects:

1. Select the objects.
2. Delete the objects by either:

   ■ Pressing the **Delete** key.

   or

   ■ From the Edit menu, choosing **Clear**.

   or

   ■ Pressing (**Alt-E, E**).

If you've selected rows or columns of data in your datasheet, Graph displays a dialog box when you choose the Clear command or press **Del**.

Figure 9.16

You can use these options to delete just the data, just the formatting, or both from your datasheet.

Table 9-5

If you want to...	*Then...*
Clear just the data, but leave the formatting information	Select **Clear Data**.
Clear just the format information, but leave the data	Select **Clear Format**.
Clear data and remove all formatting information	Select **Clear Both**.

Graph removes the objects from the display. Note that if you delete an object by mistake, choose Undo from the Edit menu *as your next step*. This restores the objects you deleted.

Deleting or Inserting Rows and Columns in the Data Sheet   You will often want to insert rows or columns or data into your datasheet. For example, you may have entered one column of data for each month of the year in your budget datasheet and find that you left out the data for the month of June. You can correct the error by inserting a column between the May and July columns. Graph automatically moves the July through December columns over one column.

Follow these steps to insert a row or column:

1. Select the number of rows or columns you want to insert. If you want to insert two columns, for example, then select the two columns where you want the new data to appear.

2. From the Edit menu, choose **Insert Row/Column (Alt-E, I)**.

    For example, suppose you want to insert two columns of data between 1st Qtr and 2nd Qtr in the spreadsheet:

	1st Qtr	2nd Qtr	3rd Qtr	4th Qtr	
East	20.4	27.4	90	20.4	
West	30.6	38.6	34.6	31.6	
North	45.9	46.9	45	43.9	

CHAP8.DOC - Datasheet

Figure 9.17

Select the two columns where you want the two new columns to be inserted:

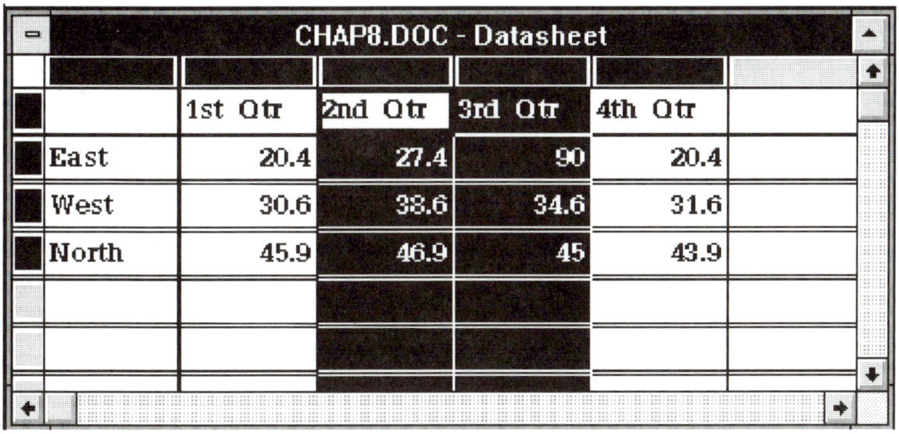

	1st Qtr	2nd Qtr	3rd Qtr	4th Qtr	
East	20.4	27.4	90	20.4	
West	30.6	38.6	34.6	31.6	
North	45.9	46.9	45	43.9	

CHAP8.DOC - Datasheet

Figure 9.18

From the Edit menu, choose **Insert Row/Column** (**Alt E, I**).

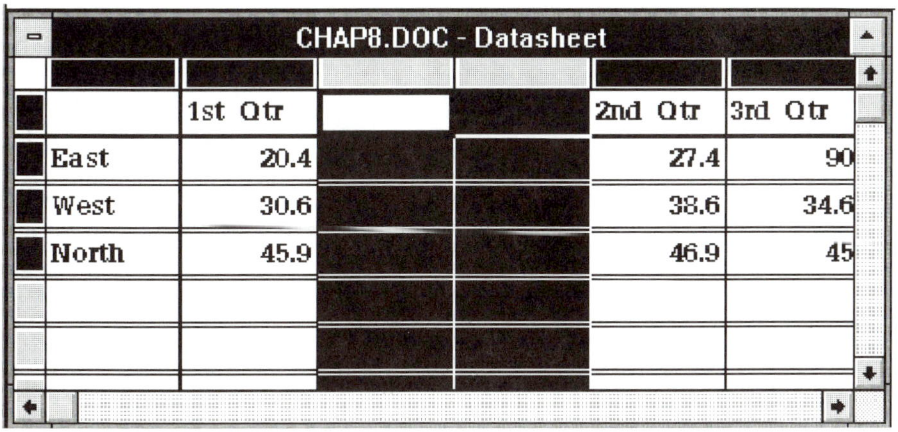

	1st Qtr			2nd Qtr	3rd Qtr
East	20.4			27.4	90
West	30.6			38.6	34.6
North	45.9			46.9	45

CHAP8.DOC - Datasheet

Figure 9.19

Graph inserts two empty columns.

You can delete rows or columns of data from the datasheet just as easily. Follow these steps to delete a row or column:

1. Select the number of rows or columns you want to delete.
2. From the Edit menu, choose **Delete Row/Column** (**Alt-E, D**).

Edit Quick Reference   Use this table as a quick guide to using the edit menu.

Table 9-6

If you want to...	*Then...*
Undo the last incorrect command.	Choose **Undo**.
Move data from one location in the datasheet to another.	1. Select the data. 2. Choose **Cut**. 3. Place insertion point. 4. Choose **Paste**.
Move objects in the chart from one location to another.	1. Select the objects. 2. Choose **Cut**. 3. Place insertion point. 4. Choose **Paste**.
Copy data in the datasheet to another location.	1. Select the data. 2. Choose **Copy**. 3. Place insertion point. 4. Choose **Paste**.
Copy items in the chart to another location.	1. Select the objects. 2. Choose **Cut**. 3. Place insertion`point. 4. Choose **Paste**.
Remove data or formatting from a row or column in the data sheet.	1. Select the row or column. 2. Choose **Clear**.
Remove one or more columns or rows	1. Select the row or column. 2. Choose **Delete Row/Column**.
Insert one or more rows or columns.	1. Select the row or column. 2. Choose **Insert Row/Column**.

DataSeries

A *dataseries* is either a row or column of data in your datasheet that produces a portion of the chart. For example, you could decide that the data in your datasheet is ordered by columns, one column of data for each month. In this case, the column of data is referred to as the *dataseries*. If you produce a bar chart from this datasheet, there will be one bar for each column (or dataseries).

You can also define your data to be ordered in rows instead of columns. The dataseries would then be the rows of information. Dataseries in rows is the default configuration.

The DataSeries menu is shown below:

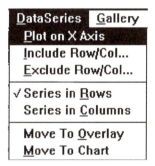

Figure 9.20

Defining Data to Use for the X Axis   You may find that you need to plot data along both the x and y axes of your datasheet. For example, you want to plot a time-versus-distance graph that shows how various members of your track team are performing. This is referred to as an XY (scatter) chart, which you can choose from one of the XY chart formats in the chart gallery.

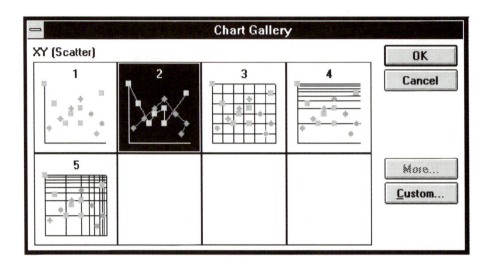

Figure 9.21

Word has a good Example Graph Help window for "Enter data for XY charts." Follow these steps to display this example:

1. From the Help menu, choose Index (**Alt-H, I**).

2. Select **How to**.

3. Under Arrange Data for the Chart, select **Entering Data for XY charts**.

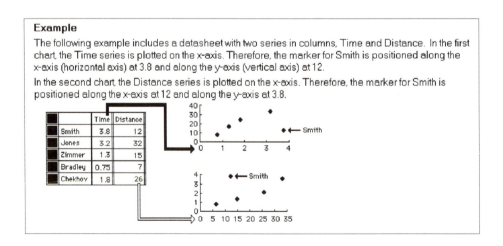

Figure 9.22

Follow these steps to create an XY chart:

1. Switch to the chart Window.

   You can click the chart window or choose **Chart** from the Window menu (**Alt-W, C**).

2. From the Gallery menu, choose the **XY** graph format (**Alt-G, S**).

3. Select the XY format you want to use, then choose **OK**.

4. Switch to the Datasheet window.

   You can click the Datasheet window, or choose **Chart** from the Window menu (**Alt-W, C**).

5. Select the dataseries you want Graph to use as the X axis.

6. From the DataSeries menu, choose **Plot on X axis** (**Alt-D, P**).

   You will see an X at the beginning of the row or column of the dataseries.

Graph uses your selection for the X dataseries to label the X axis. Graph then plots the rest of the dataseries by plotting the first value in each dataseries lined up with the first label in the X axis, then the next value in each series lined up with the second label in the X axis, and so on.

Including / Excluding Rows or Columns of Data   You may find that you don't always need to plot every dataseries contained in your datasheet. For example, suppose you have a datasheet that has a column of data for each month of the year. You may want to graph data for only the first three months of the year.

You select columns or row of data and include or exclude them using the **Exclude Row/Column** or **Include Row/Column** menu choices.

Follow these steps to include data:

If data appears black in the data sheet (not dimmed out) then it is already included. Only data that is dimmed out needs to be selected for inclusion.

N O T E

1. Select the rows or columns you want to include.

2. From the DataSeries menu, choose **Include Row/Column (Alt-D, I)** to include the selected data.

   The include data now appears in black in the datasheet.

Follow these steps to exclude data:

1. Select the rows or columns you want to exclude.

2. From the DataSeries menu, select **Exclude Row/Column (Alt-D, E)** to exclude the selected data.

   The excluded data now appears black in the datasheet.

 If data appears dimmed out in the data sheet (not black) then it is already excluded. Only data that is black can be selected for exclusion.

N O T E

Using Rows or Columns to Define the Data Ordering   Graph considers dataseries to be either rows or columns of information, with row ordering being the default. You can change the default by choosing Series in Columns from the Edit menu. To determine whether the dataseries are ordered in rows or columns, look at the datasheet. You'll see double lines between the rows of data if the dataseries are ordered in rows, and double lines between the columns of data if the dataseries are ordered in columns.

To order the dataseries in columns:

■ From the DataSeries menu, choose **Series in Columns (Alt-D, C).** Double lines appear between the columns, and a check mark appears next to the Series in Columns option.

To order the dataseries in rows:

■ From the DataSeries menu, choose **Series in Rows (Alt-D, R)**. Double lines appear between the rows, and a check mark appears next to the Series in Rows command.

Moving to Overlay or Chart You may find that you want to compare dataseries in the same chart by presenting one of the dataseries in a different format than the other. The Overlay chart does this by combining two different types of charts within a single chart.

For example, you can take the data in the default data sheet and create an overlay chart, with the first row of data plotted as a line, and the rest of the data plotted as bars:

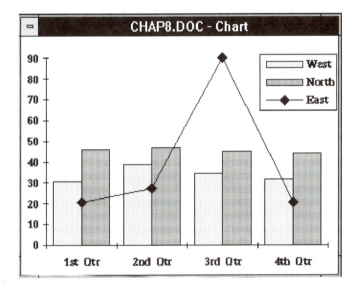

Figure 9.23

You can look at the chart and immediately see that the data for East is being compared with the data for West and North.You can also use the overlay to compare dataseries that are scaled differently. For example, suppose East had values from 100 to 1,000, but North and West had values from 1 to 10. (In the default data sheet, the values are really much closer; this is just an example.) To get the values for East to fit with North and West on the same chart, the sizes of the North and West bars would have to be so small that no meaningful trends could be observed from them. If, however, the East data was on an overlay chart, the East data could be scaled independently from North and West data, and the chart would be much more meaningful.

Follow these steps to move a dataseries to an overlay chart:

1. Make sure the current chart type is *not 3D* (a 3D chart is not compatible with the Overlay operation).

2. Click the datasheet to make it active.

3. Select the dataseries (rows or columns) of data you want to move to the overlay chart.

4. From the DataSeries menu, choose **Move to Overlay** (**Alt-D, O**).

   Graph creates an overlay chart of the default type. If you want to change the chart type, then select **Overlay** from the Format menu. See the "Format" section later in this chapter.

You can also move data from the overlay chart back to the main chart. Dataseries that have an "O" in front of them are assigned to the overlay chart. In the example pictured below, East is assigned to the overlay chart:

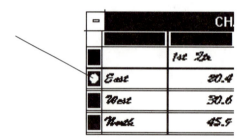

Figure 9.24

Follow these steps to move a dataseries back to the main chart:

Only dataseries that have an "O" in front of them are in the overlay and can be moved to the main chart.

N O T E

Dataseries without the "O" are already plotted in the main chart.

1. Click the datasheet to make it active.

2. Select the dataseries (rows or columns) of data you want to move to the overlay chart.

3. From the DataSeries menu, choose **Move to Chart** (**Alt-D, O**).

   Graph moves the dataseries you selected back to the main chart.

Dataseries Quick Reference

Table 9-7

If you want to...	*Then...*
Choose the dataseries to use for the X axis in an XY plot	Choose **Plot on X Axis**.
Include rows or columns from datasheet for the chart	1. Select the rows or columns you want to include. 2. Choose **Include Row/Column**.
Exclude rows or columns from datasheet for the chart	1. Select the rows or columns you want to exclude. 2. Choose **Exclude Row/Column**.
Order the dataseries in rows	Choose **Series in Columns**.
Order the dataseries in columns	Choose **Series in Rows**.
Move a dataseries from a 2D chart to an overlay chart	1. Select the dataseries to move to the overlay. 2. Choose **Move to Overlay.**
Move a dataseries from an Overlay chart back to the main chart	1. Select the series to move. 2. Choose **Move to Chart**.

Gallery

Use the Gallery command to select the format for the chart. There are many different types of chart formats. Use the following table as a guide to choosing the appropriate type:

Table 9-8

If you want to...	Then choose a chart type...
Show the contribution of different dataseries to the total over time and emphasize the amount of change	Area, 3D area
Compare values in a dataseries at particular point in time	Bar, 3D bar
Compare values of dataseries over time	Column, 3D column
Show the changes of different dataseries over time and emphasize the rate of change	Line, 3D line
Show the ratio of an element in a dataseries to the total for all the elements in the series	Pie, 3D pie
See if two variables are dependent on each other	XY (or scatter)
Compare dataseries that are scaled much differently or highlight different dataseries	Combination

Area   The area charts help you emphasize the total amount of change in one or more dataseries. The 2D Area menu appears below.

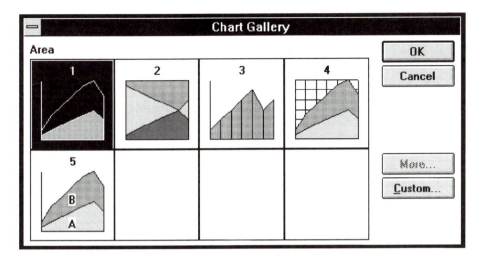

Figure 9.25

Table 9-9

If you want an area chart with...	Then choose area chart type...
No labels or gridlines	1
100% area (area equivalent of pie chart)	2
Vertical drop lines	3
Gridlines	4
Areas labeled	5

3D Area Chart The 3D area chart gives you the same emphasis on the amount of change in dataseries, but makes it easier for you to compare the different dataseries. The 3D area menu appears below.

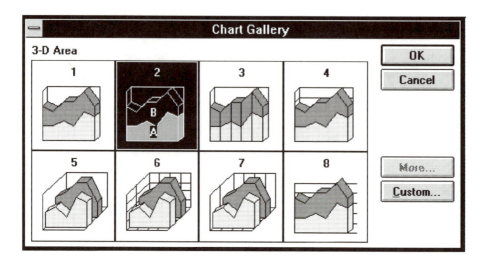

Figure 9.26

Table 9-10

If you want an 3D area chart with...	Then choose 3D area chart type...
No labels or gridlines	1
Dataseries stacked and labeled	2
Dataseries stacked with vertical drop lines	3
Dataseries stacked with gridlines	4
Dataseries separated	5
Dataseries separated with horizontal and vertical gridlines	6
Dataseries separated with horizontal and vertical gridlines	7
Dataseries stacked and horizontal gridlines	8

Bar The bar chart is useful when you want to display a set of dataseries at a particular point in time. The bar chart options follow:

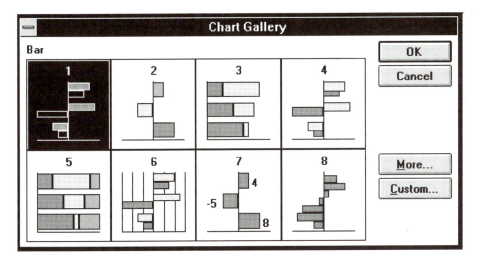

Figure 9.27

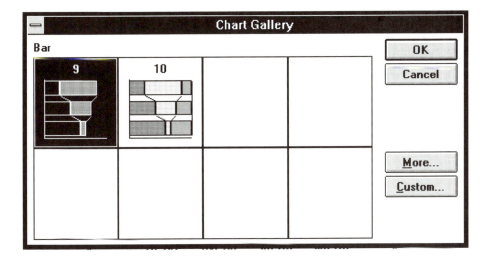

Figure 9.28

Table 9-11

If you want a bar chart with...	Then choose bar chart type...
No labels or gridlines	1
Different patterns for each bar, used with a single dataseries	2
Bars for each series stacked on top of each other	3
Bars overlapping	4
Bars for each series stacked on top of each other, all bars scaled to the same length	5
Vertical gridlines	6
Value labels	7
No spaces between bars	8
Bars for each series stacked on top of each other, with lines connecting the series	9
Bars for each series stacked on top of each other, with lines connecting the series and all bars scaled to the same length.	10

3D Bar Chart   The Chart Gallery dialog box shows the 3D bar chart options:

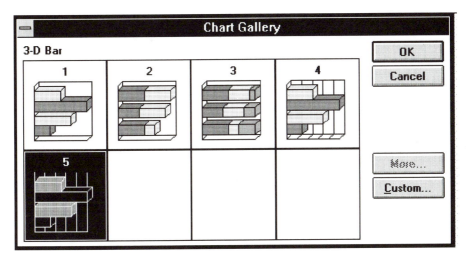

Figure 9.29

Table 9-12

If you want a chart with...	*Then choose 3D bar type...*
No labels or gridlines	1
Dataseries stacked	2
Dataseries stacked, with bar lengths the same	3
Vertical gridlines in 3D	4
Vertical gridlines in 2D	5

Column Use the column format when you want to compare the values of dataseries over time. The column chart options follow.

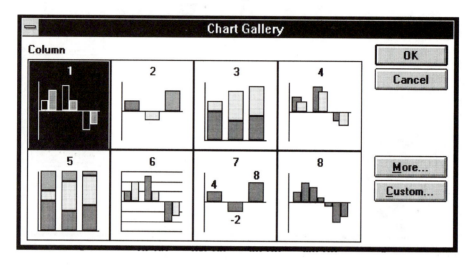

Figure 9.30

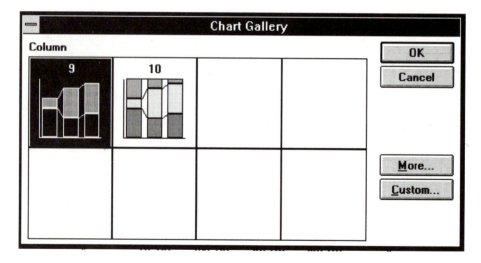

Figure 9.31

Table 9-13

If you want a chart with...	Then choose column chart type...
No labels or gridlines	1
Different patterns for each element in the series and just one dataseries charted	2
Dataseries stacked on top of each other	3
Dataseries overlapped	4
Dataseries stacked on top of each other, bar length remains constant	5
Horizontal gridlines	6
Value labels	7
No space between bars	8
Dataseries stacked with lines between series	9
Dataseries stacked with lines between series and column length constant	10

3D Chart   The options for the 3D chart follow:

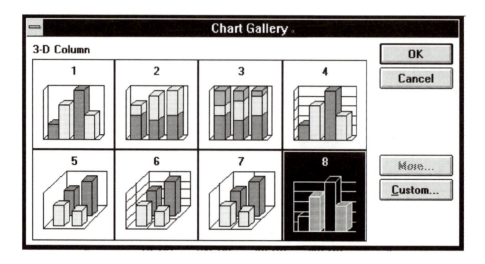

Figure 9.32

Table 9-14

If you want a chart with...	Then choose chart type...
No labels or gridlines	1
Dataseries stacked on top of each other	2
Dataseries stacked on top of each other, with column length constant	3
Vertical axis gridlines	4
Dataseries plotted side by side	5
Dataseries plotted side by side, with gridlines	6
Dataseries plotted side by side, with horizontal and y vertical gridlines only	7
2D horizontal gridlines	8

Line Use the line chart when you want to emphasize the rate of change for dataseries. The Chart Gallery dialog box shows the Line chart format:

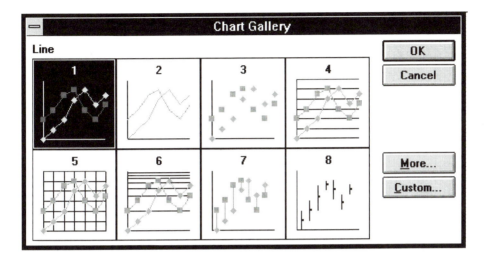

Figure 9.33

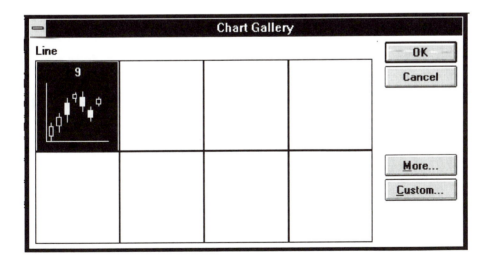

Figure 9.34

Table 9-15

If you want a line graph with...	Then choose line graph type...
Lines with data markers, but no labels or gridlines	1
Lines with no data markers, labels, or gridlines	2
Data markers with no lines	3
Lines with data markers and horizontal gridlines	4
Lines with data markers and horizontal and vertical gridlines	5
Lines with data markers and logarithmic scale and gridlines	6
High-low markers and lines	7
High-low-close chart	8
Open-high-low-close	9

3D Line Chart   The Chart Gallery dialog shows options for the 3D Line chart format:

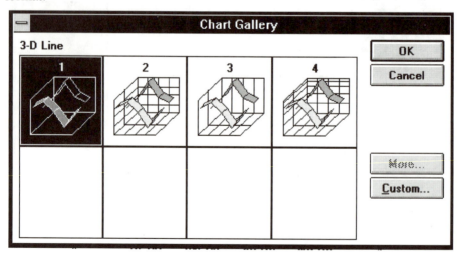

Figure 9.35

Table 9-16

If you want a 3D line chart with…	Then choose 3D line chart type…
No labels or gridlines	1
No labels with gridlines	2
No labels and horizontal and vertical gridlines	3
No labels and logarithmic gridlines	4

Pie Use the pie chart when you want to show the relationship between different elements of a dataseries to the total for all the elements of the dataseries. The pie chart shows the contribution of each element in the series to the total. The pie chart can only be used with a single dataseries. The options for the pie chart are pictured below.

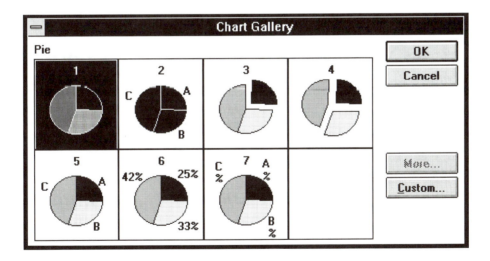

Figure 9.36

Table 9-17

If you want a pie chart with...	Then choose pie chart type...
No labels, slices have different patterns, all slices together	1
Labeled, slices have different patterns, all slices together	2
No labels, one slice exploded from rest of chart	3
No labels, all slices exploded	4
Labels for each slice	5
Percentage labels for each slice	6
Series and percentage labels for each slice	7

3D Pie Chart   The Chart Gallery dialog box shows the 3D pie chart options:

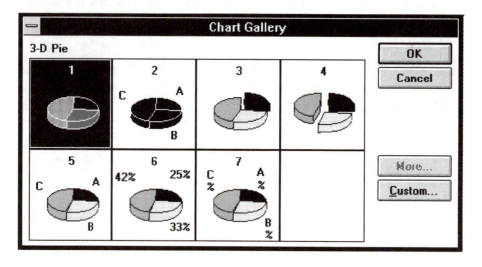

Figure 9.37

Table 9-18

If you want a 3D pie chart with...	Then choose 3D pie chart type...
No labels, slices have different patterns, all slices together	1
Labeled, slices have different patterns, all slices together	2
No labels, one slice exploded from rest of chart	3
No labels, all slices exploded	4
Labels for each slice	5
Percentage labels for each slice	6
Percentage and data labels for each slice	7

XY (Scatter)   Use the XY chart when you want to compare the relationship between two variables. The XY chart is discussed in the Dataseries section, under the heading "Defining Data to Use for the X Axis."

The scatter chart options are pictured below:

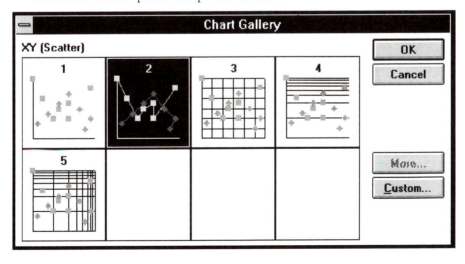

Figure 9.38

Table 9-19

If you want a XY chart with...	Then choose XY chart type...
Data markers only	1
Data markers for the same series connected by lines	2
Data markers with horizontal and vertical gridlines	3
Data markers with log scale for y axis	4
Data markers with log scale for x and y axis	5

Combination The combination chart is useful when you want to compare one set of dataseries against another set. The combination chart is essential for this type of comparison when one set of data has much larger or smaller values than the other set, requiring that the dataseries be scaled differently. The options for the combination chart are shown below.

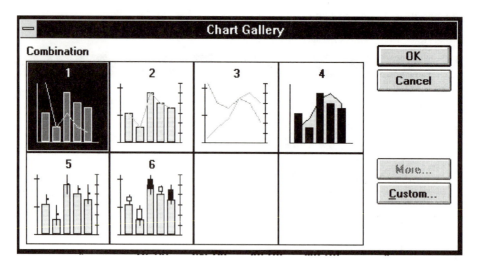

Figure 9.39

Table 9-20

If you want a combination chart consisting of...	*Then choose combination chart type...*
A column chart overlaid with a line chart with the same scaling for the y axis	1
A column chart overlaid with a line chart with independent scaling for the y axis	2
A line chart overlaid with another line chart with independent scaling for the y axis	3
An area chart overlaid by a column chart	4
A column chart overlaid by a high-low-close chart	5
A column chart overlaid by a open-high-low-close chart	6

Chart

The Chart menu allows you to:

- add titles to the chart or axes
- label data points
- add arrows to point to items of interest in your charts
- add or delete legends
- add or remove axes
- control gridlines

This is the Chart menu:

Figure 9.40

Titles   Use titles whenever you want to attach a title to the chart, or to the x or y axis on the chart or overlay chart. Note that the example title menu shows all the options available. You may not have all these options available, depending on the type of chart you are editing (for example, pie charts don't have x and y axes).

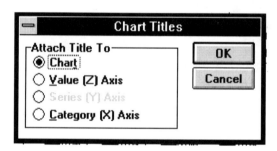

Figure 9.41

In Figure 9.42 below, titles have been added to the Chart and to the *Z axis*.

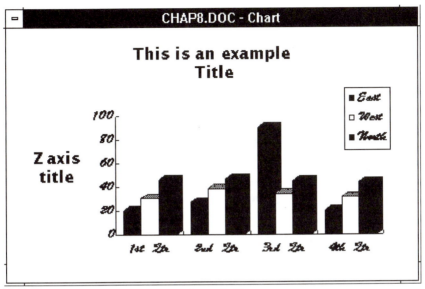

Figure 9.42

Follow these steps to add a title:

1. Make the chart the active window by clicking it.

2. From the Chart menu, choose **Title** (**Alt-C, T**).

3. Select the item that you want to title (chart, x axis, y axis) from the **Attach Title** box and choose **OK**.

   Graph places a default title next to the item you selected. Edit this text by deleting it and adding the title you want.

4. Press **Esc** when finished.

   This adds the title to your chart.

If you want to edit a title you've entered, follow these steps:

1. Position the cursor over the title you want to edit and click.

   Selection handles appear around the text.

2. Enter the new text.

3. Press **Esc** when finished.

Data Labels   You may want to label the data points in your chart with the values they represent. The Data Labels option allows you to attach:

- The values that the data point represents
- The percent of the total to each pie slice in a pie graph
- The labels from the data sheet to the data element

The following example shows the Data Labels dialog box:

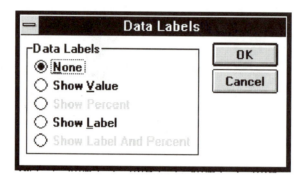

Figure 9.43

For example, suppose you have a chart and want the datapoint values displayed. You would select Show Value from the Data Labels menu to get a chart that looks like this:

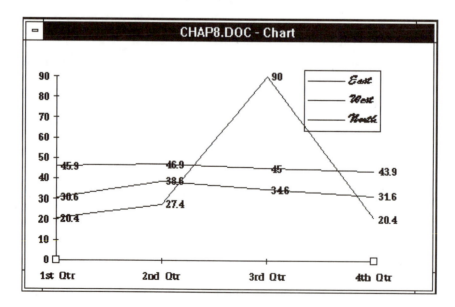

Figure 9.44

Graph isn't "smart" about how it locates label values. If you have a column chart, for example, and add labels to it, Graph may place the labels in the middle of column. Unfortunately, you can't move the labels to the top of the column, where they would be more easily visible. In this case, add text manually where you want it.

N O T E

To manually add text:

1. Ensure that no text items in the chart are selected.

2. Enter the text (don't worry about where the text is being entered, you can move it easily).

3. When you are finished entering the text, press the **Esc** key.

   Selection handles appear around the text.

4. Drag the text to the location you want.

Add Arrow You may find that you want to highlight certain datapoints in your chart—for example, maybe sales for first quarter are exceptionally good, so you want to highlight this datapoint. You can use the **Add Arrow** command to do this. The example below shows an arrow drawn to the third quarter earning, and a comment added:

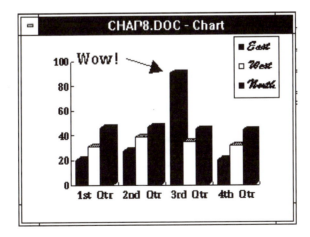

Figure 9.45

Delete Legend/Add Legend   You may decide that you do not want the legend to be displayed. In this case, select **Delete Legend**, and the legend is removed. If you have already deleted the legend, the menu command is replaced with **Add Legend**. Whenever you want to restore the legend, select Add Legend.

Axes   The Axes menu enables you to control the display of the X and Y axes. In the menu below, an "X" indicates that the corresponding axis will be displayed.

The Axes menu that you see may vary, depending on the chart type you have chosen.

N   O   T   E

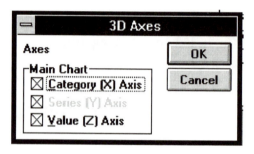

Figure 9.46

Figure 9.47 illustrates the effect of the Axes command with X axis displayed:

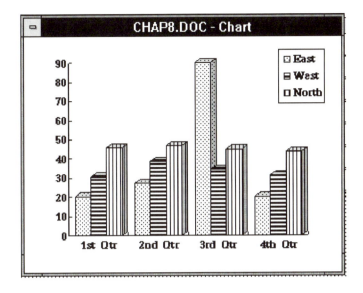

Figure 9.47

With X axis disabled:

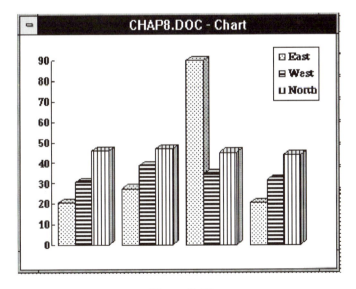

Figure 9.48

Gridlines   Gridlines are the lines along the X and Y axes that enable you to determine the values of the datapoints. You can control the display of these gridlines and also how fine the spacing is between the gridlines by enabling the **Minor Gridlines** option. Below is an example of the gridlines menu. Note that your version may differ slightly, depending on the type of chart that is active.

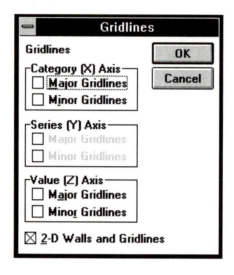

Figure 9.49

The example below shows just the major gridlines displayed for the axes.

You can determine the value that a column represents by looking along the gridlines and seeing where the top of the column is. You may find that you need more gridlines to get a more accurate estimate of the values. In this case, select the **Minor Axis** option for the axis that needs more resolution.

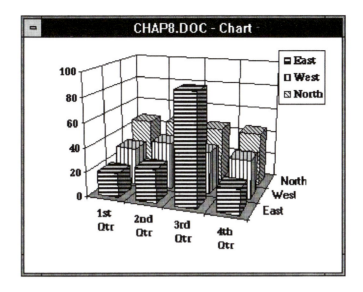

Figure 9.50

This example has the Minor Gridlines enabled for the X and Z axis.

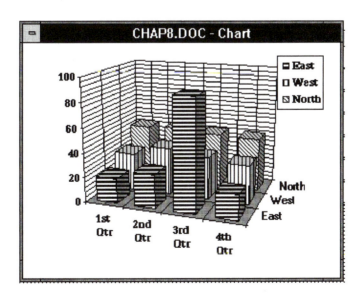

Figure 9.51

Chart Quick Reference

Table 9-21

If you want to...	Then...
Add a title to the chart, x axis, or y axis	1. Select the item you want to title. 2. Choose **Titles**. 3. Edit the default title inserted by Graph with the desired text.
Add value, percentage, or dataseries labels to the data points	1. Choose **Data Labels**. 2. Select the data label option you want.
Add an arrow to the chart	1. Choose the **Add Arrow** option. 2. Drag the arrow to the location you want.
Delete the legend	Choose **Delete Legend**.
Add the legend	Choose **Add Legend**.
Add or remove axes	1. Choose **Axes**. 2. Select the options you want.
Add or remove major or minor gridlines	1. Choose **Gridlines**. 2. Select the options you want.

Format

The Format menu presents the widest array of commands and deals with the widest array of items, from both the datasheet and the chart. At any one time, many of the commands may be grayed out, depending on the item you have selected. The commands that are grayed out cannot be applied to the currently selected item.

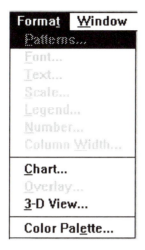

Figure 9.52

Patterns   The Patterns dialog box controls the appearance of items in the chart. With these options, you can change the border color, width, and style around almost any item, and pattern characteristics within the item. For example, you can change the pattern within columns or in the background of the legend. If you're not sure if you can edit an item's pattern, simply select the item and see if the Patterns command is grayed out on the Format menu. If it is, then this item does not have an editable pattern.

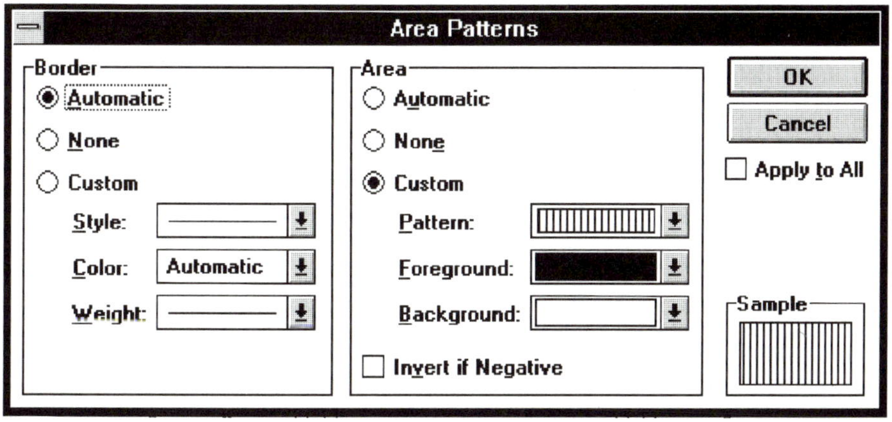

Figure 9.53

Follow these steps to change the pattern of an object in a chart:

1. Select the object within the chart.
2. From the Format menu, select **Patterns** (**Alt-T, P**).
3. Use the table below to determine the command to change the selected object:

Table 9-22

If you want to ...	*Then select...*
Change the border around an object to its default	**Automatic** in the border section
Make the border invisible	**None** in the border section
Change the color, line width, or line style of the border	1. **Custom** 2. The characteristic you want to change 3. The new characteristic from the menu
Change the pattern of an object to its default	**Automatic** in the pattern section
Make the pattern invisible	**None** in the pattern section
Change the color, line width, or line style of the border	1. **Custom** 2. The characteristic you want to change 3. The new characteristic from the menu

Font   You can change the characteristics of text in your chart. By selecting the text you want to change and choosing the **Font** command from the Format menu, you can change such characteristics as:

▪   Font
▪   Color

- Size
- Style
- Background

Any text you can select in the chart, such as axis text, legends, or titles, can be changed through the Font dialog box, as shown below:

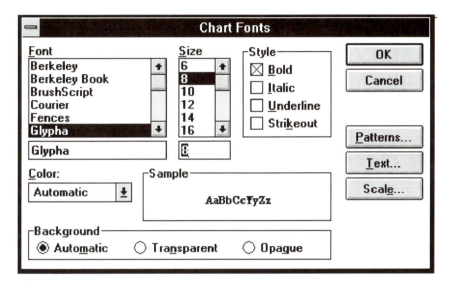

Figure 9.54

To change the text characteristics:

1. Select the text.
2. Select the appropriate option within the Fonts dialog box:

Table 9-23

If you want to change...	*Then...*
Font	Click the font you want within the font window.
Text size	Select the font size within the size window.

Table 9-23 (Continued from previous page)

If you want to change...	Then...
Text style	Select the style (bold, italic, underline, or strikeout) from the Style window.
Color	From the color window, select **Automatic** for the default color, or select another color.
Background (this is the area surrounding the text)	■ Select **Automatic** for the default background **or** ■ Select **Transparent** for a transparent background. **or** ■ Select **Opaque** for an opaque background.

Text　You can change the alignment of text in the chart. The default is text that flows from left to right, but you can change this to top to bottom (two choices), and bottom to top.

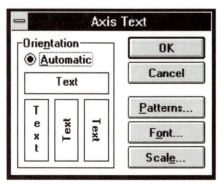

Figure 9.55

After you change the orientation of the text, you can change the characteristics of the object the text is attached to:

Table 9-24

If you want to change the...	Then...	For more information, refer to the Format section under..
Pattern of an object to which the text is attached	1. Click **Pattern** 2. Complete the Patterns dialog box.	Pattern
Font	1. Click **Font** 2. Complete the Font dialog box.	Font
Scale, if the text is attached to an axis	1. Click **Scale** 2. Complete the scale dialog box	Scale

Scale   You may want to change characteristics of the scale for a particular axis, such as changing the scale from linear to logarithmic, for example. The scale dialog boxes are shown below. The dialog boxes are different, depending on whether you have an x, y, or z axis selected. The first example shows the dialog box if the Z axis is selected:

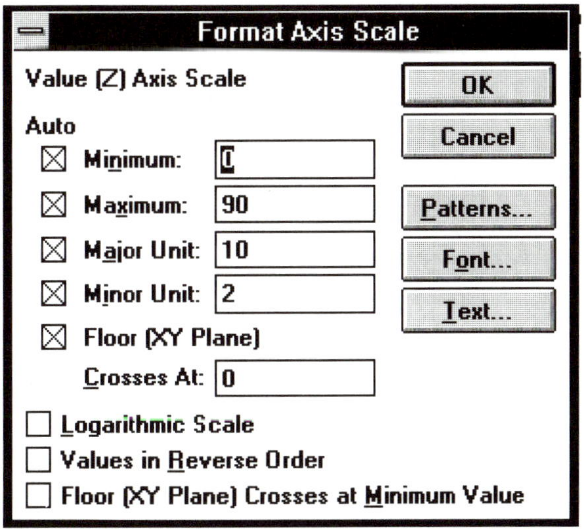

Figure 9.56

The next example shows the dialog box with the X axis selected:

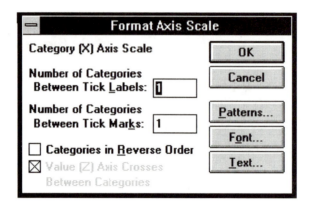

Figure 9.57

To scale an axis, click on the axis, then choose **Scale** from the format menu (**Alt-T, S**)

Use the following table to help you decide the options to use when scaling axes:

Table 9-25

If the chart type is...	And you want to	Then...
Any	Change how many labels are skipped between categories (x axis)	Enter the skip value in **Number of Categories between Tick Labels**.
3D	Change how many labels are skipped between series (on y axis)	Enter the skip value in **Number of Series Between Tick Labels**.
Any	Change how many categories (on x axis) occur between tick marks	Enter the skip value in **Number of Categories between Tick Marks**.
3D	Change how many series (on y axis) occur between tick marks	Enter the skip value in **Number of Series between Tick Marks**.

Table 9-25 (continued from previous page)

If the chart type is...	And you want to	Then...
Any	Place the categories (on x axis) in the reverse order in which they appear in the datasheet	Select **Categories in Reverse Order**.
3D	Place the series (on y axis) in the reverse order in which they appear in the datasheet	Select **Series in Reverse Order**.
Any	Control the smallest value displayed on chart (may exclude items from chart)	Enter value in **Minimum** or Click **Auto** to choose automatically.
Any	Control the largest value displayed on chart (may exclude data items on chart)	Enter the value in **Maximum**. or Click **Auto** to choose automatically
Any	Change the increment between major tick marks	Enter a value in **Major Unit**. or Click **Auto** to choose automatically
Any	Change the increment between minor tick marks	Enter a value in **Minor Unit**. or Click **Auto** to choose automatically
3D	Change where the floor (bottom part of 3D chart) crosses the value axis (z axis)	Enter a value in **Floor (XY Plane) Crosses At**

Table 9-24 *(continued from previous page)*

If the chart type is...	And you want to	Then...
2D	Change where the value axis (y axis) crosses the category axis (x axis)	Enter a value in **Value (Y) Axis Crosses At**.
2D	Change where the category axis (x axis) crosses the value axis (y axis)	Enter a value in **Category (X) Axis Crosses At**.
Scatter (XY)	Change where the y axis crosses the x axis	Enter a value in **Category (Y) axis Crosses At**.
3D	Plot the floor (XY plane) on the minimum value	Select **Floor (XY Plane) Crosses At Minimum Value**.
2D (except scatter or XY format)	Plot the Category axis (x axis) at the highest point on value (y) axis	Select **Category (X) Axis Crosses At Maximum Value**.
Scatter (XY)	Plot the value (y) axis at the highest point on the category (x) axis	Select **Value (Y) Axis Crosses At Maximum Category**.
3D	Plot the value (z) axis between categories	Select **Value (Z) Axis Crosses Between Categories**.
2D	Plot the value (y) axis between categories	Select **Value (Y) Axis Crosses Between Categories**.
2D	Plot the value (y) axis at the last category	Select **Value (Y) Axis Crosses at Maximum Category**.
2D	Plot the value (y) axis at a specified category	Enter value in the **Value (Y) axis Crosses at Category Number**.

Legend The *legend* is the portion of your chart that shows you what symbols identify the different categories. In the example below, the legend is showing the different colors for the East, West, and North categories.

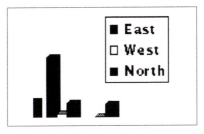

Figure 9.58

The Legend menu, shown below, allows you to place the legend at one of five different locations within the chart, to change the font for the legend, and to change the patterns used within the legend box.

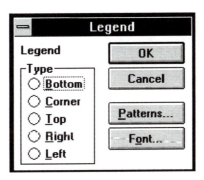

Figure 9.59

Follow these steps to move the legend:

1. Select the legend in the chart.

2. From the Format menu, choose **Legend** (**Alt-T, L**).

3. From the **Type** box, select the position you want for the legend.

    The legend is moved to the new location.

Note that you can also move the legend with the mouse by clicking the legend and dragging it to the new location.

To change the font, click the font button (**Alt-O**). Refer to the "Font" section earlier in this chapter for instructions on using the Font menu.

To change the patterns within the legend, select the pattern button (**Alt-P**). Refer to the "Patterns" section for instructions on using the Patterns menu.

Number   There are also formatting options with the datasheet as well as the chart. You may want to control how values are displayed within the datasheet by specifying how many places are used after the decimal point, for example. Using the Number formatting option, you can specify:

- The number of places to add after the decimal point, including none

- Commas to be used every three decimal places

- Dollar signs to be used for numeric amounts

- Negative amounts to be enclosed within parentheses (and optionally displayed as red)

- Many other different ways of displaying data information

The number menu follows.

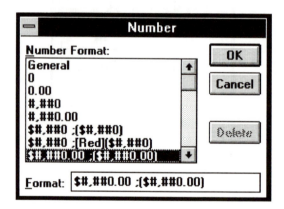

Figure 9.60

The Help system for Graph has a good explanation and examples of the different types of number formats.

Follow these steps to get the Help display on number formats:

1. Select the Help menu (**Alt-H**).

2. Choose How To....

3. Select **Format Data**.

4. Select **Formatting Numbers**.

This displays a help window with examples of the different types of numbering formats.

Follow these steps to format a number or group of cells in the datasheet:

1. Select the cell or cells in the datasheet.
2. From the Format menu, choose **Number**.
3. Select the format type you want to use.
4. Choose **OK**.

The formatting you specified is applied to the selected cells.

Column Width   You can change the width of columns in your datasheet by using the Column Width command. When a column in the datasheet isn't wide enough, Graph displays ### in the column, which means that there are too many characters in the data to fit in the present column width. You may also have columns where the data is only a few characters wide, and much of the space is wasted. In this case, you may want to make the column narrower. The example below shows what your datasheet looks like when you have a column that is too narrow for the data:

	1st Qtr	2nd Qtr	3rd Qtr
East	#########	27.4	90
West	30.6	38.6	34.6
North	45.9	46.9	45

Figure 9.61

To fix this problem, you can simply make the column wider. You can do this using the Column Width dialog box:

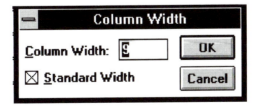

Figure 9.62

To change the column width:

1. Select the column that you want to change (or any cell within the column).

2. From the Format menu, choose **Column Width** (**Alt-T, W**).

3. Enter the new width of the column in the **Column Width** box, or select **Standard Width**, if you want to return to the default settings.

   The selected column is resized to the width you specify.

Chart   The Chart command from the Format menu is what you use to customize the chart appearance. You can duplicate any chart format from the Gallery menu through use of the Format menu, or customize a chart in many different ways. Because using the Gallery command is a much easier way to format the chart, you should use the Chart command only when you can't get the appearance you want by using the predefined formats in the Gallery.

With the Chart command, you can can:

- Choose a different display type (for example, switch from bar to column)

- Choose a display format (for example, stacked bars versus side by side)

- Control various characteristics of the chart (for example, bar depth and width)

The Chart menu is shown below. Note that this menu may vary, depending on the type of chart, such as bar or column, that you have selected.

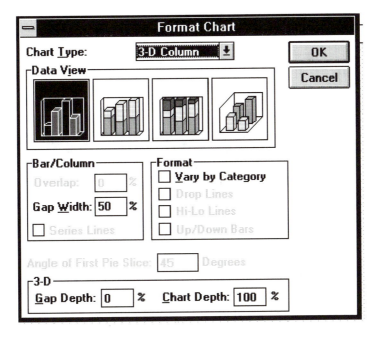

Figure 9.63

To get more information on the what the various options mean, use the help menu:

1. From the Help menu, choose **Commands and Menus**.

2. Select **Format Chart**.

This displays a help window, that explains the different options within the chart format command.

Overlay   The Overlay menu allows you to customize the overlay graph, in the same way that the Chart command allows you to customize the charts. You can duplicate any overlay format from the Gallery menu or customize a chart in many different ways by using this command. Since using the Gallery command is a much easier way to format the chart, use the Overlay command only when you want a format that is unavailable using the Gallery command.

With the Overlay command, you can

- Choose a different overlay type (for example, switch from line to bar)

- Choose a overlay format (for example, stacked bars versus side by side)

▪ Control various characteristics of the overlay (for example, bar depth and width)

The Format Overlay dialog box is shown below. Note that this menu varies, depending on the type of Overlay such as, bar, column or line that you have chosen.

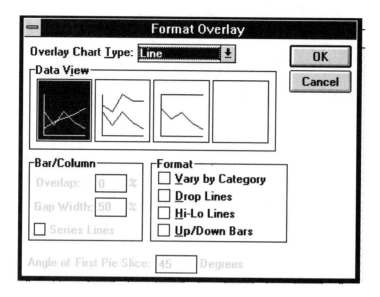

Figure 9.64

3-D View   You can customize the 3D display of any chart by using the Format 3D View menu. With this menu, you can rotate the chart around the vertical and horizontal axes, change perspective, and more. The menu command is shown below:

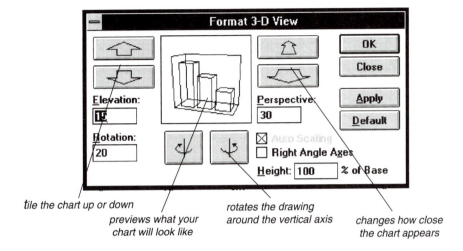

tile the chart up or down

previews what your
chart will look like

rotates the drawing
around the vertical axis

changes how close
the chart appears

Figure 9.65

In the center of the dialog box, you can see a preview of how your chart will look after you apply a command. A brief summary of how to use the menu follows:

Table 9-26

If you want to...	Then...
Rotate the chart around the vertical axis	Use the rotation controls in the bottom center of the dialog box.
Tilt the chart up or down	Use the tilt controls in upper-left of the dialog box.
Change the perspective of the chart	1. Make sure the Right Angle Axes box is not checked. 2. Use the arrows in the top right of the dialog box.

For a detailed explanation of what each of the commands means, refer to the Help menu for the 3D chart:

1. From the Help menu, choose Commands and Menus.
2. Select Format Chart.

Format Quick Reference

Table 9-27

If you want to...	Then...
Edit the pattern within or bordering an item in the chart	1. Select the item. 2. Select the **Pattern** option. 3. Select the configuration you want.
Change characteristics of the font, such as the font, size, color, bold, italic, underlined, or background	1. Select the text. 2. Select the **Font** option. 3. Select the font characteristics you want.
Change the alignment of text (vertical or horizontal)	1. Select the text. 2. Select the **Text** option. 3. Select the text orientation you want.
Change the scale of one or more axes (from linear to logarithmic, for example)	1. Select the axis to change. 2. Select **Scale**. 3. Select the scale you want.
Change the position of the legend	1. Select the legend. 2. Select the **Legend** option. 3. Select the new position from one of the standard positions. or 1. Select the legend. 2. Drag the legend to the new position.
Change the format of numbers within the datasheet (adding dollar signs, for example)	1. Select the cells to be formatted. 2. Select the **Format** option. 3. Select the format you want.

Table 9-27 (continued from previous page)

If you want to...	Then...
Change the width of a column in the datasheet	1. Select the columns to be changed. 2. Select Column width. 3. Enter the new value for the width.
Customize the chart	1. Select the **Chart** option. 2. Select the new characteristics.
Customize the overlay	1. Select the **Overlay** option. 2. Select the new characteristics.
Change characteristics of a 3D chart, such as how it is rotated	1. Select **3D View**. 2. Select the new characteristics.

SUMMARY

Now you have the skills necessary to prepare sophisticated graphs and incorporate them into your final document. Word provides you with an advanced graphing tool that can be used while preparing text documents. You can take a set of data and prepare attractive 2D and 3D charts, which will greatly enhance any document that needs to present a large amount of numerical information.

CHAPTER 10

USING THE
EQUATION EDITOR

T his chapter includes the following Equation Editor topics:

- *an overview of how to use the Equation Editor*

- *the key features*

- *the Equation Editor Window*

- *the symbol and template palettes*

- *instructions for creating basic mathematical building blocks*

The Equation Editor enables you to create equations, from simple to extremely complex, and import them into your Word document. The Equation Editor has a built-in range of styles for different types of mathematical constructs, which allows you to enter a wide range of functions and symbols and have them appear correctly formatted in your final equation. Although the default formatting provided by the Equation Editor is probably adequate, you can always adjust the appearance of the final equation by using the custom formatting options.

USING THE EQUATION EDITOR TO CREATE AN EQUATION

To create an equation using the Equation Editor, you will generally use the following process:

1. Invoke the Equation Editor from within your Word document.
2. Begin the process of building your equation:

    a. Select a template.

    b. Enter symbols or text.

3. Adjust formatting, if required.
4. Exit the Equation Editor, and import the equations into your Word document.

Invoking the Equation Editor

Invoking the Equation Editor follows the standard Word procedures:

1. From the Insert menu, choose Object (**Alt-I, O**).
2. Choose Equations from the Object dialog box.

The Equation Editor window is displayed on top of your Word document window. At this point, you are in the Equation Editor, and can begin entering equations.

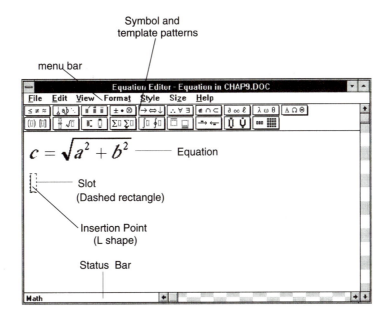

Figure 10.1

This table shows the main features of the Equation Editor Window:

Table 10-1

Feature	Description
Menu Bar	The place where you choose menu options.
Slot	The location for text that is logically grouped together (an index, for example, or the integrand of an equation.)
Insertion point	Identifies which slot you are in, and where text you type will appear.
Symbol palette	The choices for mathematical symbols.
Template palette	The choices for mathematical expressions.
Status bar	Shows the formatting currently in effect.

KEY FEATURES

This section gives you a brief overview of the Equation Editor's key features.

Embedded Object

Equations created with the Equation Editor are stored as *embedded objects*. This means that you can double-click an equation stored in your Word document to invoke the Equation Editor with the selected equation entered and ready for editing.

The Slot

The *slot* is the "building block" for the equation editor. All equations are made up of slots, which are filled with text, symbols, or even other slots. These slots contain related blocks of information that have the same formatting character-istics, such as font size. When you first invoke the Equation editor, you see a single dashed box. The dashed box represents the empty slot. When you type text, select a symbol, or select a template, the results of your action will be placed within the slot.

An equation may consist of many different slots. These slots can be nested, one slot inside of another slot, which is inside of another slot, and so on, enabling you to make extremely complex equations. An example of a complex equation that nests slots is shown below, with the slots enclosed in rectangles:

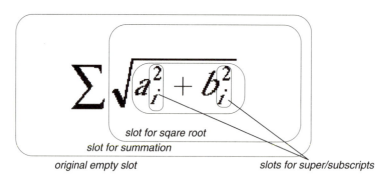

Figure 10.2

Templates consist of one or more slots, depending on the different formatting requirements. For example, there is an integral template that has both upper and lower limits. The upper and lower limits each have their own slots, since the limits require smaller characters than the contents of the integral.

Note that you can insert new templates into the slots of existing templates. For example, look at the definite integral shown below, with the limits of integration left as empty slots:

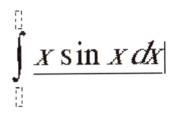

Figure 10.3

You can insert a new template into these empty slots. For example, you could insert summation templates into the empty slots of the definite integral template:

The Insertion Point

The insertion point indicates the current slot. Examples of the insertion point are shown below:

Next character will be inserted before the x	**Next character will be inserted before the y**	**Next character will be inserted after the y**
$\sum\sum x_i y_j$	$\sum\sum x_i y_j$	$\sum\sum x_i y_j$

The horizontal bar runs the length of the current slot. The vertical bar runs from the top to the bottom of the slot and indicates where the next inserted item will appear.

Moving the Insertion Point

Use Table 10-2 as a guide to moving the insertion point:

Table 10-2

If you want to move...	*Then press...*
To the end of the slot or to the end of the next slot if already there	Tab or Enter
To cycle through all the choices	Tab (press repeatedly)
To end the end of the previous slot	Shift-Tab
Right one character	Right Arrow
Left one character	Left Arrow
Up one line	Up Arrow
Down one line	Down Arrow
Beginning of slot	Home
End of slot	End
Previous screen	Page Up
Next screen	Page Down

Selecting an Item

Before you can copy or delete an item, you must select it.

Table 10-3

To select...	Do this...
Part of an equation or matrix	Position the cursor at the start of the equation, hold down the mouse button, and drag to the end of the item you want to select.
A symbol	Hold down **Ctrl**. When the cursor changes, click the symbol.
Everything in a slot	Position the cursor in the slot and double-click.

Deleting Selected Items

Table 10-4

To delete...	Do this...
The character to the left of the insertion point	Press Backspace.
The character to the right of the insertion point	Press **Del**.
The slot	1. Delete its contents. 2. Press **Backspace**. **NOTE:** You cannot delete some slots (for example, the integrand in the integral template).
The selected items	From the Edit menu, choose **Clear**. or Enter the new text.

You can always restore a deleted item by selecting Undo from the Edit menu (**Alt-E, U**) immediately after deleting.

N O T E

Nudging Text

You may want to "fine tune" spacing (called *nudging*) by moving an selection one pixel at a time. You use nudging to:

- move embellishments to better alignment with other embellishments
- form overstrikes or other special characters
- adjust kerning

First, select the item(s) you want to move. Then perform the appropriate action from the table below:

Table 10-5

If you want to move one pixel...	Press...
Left	Ctrl-Left Arrow
Up	Ctrl-Up Arrow
Down	Ctrl-Down Arrow
Right	Ctrl-Right Arrow

Vertically Aligning Equations (Piles)

You may want to enter a series of equations in successive lines and align the equations vertically. Enter a carriage return after each equation, then choose the alignment method from the table below:

Table 10-6

To align the equations…	Do this…	Example
With left alignment	From the Format menu, choose **Align Left** or Press **Ctrl-Shift, L**.	$a = \sin x$ $b = \cos x + y \sin z$
With right alignment	From the Format menu, choose **Align Right** or Press **Ctrl-Shift, R**.	$a = \sin x$ $b = \cos x + y \sin z$
With center alignment	From the Format menu, choose **Align Center**.	$a = \sin x$ $b = \cos x + y \sin z$
With the equals sign (=)	From the Format menu, choose, **Align At =**.	$a + b = \sin x$ $b = \cos x + y \sin z$
With the decimal point (.)	From the Format menu, choose **Align At**.	$a + b = 15.75$ $b + c = 172.1$
With a different point in each equation	From the Space/Ellipses palette, choose the alignment symbol, and insert in each equation where you want to alignment point to be. (The example shows alignment with the "b" variable.)	$a + b_{\triangle} = 15.75$ $b_{\triangle} + c = 172.1$

Status Bar

The Status bar appears at the bottom of the Equation Editor Window, and indicates the current formatting style (for example, **Math** indicates that the math style is being applied to any text you enter).

SYMBOL AND TEMPLATE PALETTES

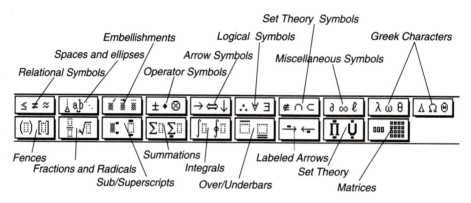

Figure 10.4

Relational Symbols

Description: Contains symbols to express relationships between two quantities, such as greater than, less than, or equal to.

Comments: The less than (<) and greater than (>) symbols are available on the keyboard and are not included in this palette.

Spaces and Ellipses

Description: Contains the alignment symbol, ⚓ the spacing symbols and the 𝖺𝖻 ellipses symbol ▮▮▮

Comments: Use the alignment symbol when you align equations vertically (see section, "Vertically Aligning

Equations"). The spacing symbol overrides the Equation Editor's default spacing. Use the ellipses when you want to indicate items that have been omitted (see section on Matrices).

Embellishments

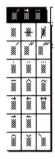

Description: Lets you add embellishments, such as prime symbols, hats, dots, and so on, to a symbol.

Comments:

■ You can put a slash through any symbol by using the slash embellishment at the end of the first row.

■ If you want to remove embellishments from a symbol, choose the first embellishment in the first row.

■ Change the height of all embellishments by using the Spacing command from the Format menu.

■ Change the height of a single embellishment by using the Nudge commands (see the section on Nudging later in this chapter).

Operator Symbols

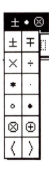

Description: Denotes mathematical operators.

Comments: The angle brackets ⟨ ⟩ are a fixed size (one symbol in height). If you need angle brackets that expand to fit the expression, choose the brackets from the Fences template .

Arrow Symbols

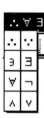

Description: Indicates convergence or implications.

Comments: Use the last symbol ↵ to indicate a carriage return.

Logical Symbols

Description: Contains shorthand symbols for logic expressions such as "not," "and," "such that," and so on.

Set Theory Symbols

Description: Contains symbols for set union, intersection, membership, containment, and elements.

Comments: Note that the second and third rows contain the same symbols, with the third row being a heavier font. The heavier style looks better with summation signs.

Miscellaneous Symbols

Description: Contains symbols that don't fit into other categories.

Greek Characters

Description: Two palettes are included, one for uppercase Greek letters, another for lowercase.

Comments: You can also enter Greek characters by using the keyboard. To enter a Greek letter using the keyboard, press **Ctrl-G**, then enter the corresponding English character. Enter the uppercase English character for the uppercase Greek letter, lowercase for the lowercase Greek letter.

Fences

Description: Encloses expressions.

Comments:

- Fences expand to accommodate equations that span several lines.
- If you want to increase overhang for all fences(the amount of the fence that extends above and below the expression) use the Spacing option from the Format menu. If you just want to change the overhang for the selected fence, use the Size menu.

Fractions and Radicals

Description: Contains templates for fractions and radicals.

Comments:

- Templates with slots that are dotted boxes will be normal size. Templates with solid black boxes for the slots will have the slots smaller size (suitable for sub/superscripts).

- You can nest radicals; the radical sign will be resized to fit correctly:

$$\sqrt{x + \sqrt{y + \sqrt{z}}}$$

Figure 10.5

Sub/Superscripts

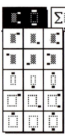

Description: Provides templates for subscripts and super-scripts.

Comments:

- The small black dots indicate the location of the super-scripts and subscripts.

- To attach a superscript or subscript to an existing expression, use the solid blocks (first two rows). Use the dotted blocks to bring up a slot with a superscript slot attached to it. For example, the solid block gives you:

$a \sin x^{\Box}$ where the dotted block gives you:

$a \sin x \Box$

- To change the spacing between the radical and the expression choose Spacing from the Format menu.

Summations

Description: Contains a variety of different summation sign formats. The dotted boxes are the slots for the summation expressions, the small solid boxes are the slots for the limits.

Comments:

■ To create a repeated sum such as this:

$$\sum_{x}\sum_{y}\sum_{z} a_{xyz}$$

insert the summation in the slot of the previous summation, as many times as needed.

■ To create a two-line limit, such as:

$$\sum_{\substack{0<j<10 \\ 0<i<100}} a_{ij}$$

simply enter a carriage return after entering the first line of the limit, then enter the second line.

■ To change the default spacing of all summations, use the **Define** option from the **Size** menu. To change the spacing of the current summation, use the **Spacing** option from the **Format** menu.

■ The size of the summation sign does not change with the size of the summand. To change the size of the summation sign, press **Ctrl**, and select the expression, then use the **Size** menu to choose the size you want.

Integrals

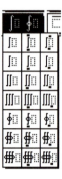

Description: Includes a variety of different integral formats.

Comments:

■ To create repeated integrals, insert the new integral in the slot of the previous integral, as many times as needed as shown below.

■ If you want the integral sign to expand to meet the height of the expression, hold down **Shift** when selecting the integral template.

Over/Underbars

Description: Insert single or double bars above or below expressions.

Labeled Arrows

Description: Labeled arrows indicate convergence to a limit, or properties of a function.

Comments: The small black box indicates the position of the label with respect to the arrow. For example, ⬚→ will let you generate a labeled arrow like this: $\xrightarrow{\text{Label}}$

Set Theory

Description: Symbols for relationships between sets (unions and intersections), products, and coproducts.

Comments: The small black box indicates where indices are; the dotted box indicates the primary slot.

Matrices

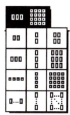

Description: Create vectors and matrices.

Comments:

■ The first row has templates for vectors and matrices of width two.

■ The second row has templates for vectors and matrices of width three.

■ The third row has templates for vectors and matrices of width four.

■ The fourth row has template for vectors and matrices of arbitrary size. When you select a template from this row, a dialog box appears (see discussion below).

Insert the matrix inside of a Fences bracket or template to enclose the matrix using conventional notation:

$$\begin{pmatrix} a & b & c \\ d & e & f \\ g & h & i \end{pmatrix}$$

The Matrix Dialog Box

Whenever you select a template from the last row, the program displays the Matrix dialog box as shown in Figure 10.6.

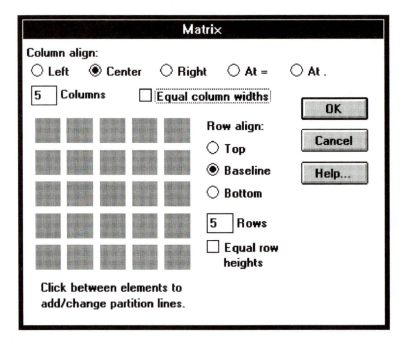

Figure 10.6

This dialog box allows you to:

■ Choose the number of rows or columns in your matrix or vector.

■ Control the alignment of the columns and rows.

■ Create tables or boxes around the equations.

Aligning Column Entries   You can control how equations are aligned horizontally within the columns.

Table 10-7

If you want to the column entries to be...	Click...
Left aligned	Left
Center aligned	Center
Right aligned	Right
Aligned with the equal (=) sign	At =
Aligned with the decimal point (.)	At (.)

Controlling Column Width   If you want all the columns to be the same width, click the Equal Column Widths box. The Equation Editor takes the width of the widest column and changes all other columns to this width. If this box is left blank, the Equation Editor adjusts the space of each column to fit the widest equation in the column.

Aligning Equations Along the Rows   You can choose whether rows are aligned with the tops of the equations, bottoms, or baselines (bottom) of text in the equations:

Table 10-8

If you want rows to be aligned with...	Then choose the Row Align option...
The top of the equation	Top
The bottom of the *text*	Baseline
The bottom of the *equation*	Bottom

Cutting and Pasting Templates

You may often find that you need to put an equation you've created "inside" of another template. For example, suppose you're calculating the length of a line using the quadratic formula, for some set of points:

$$\sqrt{\left(X_{i+1} - X_i\right)^2 + \left(Y_{i+1} - Y_i\right)^2}$$

Figure 10.7

After you create this equation, you realize that you need to put it inside of a summation sign to indicate that you're going to sum the lengths of the lines over the index "i." You cannot just select the summation sign and have it inserted in front of the expression, because you want this expression *inside* of the summation sign's slot, instead of *outside* the summation sign slot.

To insert the expression inside of the summation sign, select the expression (from the Edit menu, choose **Select All**, or drag the cursor over the entire expression with the mouse button pressed). The expression will appear in reverse video, indicating it is selected:

$$\sqrt{\left(X_{i+1} - X_i\right)^2 + \left(Y_{i+1} - Y_i\right)^2}$$

Figure 10.8

From the Edit menu, choose **Cut**. This places the expression in the Clipboard, and removes it from the Equation Editor window. Next, choose the summation sign template:

$$\sum_{i} \square$$

Figure 10.9

Place the cursor inside of the insertion slot (the dotted box) for the summation sign and from the Edit menu select **Paste**. The expression is now pasted inside of the summation sign slot.

$$\sum_{i} \sqrt{\left(x_{i+1} - x_i\right)^2 + \left(y_{i+1} - y_i\right)^2}$$

Figure 10.10

SUMMARY

This completes the section on use of the Equation Editor. Now you have acquired the necessary skills to enter simple-to-complex mathematical expressions in the Equation Editor. You can accept the default formatting provided by the Equation Editor, or you can alter the formatting as desired. The Equation Editor has a different look and feel to it than the other options within Word. The best way to gain familiarity with the Equation Editor is to use it. Once you get comfortable with the user interface, you'll find that the Equation Editor is an indispensable tool to have when you need to express mathematical equations.

CHAPTER 11

MACROS

This chapter includes these topics:

- *what are macros?*

- *why use macros?*

- *how to create macros*

- *how to save macros*

- *how to invoke a macro*

- *how to record a macro*

- *how to run a macro*

- *how to test a macro*

- *macro tutorial*

This chapter discusses one of the most powerful features in Word for Windows—the ability to automate a complex series of operations into a single operation called a *macro*.

WHAT ARE MACROS?

Macros are programs for Word. They contain a sequence of steps that you need to perform repeatedly. They can be as simple as a series of keystrokes, or as complex as a several-hundred-line WordBasic program.

WHY USE MACROS?

Instead of forcing you to repeat the same steps at the keyboard, macros allow you to save time and only enter a single command to perform these actions.

The following example shows the power of macros. Suppose you find yourself changing the order of columns in a table, switching the first column, for example, with the last. This can be a time consuming process to perform manually. A macro called RotateTableColumn (included in the NEWMACROS.DOC file in your Word package) can automate this process for you.

This is the example table:

a	b	c
d	e	f
g	h	i
j	k	l

Suppose you want to swap the first column (a, d, g, j) with the last (c, f, i, l). If you installed RotateTableColumn as a macro in the Table menu, you can perform this operation easily. You can select the macro from the Table menu:

```
┌─────────────────────────────────────────┐
│ Table    Window    Help                   │
│ ┌───────────────────────────────────────┐│
│ │ Insert Cells...                        ││
│ │ Delete Cells...                        ││
│ │ Merge Cells                            ││
│ ├───────────────────────────────────────┤│
│ │ Convert Text to Table...               ││
│ ├───────────────────────────────────────┤│
│ │ Select Row                             ││
│ │ Select Column                          ││
│ │ Select Table   Alt+NumPad 5            ││
│ ├───────────────────────────────────────┤│
│ │ Row Height...                          ││
│ │ Column Width...                        ││
│ ├───────────────────────────────────────┤│
│ │ Split Table                            ││
│ │ √ Gridlines                            ││
│ │ RotateTableColumn                      ││
│ └───────────────────────────────────────┘│
└─────────────────────────────────────────┘
```

Figure 11.1

After selecting this macro, Word rotates the columns of the table automatically:

b	c	a
e	f	d
h	i	g
k	l	j

When you select the table menu, you most likely won't see RotateTableColumn as one of the options. That's because we installed RotateTableColumn as a menu option on our version of Word. Customizing Word menus is just one of the many ways you can configure Word to your exact liking.

N O T E

Macros are not limited to just operations on tables. As you gain more experience with Word macro capability, you may find yourself creating more and more sophisticated macro applications.

HOW TO CREATE MACROS

There are several different ways to create macros. You can

- capture a series of keystrokes
- create a WordBasic program
- edit an existing macro

You capture a series of keystrokes by using the Record Macro command, from the Tools menu (for details, see the section "How to Record a Macro" later in this chapter). This feature of Word lets you type a series of keystrokes that you find yourself performing repeatedly, save them as a macro, then have Word repeat the same sequence of keystrokes whenever you choose to run the macro.

Recording keystrokes is not always the easiest way to proceed, however. You may find that you need to perform basically the same thing over and over, but some of the details change. In this case, you need to create or edit a macro using WordBasic. (WordBasic is a programming language in which *all* macros are stored in—even macros you create by recording keystrokes are converted to the WordBasic language.) You can do this by creating your macro "from scratch" in the WordBasic language, or you can record the series of keystrokes that you perform for a specific document, then edit that macro to add the features you want for the general case. For a novice, it's probably better to take the first approach: record a series of keystrokes to get a rough idea of how to create your macro, then customize it later using your knowledge of WordBasic. Details of programming in WordBasic are explained in Chapter 13, "WordBasic".

HOW TO SAVE MACROS

There are two basic types of macros—macros that are available only for a particular template (template macros), and macros that are available for every document (global macros). At first, you might think that every macro should be saved as a global macro, since you could then access it from any document. If you're going to create only a few macros, this approach may be acceptable. But once you start adding a lot of macros to your global library, you'll find that giving all of them unique names can become confusing. Also, you may find that one type of template requires a slightly different version of a macro than another template. By associating a macro with a particular template, you can avoid this confusion, and customize each macro to the template you need.

Table 11-1

If you plan to use the macro that is...	Then select...
Unique to a particular template	**Template**
Used by many different templates	**Global**

Using the Macro in a Template

Each document has a template associated with it. When you first open a document, Word assigns it the Normal template by default. The Normal template is a general-purpose template, and is designed to meet only the basic document formatting needs. Whenever you create macros in a document that is assigned to the Normal template, the macros are saved as global macros. Any other template allows you to choose whether you want the macros to be global or assigned to the current document template. You can easily check which template you are currently using.

1. Choose **Template** from the File menu (**Alt-F,T**).

2. In the Template dialog box, look in the Attach Document To box, which contains the name of the template you are using.

Figure 11.2

Note that the figure indicates that the Normal template is being used (it appears in the Attach Document To: window). If you want your macros to be saved as something other than global macros, you'll need to change to a different template.

To determine if macros will be stored as global or with a template (if you're not using the Normal template), use the following procedure:

1. From the File menu, choose **Template (Alt-F, T)**.

    Word displays the Template dialog box.

2. In the **Store New Macros and Glossaries as box**, choose the appropriate action from the table below:

Table 11-2

If you want to...	Select...
Make all new macros you create local to this template	**With document template**
Choose whether a new macro is to be global or local at the time you create it	**Prompt for Each New**
Make all new macros global	**Global**

Using the Macro Globally

A global macro will be accessible to every document and does not depend on a particular template. By saving your macro as a global macro, you will be able to run it from any document. There are two ways to do this, either by using the Normal template for your document, or by choosing the **Global** or **Prompt for Each New** options within the Template window.

Table 11-3

If your template is...	And...	Then...
Normal	you want all new macros to be global	no action is necessary. All macros you save in a document using the Normal template will be global.
Other than the Normal template	you want to choose which macros are global or assigned to your current template	change the Template option to Prompt for Each New.
Other than the Normal template	you want all new macros to be global	change the Template option to Global.

HOW TO INVOKE A MACRO

Word allows you to pick the best way to select and run your macro. You can:

- Select the macro from the list of macros in the Tools/Macros command.
- Select a special key combination to run your macro automatically.
- Assign the macro to one of the pull-down menus.
- Place an entry for the macro in the toolbar.

In general, using the list of macros from the Tools/Macro command gives you the greatest flexibility, with nearly unlimited choices for the macro name. You can select any macro using this method, as any macro saved for the current template and all global macros are visible. Key combinations, while providing faster access, provide a more limited set of possible macros, as there is a more limited set of unique key combinations available. You can also insert a macro in one of the pull-down menus as an option. The quickest way to find and invoke your macro is by using the Toolbar option, which allows you to associate an icon on the Toolbar with the macro. There are, however, only a very limited number of spaces for new icons, and you may be forced to remove existing icons to accomodate your macro-naming scheme.

This gives you some idea of how to proceed—use the Toolbar option only for the very few macros that you expect to use very often, key combinations for macros that will see a fair amount of use, and simply use the default method of selecting through the Tools/Macro macro list for macros that you will use infreqently.

Table 11-4

If you expect to use the macro...	Then...
Very frequently	assign it as a Toolbar icon.
Frequently	assign it as a keystroke combination.
Somewhat often	assign it as a menu option.
Occasionally	use the macro list from the Tools/Macro command (that is the default, no action on your part is required).

Assigning the Macro as a Toolbar Icon

This procedure explains how to assign a macro to a Toolbar icon. You can assign a Toolbar icon to a macro, then invoke and run the macro simply by clicking the appropriate icon on the Toolbar.

1. From the Tools menu, select **Options** (**Alt-O, O**).

    Word displays the Options dialog box.

2. Select the **Category** column on the left side (**Alt-C**), then click
    Toolbar. (If you don't see the Toolbar option, then scroll the selections
    up and down by using the scroll arrows or button).

    Word displays the Toolbar options dialog box.

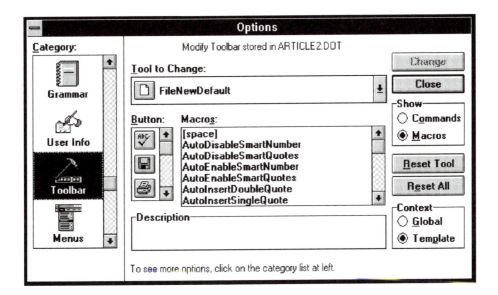

Figure 11.3

3. In the Show box, select Macros (**Alt-M**).

4. In the Context box, click either **Global** (**Alt-G**) or **Template** (**Alt-P**),
    depending on whether you want the macro to be global or assigned to
    the current template. (Note that if you are using the Normal template,
    only the Global option is available).

5. Scroll through the list in the Macros box until you see the macro you
    want to assign to a Toolbar icon.

6. Select the macro name.

7. Now decide on whether to replace an existing button on the toolbar or
    add a new button to those already on the toolbar.

Table 11-5

If you want to...	Then...
Replace an existing button	Go to the Tool to Change box (**Alt-T**) and scroll through the list of tools and buttons (the button appears on the left, the tool name on the right) until you get to the button you want to replace. Click this selection.
Add a new button	Select the Macros box (**Alt-S**), then select [space] (this is the first entry in the list).

8. Select the button you want to appear in the toolbar. Go to the button window (**Alt-B**) and select the button type you like.

   There are many different styles of buttons. Scroll through the list to get to the style you like. Click on the button style you want.

9. If you are satisfied with your choices, select **Change**, then select **Close** to add your button to the Toolbar.

You will now see the button you chose appear on the Toolbar, and you will be able to run your macro by clicking this button.

Assigning a Key Combination to a Macro

This procedure shows you how to assign a key sequence to a macro. After using this procedure, you will be able to invoke your macro with a key sequence such as **Ctrl-Shift-A**.

1. From the Tools menu, select **Options** (**Alt-O, O**).

Word displays the Options dialog box.

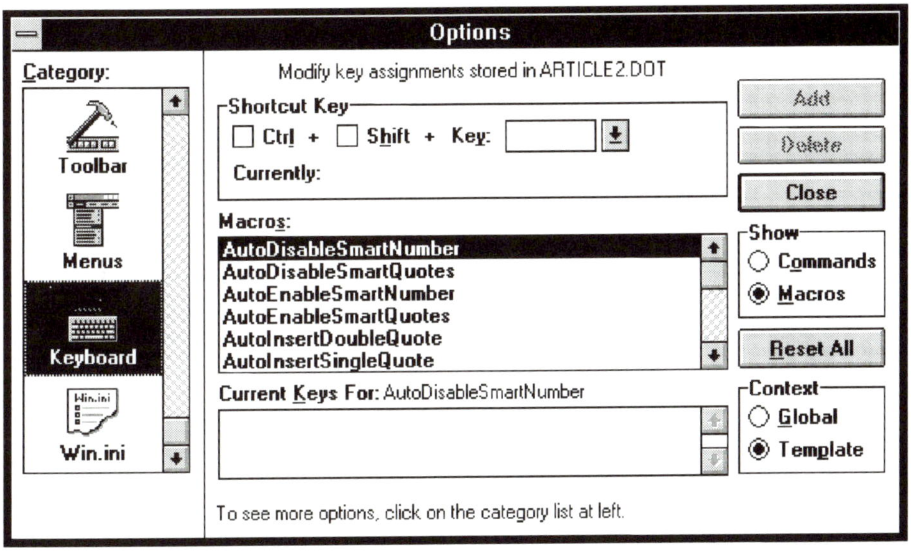

Figure 11.4

If you don't see Keyboard, then scroll the selections up and down by using the scroll arrows or button. Now you will see the keyboard options.

2. In the Show box, select **Macros** (**Alt-M**).

3. In the Category column on the left side, choose **Keyboard**.

   Word displays the Shortcut Key box in the open window.

4. In the Context window, choose either **Global** (**Alt-G**) or **Template** (**Alt-P**), depending on whether you want the macro to be global or assigned to the current template. (Note that if you are using the Normal template, only the Global option is available).

5. Scroll through the list in the Macros box (select the Macros box with **Alt-S**) to get to the macro you want to access through a key combination.

6. Select the macro name.

7. In the **Shortcut Key** box, enter the key combination you want to use to run the macro.

The key combination can have the Control key, the Shift key, plus an alphanumeric key (A through Z, 0-9), a function key (the F1-F12 keys on your keyboard), the Insert key, or the Delete key.

You can toggle whether the Control or Shift key is used (an **x** is in the box) or not (the box is blank). Do this by either clicking the box or entering **Alt-L** for the Control key, **Alt-H** for the Shift key.

WARNING

Do not use a key combination that you use for another purpose. You will overwrite it. Word will tell you if you are using a key combination that has already been assigned. The Currently field in the Shortcut Key box will tell you if the key assignment has already been assigned to another macro.

Note that you can return to the old assignment by using the Reset Tool or Reset All options, or by simply reassigning the keystroke to the old command. If you use the Reset Tool option, then Word will restore all the default assignments for that tool (the keyboard assigments as they existed when you first installed Word). This means that any assign-ments you made for this tool (the keyboard) will be removed. If you choose the Reset All option, then the default assignments for all the tools will be restored.

WARNING

Be careful when selecting a key combination that does not require you to press the Control key, and uses only the Shift key plus some alphabetic key. Suppose you choose **Shift-A** to be the name of your macro. From this point on, whenever you press **Shift-A**, even when you're just capitalizing the first letter of word begin-ning with **A**, the macro will be executed. This probably is not what you intended.

8. To save this key combination, click the **Add** button, then the **Close** button.

Adding a Macro to a Menu

The following procedure shows you how to put your macro name into one of the pull-down menus in Word.

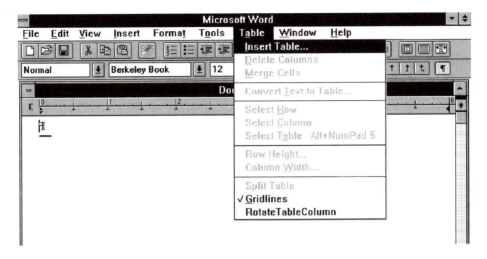

Figure 11.5

1. From the Tools menu, select **Options** (**Alt-O, O**).

   Word displays the Options dialog box.

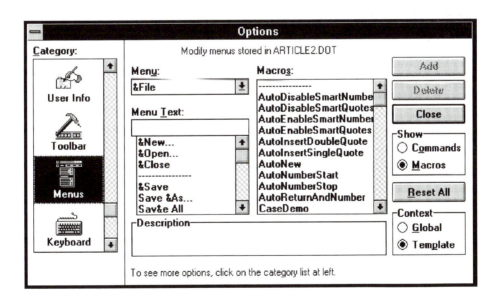

Figure 11.6

2. In the Category column on the left side, choose Menus.

   If you don't see Menus, then scroll the selections up and down using the scroll arrows or button. Word displays the Menus options.

3. In the Context box, select either **Global** (**Alt-G**) or **Template** (**Alt-P**), depending on whether you want the macro to be global or assigned to the current template.

   (Note that if you are using the Normal template, only the Global option is available).

4. Select **Macros** in the Show box (**Alt-S**).

5. Scroll through the list in the macro window to find the macro you want to access through a menu choice.

6. Select this macro name.

7. In the Menu box, select the name of the menu where you want your macro name to appear.

You'll see that the macro name is now in the menu text box, along with an ampersand (&) imbedded in the name. The character following the ampersand is the *access key*—which indicates that you can select this menu item by pressing **Alt** and the character following the ampersand at the same time. (This is same principle Word uses to let you select the Macro box by entering **Alt-S**, for example.)

Initial Access Key Assignment

Figure 11.7

You can change the access key by editing the name in the Menu Text box. For example, if you want to change the access key for Macro5 from its initial assignment of "m" to "o" you would use the following procedure:

Changing the Default Access Key Assignment

1. Go to the Menu Text box (**Alt-T**).

2. Delete the "&" sign.

3. Insert the "&" in front of the access key you want.

Modified Access Key Assignment

Menu Text:

Macr&o5
&New...
&Open...
&Close

&Save
Save &As...
Sav&e All

Figure 11.8

If you've chosen an access key that is used elsewhere in the same menu, then Word will highlight the menu choices with the same access key with each entry of the access key. In our example, we saved Macro5 in the file menu with "O" as the access key, but the "Open" selection choice also has "O" as its access key. Word will step through the choices by highlighting Open the first time you press **Alt-O**, and Macro5 the second time you press **Alt-O**.

N O T E

4. When you're satisfied that everything is correct, choose **Add**, then **Close**.

Choosing Macros from the Macro List

You can decide to use the default way of accessing macros, which is by using the macro list from the Tools/Macro command. Whenever you save a macro and give it a name, that name will appear in the list of macros.

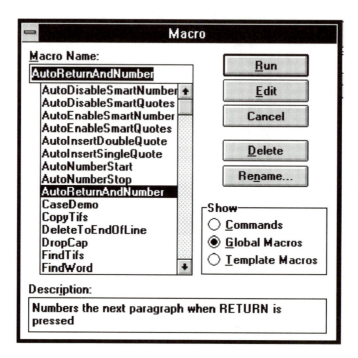

Figure 11.9

To access the macro list, use the following procedure:

1. From the Tools menu, choose **Macros** (**Alt-O**).
2. Choose **Global** (**Alt-G**).

    Word displays a list of global macros.

    or

    Choose **Template** (**Alt-T**).

    Word displays a list of macros assigned to the current template.
3. Choose the macro name you want to run
4. Choose **Run**.

HOW TO RECORD A MACRO

Now that you understand the different ways that you can name your macros, you can go through the procedure for recording a macro. This is a process where Word starts recording every keystroke you enter, until you indicate that you want it to stop recording. You may find that you often want to make your macro more flexible—you will learn about both ways to do that later. First, you will learn about the basics of recording a macro.

Starting Macro Recording

The first step in recording a macro is selecting the **Record Macro** command from the Tools menu. Note that Word automatically assigns a name for the macro in the Record Macro Name box. If you don't like the macro name assigned, you can type another one over it.

You can also assign a shortcut key combination to start recording a macro. You'll see that the default is for a key combination that simultaneously requires the Control key, the Shift key, and any other alphabetic key (a, b, c) combination. If you don't want the Control key or the Shift key, simply click on the corresponding box to remove the X.

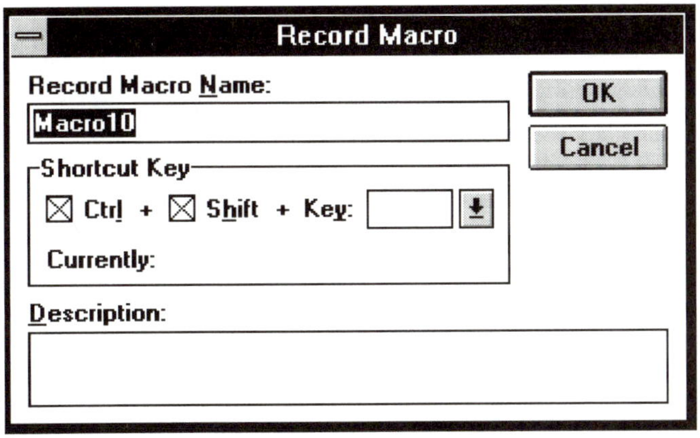

Figure 11.10

WARNING

Be careful when selecting a key combination that does not require you to press the Control key, and only uses the Shift key plus some alphabetic key. Suppose you choose Shift-A to be the name of your macro. From this point on, whenever you press Shift-A, even when you're just capitalizing the first letter of word beginning with A, the macro will be executed. This probably isn't what you intended.

N O T E

Word tells you when you are in macro record mode. Look at the bottom line in your Word window, the status bar. You will see **REC** in the right-hand side when the macro recorder is on.

Recording Your Keystrokes

After you've started the macro recording feature, all keystrokes that you enter will be recorded into the macro until you stop recording. Note that you cannot use the mouse to select text or move the cursor because the macro recorder cannot record mouse movements. This really isn't a disadvantage, when you stop to think about it. Since macros will probably be used in a variety of different documents, the location of the affected text will change as well. You can, however, use the mouse to select menu items, as you normally do.

If You Make Mistakes while Recording Keystrokes

If you're recording a fairly short macro, then it is a simple matter to stop the recording and restart again under the same name. If you're recording a long macro, chances are that you will make at least one mistake, and it is impractical to go back and re -record your macro each time. Depending on the nature of the mistake, you can simply use the Undo command (click the Undo button in the Toolbar), or press **Alt-E, U**, to remove your last entry. After you choose the Undo command and see that the mistake is corrected, enter the correct keystrokes.

Note that the macro recorder is simply recording all of these actions, the incorrect keystrokes, followed by the Undo, followed by the correct keystrokes. This means that you have not removed the incorrect action from the macro. When your macro runs, the incorrect keystrokes will be executed, followed by the Undo command, which will reverse their actions, followed by the correct keystrokes.

You may find that you've made mistakes that you can't undo easily, or there are other changes you'd like to make to your macro once you're finished. Word has a macro editor that allows you to edit an existing macro or create a new macro. You can use this to remove commands or add new ones. You can edit a macro that has incorrect keystrokes followed by Undo commands and remove the incorrect statements and Undo command to make your macro run more efficiently. You use the macro editor after you finish recording your macro, since you cannot correct your mistakes with the editor while recoding. The macro editor is discussed in more detail in a later section of this chapter.

Stopping Macro Recording

To stop macro recording, choose the **Stop Macro** command from the Tools menu. Word saves the macro with the naming convention you specified.

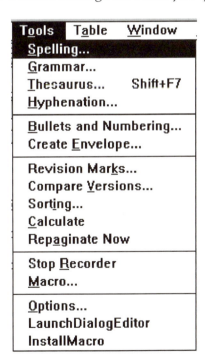

Figure 11.11

RUNNING YOUR MACRO

There are four ways that you can run a macro:

- with a macro name
- with a keystroke combinations
- from a pull-down menu
- with a button on the Toolbar.

The following table shows how:

Table 11-6

If your naming method is...	Then run your macro by...
A name	choosing **Macro** from the Tool menu, then selecting the name (**Alt-T, M**, **name**)
Keystroke	typing the keystroke combination you assigned to the macro
Menu	choosing the macro name from the pull-down menu
Toolbar button	clicking the button on the Toolbar

If You Forget How You Named Your Macro

It is easy to forget the name you've used for your macro. By use of Word's display options, finding your macro is an easy task.

Table 11-7

If you're trying to find a macro by...	Then...
Name	1. From the Tools menu, choose **Macro** (**Alt-O, M**). 2. Ensure that either the global or template macro option is checked. 3. Check the list of macros to find the one you need.
Keystroke	1. From the Tools menu, choose **Options** (**Alt-O, O**). 2. Select **Keyboard**. 3. Check the list of macros to find the one you need.
Menu	1. Choose a menu. 2. Check the list of menu options. 3. Continue steps 1 and 2 until you find the one you need.
Toolbar	1. From the Tools menu, choose **Options** (**Alt-O, O**). 2. Select **Toolbar**. 3. Press **Alt-T** to see a list of all the macros assigned to a Toolbar.

HOW TO TEST A MACRO

Once you've created your macro, the next step is to verify that it works correctly on the documents in which you want to use it. The basic testing procedure is as follows:

1. Create a copy of the document on which you want to test the macro.

2. Run the macro on the document.

3. Verify that the changes are correct.

4. If the macro isn't performing as you expected, then use the Step option through the Macro Edit dialog box to run your macro, one line at a time, until you see where the problem is occuring.

5. Edit and correct the macro.

The following sections explain each of these steps in more detail.

Creating a Copy of Your Document

Creating a copy of the document you want to test your macro on is an important first step. After all, you're testing your macro for the first time, and you really don't know if the macro will do what you intended, or if it's going to damage the document.

Copying your document is an easy process in Word.

1. From the File menu, choose **Save As** (**Alt-F, A**).

   Word displays the **Save As** dialog box:

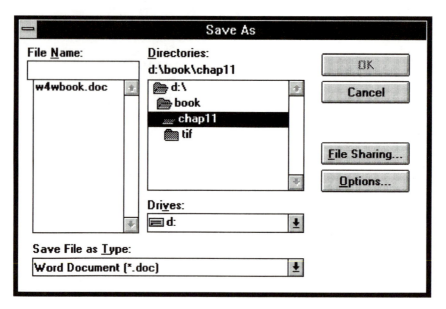

Figure 11.12

2. Enter a new name for the document in the File Name box, and choose **OK**. Now the new document is the one you're currently editing, and the macro will be run on this copy. Remember to go back to your original document when you are finished testing.

Running the Macro

After you've made a copy of your document, the next step is to actually run the macro on your new copy and verify that the macro performed as you intended.

Table 11-8

If you're trying to run a macro by...	Then...
Name	1. From the Tools menu, select, **Macro** (**Alt-O, M**).
	2. Ensure that either the **Global** or **Template** macro option is checked, depending on how you saved your macro.
	3. Check the list of macros to find the one you need.
	4. Select the macro name you want to run.
Keystroke	Enter the keystroke combination for your macro.
Menu	1. Choose the menu that contains the macro.
	2. Select the macro name or use the access key (the underlined character).
Toolbar	Select the Toolbar icon for your macro.

Verifying the Changes

After your macro finishes running, examine your document. Did the macro make the changes you intended? If not, then you'll need to enter the next phase of macro design—the debugging phase. In this next step, you will see how to run a macro one instruction at a time, to see exactly where the error is in the macro.

Using Macro Edit to Step through Your Macro

To single-step through a macro, use the Macro Editing option within the Tools window:

1. From the Tools menu, select **Macro (Alt-O, M)**.

2. Select the Macro name you want to step through.

3. Select the Edit button

Word displays the macro editing window.

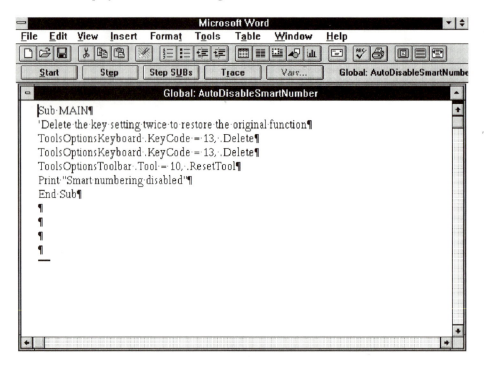

Figure 11.13

You will see several option buttons across the top of the macro edit window:

- Start
- Step
- Step Subs
- Trace
- Vars

Choose a button based on the following criteria:

Table 11-9

If you want to...	Then select...
Perform one line of the macro, entering any other macros that are called, then stop	Step
Perform one line of the macro (without stepping through any of the other macros called) then stop	Step Subs
Run the entire macro in "slow motion"	Trace
Look at the values of any variable in the macro	Vars

Notice that we've introduced some new concepts. A macro may call other macros to avoid making you duplicate instructions that have already been saved as a macro. Your macro, for example, may call other macros that you created earlier. If you already debugged these other macros and know that they are functioning properly, then there is no need to waste time debugging them. This is the reason for the Step and the Step Sub options. Use Step Sub when you want to simply execute the instructions in a called macro without tracing through them, and Step when you want to trace through every macro called.

One thing you'll want to do while debugging your macro is to have both the macro and your test file visible. This way you can actually see the changes your macro is making to the document as you step through the macro, one line at a time.

To split the screen into two windows, one for the macro, and the other for the test file, follow this procedure:

1. Bring up your macro in the macro edit window by

   ■ Pressing **Alt-O, M** to display the list of macros.

   ■ Selecting the macro in the macro list.

   ■ Selecting Edit.

2. Choose the **Arrange Windows** option from the Windows menu (**Alt-W, A**). You'll see something similar to the figure below:

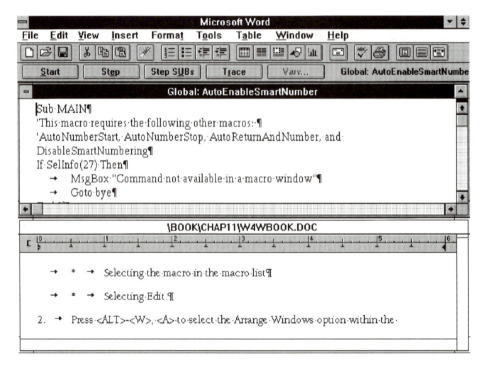

Figure 11.14

To start stepping through your macro, click the document window to make it active, then select the **Step** or **Step Subs** option, and watch the changes to your original text file as your macro runs.

Editing Your Macro with the Macro Editor

As you might have suspected, you can also use the macro editor to edit existing macros, and create new macros. You'll find the editing process quite similar to normal document editing, with a few exceptions. Formatting rules don't apply to macros, since you're not creating a document to be printed.

If you want to learn about the WordBasic macro language as you modify existing macros, place the insertion point at the beginning of any statement in your macro that you want to understand, then press F1. You'll get a help window explaining the function.

N O T E

MACRO TUTORIAL

Now that you've learned the basics of creating, invoking, editing, and debugging macros, you can go through the actual process of creating a macro. The tutorial draws on information you learned in the previous sections, so if you need more information at any point than is contained in this tutorial, refer to the information presented earlier.

Often when you create tables, you perform two steps: the first step is the creation of the table, the next step is drawing a border around the table. As you repeat these operations frequently, it would make sense to put both of them in the form of a single macro. You've also seen that you need to perform these operations in a variety of different templates, which gives you a hint to use later on when deciding the best way to store and invoke your macro.

There are two basic ways to proceed in creating the macro—you can record the macro as a series of keystrokes or you can create it "from scratch" in WordBasic. Since you may not be an expert in WordBasic at this point, this section discusses the keystroke recording method.

First, follow these instructions for stepping through the process of creating a table and drawing a border around it. Then you can start recording the keystrokes as a macro. Gaining a little familiarity with the mechanics of how to create a table with borders will help you avoid entering errors into our macro as you record. Since the macro recorder cannot record mouse movements, you need to use the pull-down menus to create the table, not the Table button on the Toolbar. (The Toolbar icon requires use of the mouse to define the size of the table.)

1. From the Table menu, choose **Insert** (**Alt-A, I**) to create a table.

   For now, assume a fixed table size of two columns by three rows. You will fill in those values in the Insert Table dialog box, which requests table size information.

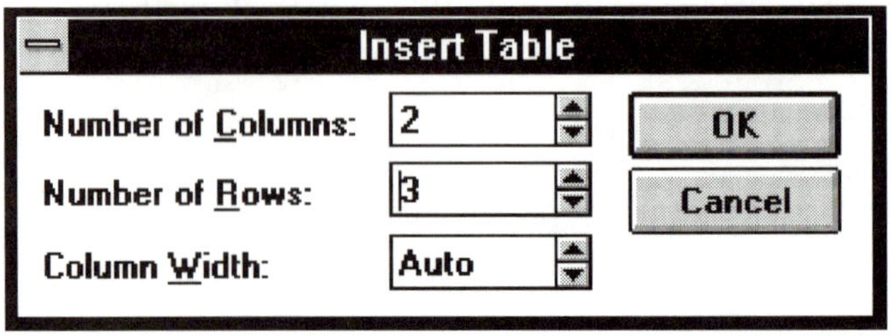

   Figure 11.15

2. Choose **OK**.

   Word inserts an empty table, two columns by three rows, at the current insertion point.

3. From the Table menu, choose **Select Table** (**Alt-A, A**) to select the entire table.

   Remember that the macro recorder cannot record mouse movements, so you cannot use the mouse to select the table.

4. From the Format menu, choose **Border** (**Alt-T, B**).

   Word draws a border around the table.

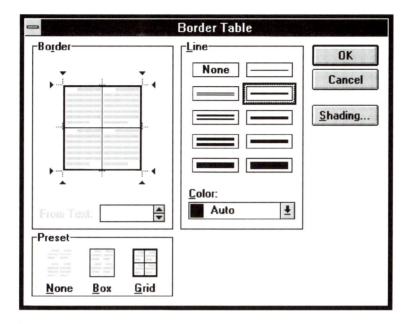

Figure 11.16

5. Select the **Grid** option (**Alt-G**), and select **OK**.

    Word draws a border around the table, and lines between each of the cells.

Now that you understand the mechanics of the table creation process, you can go about the process of recording the keystrokes into a macro. You will need to be able to use this macro with a variety of different templates. This means that you will need to save the macro as a *global macro*.

Follow these steps to make this process easy:

1. Open a new file.

   The Normal template is attached to it by default, and all macros created will be global.

2. From the Tool menu, choose **Record Macro**.

   Word assigns a default name to the macro, such as **macro1**. You will probably want a more meaningful name.

3. In the **Record Macro Name** box change the name to **TableWithBorder**.

4. In the **Description** box, assign a meaningful description to the macro, so when you choose the macro name later on, you can look at the description and remember what it is supposed to do.

   Move to the description window, and enter a description, such as **Create a table with borders**.

5. Select **OK** to start macro recording.

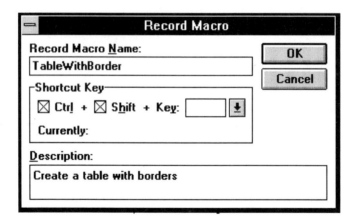

Figure 11.17

Word tells you when you are in macro record mode. Look at the bottom line in your Word window, which is the status bar. You will see **REC** in the right hand side when the macro recorder is on.

N O T E

Pg 17   Sec 1   17/ 32   At 7.8"   Ln 18   Col 1   100%   REC

Now repeat the process you used earlier to create a table with borders: create the table, select the table, then draw the border around the table. After you finish, and the table with borders is created, choose **Stop Recorder** from the Tools menu. The keystrokes you used to record the macro are now saved under the name TableWithBorder. Also note that the REC message disappears from the status bar.

Now verify the operation of your macro. Before you assign the macro to a menu, try it out. Follow these steps to see how to use the various macro debugging features.

1. From the Tools menu, choose **Macro** (**Alt-T, M**).
2. Select your macro (**TableWithBorder**).
3. Select **Run**.

    You should see a table with a border created at the position of insertion point.

Now suppose that your macro didn't work as intended. To debug the macro, you create two windows, one which contains the macro, and another which has the file you're working on. Follow these steps:

1. From the Tools menu, choose **Macro** to create the macro debugging window (**Alt-O, M**).

    Word displays the Macro dialog box.
2. From Word's main Menu bar, choose **Windows**, then **Arrange All**.

    You'll see the macro in one window, and the document in another.
3. Position the insertion point on the Step option in the macro window, and click.
4. Click this option repeatedly, noticing the line of the macro that is highlighted, and the action the macro performs on the document.

The highlighted line shows you the *next* line to be executed when you choose the Step option. This debugging process is valuable when you are trying to determine why a macro isn't working properly.

Now, if you're satisfied that the macro is working properly, decide how to invoke it. Because you want to use this macro in a variety of different templates, this should be a *global macro*. Otherwise, you would need to recreate the macro for every template in which you might use it. This is something you are doing frequently—but not so often you need to insert it as a button on the Toolbar. Instead, you'll add the macro to the Table menu, so you can access it easily.

Follow these steps to add the macro to the Table menu:

1. From the Tools menu, select **Options** (**Alt-T, O**).
2. In the Categories window, select **Menus**.
3. In the Macros window, select **TableWithBorders**.
4. Choose the **Add** button (on the right-hand side of the window).
5. Select **Close** to exit this option.

Now you can invoke this macro from the Table menu. Select the Table menu, and TableWithBorders will appear as one of the last menu choices. Now you can invoke your macro just like any of the Word menu choices.

SUMMARY

Now you can create and edit Word macros and customize the Toolbar and menus with functions you design just for your applications. Chapter 13, "WordBasic" will help you to understand the language in which the macros are written so you can edit and enhance them more easily.

CHAPTER 12

PRINT MERGE: CREATING FORM LETTERS, FORM DOCUMENTS AND MAILING LABELS

This chapter will discuss the basics of Print Merge. You will learn how to:

- *create form letters and documents*
- *create and edit the data file and header files*
- *import data files from other applications*

The chapter finishes with a tutorial that walks you through the print merge process, using example data files and print merge documents from the example floppy disk.

If you've ever found yourself printing several versions of the same letter that differ in only a few areas, or building documents from "boilerplate" text, or you need to create mailing labels, then Word for Windows can help eliminate a lot of this drudgery. By allowing you to create a "master" copy of a document, along with a "data file" which contains the frequently changing information, Word can automate the tedious process of creating form letters and documents.

WHAT ARE FORM LETTERS AND DOCUMENTS?

The term *form letter* refers to a letter that has a few sections of it that change often, but the bulk of which stays constant. One example would be a letter that is part of a mass mailing. The copy you get has your name and address on it, but the rest of the text stays the same for everyone who gets the letter.

Form letters are not restricted to simply having a customized name and address, however. Word allows you to embed decision-making fields in your form letters to make them even more personalized. For example, suppose that you were marketing a product for both men and women, but wanted to stress different aspects of the product, depending on whether the recipient of the letter was male or female. Word would allow you to create a form letter that used different paragraphs, depending on the gender of the recipient.

Form documents use exactly the same concept. Suppose there is a basic contract that you send out to clients, but some of the specific sections within the document change, depending on the type of service the client is being provided. Word allows you to insert other documents into these sections, on the basis of some decision-making fields that are included. For example, if a client is a Medicare patient, you could code instructions into your document to insert another document that deals with Medicare patients. If the client is privately insured, then you could code instructions to insert another document directed privately insured patients.

THE BASICS BEHIND PRINT MERGE

Now that you've gotten an idea of how print merge can be useful, look at the process in some more detail. As mentioned at the beginning of the chapter, there are two files used in the print merge process: the *data file* and the *main document*. The data file will contain all the variable information in your document, and the main document contains the text that remains constant, and instructions (referred to as *fields*) about how to fill in the variable information. You can also can select only portions of the data file to be used at print merge time, by using the Print Merge / Merge / Record Selection menu commands. For example, suppose you just want to send the documents to customers who live in Oregon. You could tell Word to pull only the records from the data file that have Oregon in the state field.

The Data file

The data file can be either a Word document you create yourself, or a Microsoft Excel, dBase, Lotus 1-2-3, or WordPerfect file.

If you create the data file in Word, the file contains two basic sections: a header section, and the record section. Both the header and record sections are made up of fields. If the concept of records and fields is new to you, the next paragraph will help. Most of time, you will not need to understand how the data file is structured. Word has macros to help you create and edit the data file when the data file is created at the same time as the main document.

Think of a file as consisting of lines of information, with each line containing all the information on a particular item. Each distinct piece of information on the line is considered a field. For example, suppose your data file was a list of all the employees in the company, one employee per line, and each line consisting of information like the employee name, home address, social security number, phone, and emergency contact. The line of information associated with the individual employee is called a *record*. The individual items within the record, such as the phone number and social security number, are the *fields*.

The first record, or line, in the data file is the *header record*. Each field in the header record is the name of the corresponding information below it. Using our previous example, the header record would consist of employee name, home address, social security number, phone, and emergency contact. The header record has the names for the columns of information underneath it. These names are what you use in the main document fields to extract information from the data file.

The header section is only the first line of the data file. The second through last records in the data file are the actual data. In the following example, this might be information like "John Smith," "13079 SW Pickleberry Way," "508-83-4171," "555-2025," "Mrs. Adolphus Smith," and so on, one line for each employee.

The data file would then look something like the following:

Table 12-1

name	address	ssnumber	phone	contact
John Smith	13079 SW Pickleberry Way	508-83-4171	630-2025	Mrs. Aldophus Smith

Again, don't be too concerned about how the data file is structured. You can use Word's built-in macros to guide you through the creation and editing process. The following chapters describe in detail how to use these macros.

You can leave out the header record information if you create a separate header file (see "The Header File" in this chapter for more information). However, this is really only needed for data files that come from other applications. If you are creating a data file from Word, it would probably be most convenient for you to have the header and data information in the same data file.

The Header File

You may want to use a data file created by another application, and this data file may not have a header record at the beginning of it. You then have two choices: either edit the data file and add a header record manually, or create a separate header file that contains all the field name information. If the data file you're getting from another application may be changing frequently, then you won't want to edit the file continually and add a header record with each revision. In this case, it is much simpler to create a separate file called a *header file*, where the field name information is entered once, and doesn't need to be updated with each new version of the data file. Use of the header file will be explained in the following sections.

The Main Document

The main document will contain all of the text that you want to appear in all documents plus one or more of the following type of fields:

- merge
- if
- ask, prompt, fillin, quote
- mergerec
- next
- skipif, nextif

The **merge** fields are what you use in place of variable text in your main document. In the case of a form letter, a merge field might be the recipient's name and address. The **if** fields allow you to make decisions based on values of text, such as using a record only if the state in the address is Oregon. The **ask**, **prompt**, **fillin**, and **quote** fields insert information that is not available in the data file, either as information that the user enters for each version of the main document or as constant information that appears the same way in every version of the document. The **mergerec** field prints the record number being used in the current version of the document (you can use this to see where information is coming from in the data file). The **next** field pulls information from the next record in the data file, without starting another version of the document. This is useful in situations where you might want to generate a list of names in the document, for example, all the employees who live in Washington. The **skipif** field skips a record that does not meet your requirements, such as skipping any employee records that have a blank entry in the emergency contact field. The **nextif** field merges the next record if a condition you specify is satisfied, like the **next** field, but it allows you to specify conditions for its use.

A Simple Form Letter Example

Suppose you're trying to find a job, and you want to send out dozens of cover letters, but you need to customize the letter in some areas, such as the name of the company and the contact person. First, you would develop a general cover letter and think about what information might change:

13079 SW Easy Street
Tigard, OR 97224
(503)555-2000
January 29, 1992

Mr. Elmer Fudd
Fudd's Factory
12 Fuddy Duddy Rd.
Marmot, OR 97666

Dear Mr. Elmer Fudd:

I read in the *Marmot News* about an opportunity for a NitPick. I feel that I am well-qualified for a position as a NitPick, and would like to submit my resume for your consideration.

I have a great deal of experience in NitPicking, having done almost exactly this kind of work for the past several years. Additionally, I am a wonderful and entertaining employee. My coworkers are constantly entertained by my incessant joking and my prying into their private lives.

Sincerely,

Mr. Wonderful

Figure 12.1

Looking at our (facetious) cover letter, you can see a few things that will change from letter to letter, for example:

- The data under the address
- The person and company to whom the letter is directed
- Where you read about the position
- The nature of the position advertised

The date can be inserted as a date field, which has nothing to do with print merge (simply place the cursor where you want the data, then press **Alt I, T**, and select the appropriate date option). For the rest of the information, you would replace the text in the letter with the names for the fields in the data file. Because you can name the fields in the data file anything you want, you can make the names meaningful. Here's how the example letter looks after the field codes are inserted:

13079 SW Easy Street
Tigard, OR 97224
(503)555-2000
{date \@ "MMMM d, yyyy" }

{mergefield towhom}
{mergefield compname}
{mergefield compaddr }
{mergefield compcsz }

Dear **{ mergefield towhom}**:

I read in the **{mergefield wherefound }** about an opportunity for a **{mergefield jobdesc}**. I feel that I am well-qualified for a position as a **{mergefield jobdesc}**, and would like to submit my resume for your consideration.

I have a great deal of experience in **{mergefield jobdesc}**ing, having done almost exactly this kind of work for the past several years. Additionally, I am a wonderful and entertaining employee. My coworkers are constantly entertained by my incessant joking and my prying into their private lives.

Sincerely,

Mr. Wonderful

Figure 12.2

For this type of letter, you need to create a data file with a column for each of these items. Here's an example:

Table 12-2

towhom	compname	compaddr	compcsz	wherefound	jobdesc
Mr. Smithers	IRS	1099 Taxfield Lane	King City OR 55555	Oregon Fishwrapper	Gopher
Gomer Pyle	Gomer's Service Station	01 Brambleberry Lane	Mayberry, NC 66655	Mayberry Scream n' Tattler	Pump Jockey

When you perform the print merge, Word reads from the data file and inserts the information into a copy of your master document. Your letters will look something like this:

13079 SW Easy Street
Tigard, OR 97224
(503)555-2000
January 31, 1992

Mr. Smithers
IRS
1099 Taxfield Lane
King City, OR 55555

Dear Mr. Smithers:

I read in the Oregon Fishwrapper about an opportunity for a Gopher. I feel that I am well-qualified for a position as a Gopher, and would like to submit my resume for your consideration.

I have a great deal of experience in Gophering, having done almost exactly this kind of work for the past several years. Additionally, I am a wonderful and entertaining employee. My coworkers are constantly entertained by my incessant joking and my prying into their private lives.

Sincerely,

Mr. Wonderful

Figure 12.3

13079 SW Easy Street
Tigard, OR 97224
(503)555-2000
January 31, 1992

Gomer Pyle
Gomer's Service Station
01 Brambleberry Lane
Mayberry, NC 66655

Dear Gomer Pyle:

I read in the Mayberry Scream n' Tattler about an opportunity for a Pump Jockey. I feel that I am well-qualified for a position as a Pump Jockey, and would like to submit my resume for your consideration.

I have a great deal of experience in Pump Jockeying, having done almost exactly this kind of work for the past several years. Additionally, I am a wonderful and entertaining employee. My coworkers are constantly entertained by my incessant joking and my prying into their private lives.

Sincerely,

Mr. Wonderful

Figure 12.4

This is an easy, but practical, example of what you can do with print merge (remember the last time you sent out dozens of cover letters?). No complicated decision-making fields were used, just simple print merge fields, which will probably be adequate for most purposes.

An Overview of the Print Merge Process

When you develop a print merge application, you will probably follow a path like the following:

1. Design your main document.

2. Analyze what information will be changing, and if you will want to select all of the records from the data file or just some of them.

3. If you already have a data file, then you will simply attach the data file to your document and create a header record for the data file, if one doesn't exist (for example, if you are importing spreadsheet data).

Otherwise, if no data file exists, then you will use Word's built-in data file creation macros to define and edit your data file.

4. Insert the fields into your main document. Word checks the field codes against the field names in the data file. You can use Word's built-in macros to make this easier.

5. Perform the print merge with the option of selecting only certain records to be pulled from the data file.

This gives you a "big picture" view of how the print merge process works. The next sections in this chapter explain this process in more detail.

How to Use Print Merge

You probably understand the fundamentals of print merge at this point—how you can create a document with fields that are filled with information from the data file. Now you need to understand in more detail the process you use to develop a print merge letter or document.

The first step is to understand what your final document is going to look like. Make sure you know what portions of your document will change. For example, if you're sending a cover letter to prospective employers, the company, job position, and person to whom you address the letter will certainly change.

Once you've gotten a clear picture of your final document, then start looking at the individual fields that will be changing, and see if you can structure the documents and fields in such a way as to reduce duplicated information.

One example of duplicate information might be in a typical form letter. Suppose your letter started like this:

Ms. Ima Bigshot
SuperMega Electronics
San Hose, CA 97203

Dear Ms. Bigshot:

Blah, blah, blah, please buy our product.

Figure 12.5

If you were going to use this letter for a print merge main document, you would probably replace the name and address section at the beginning with fields, as well as the salutation. But notice that the salutation ("Dear Ms. Bigshot") uses the *last* name from the name in the address section (Ms. Ima Bigshot). If you used one field for the name in the address and another for the name in the salutation, you'd have to enter the same last name information twice in your data file. Instead, structure your data file so the name is broken into two separate fields for the first and last name. The name in the address section would be something like "Ms. {mergefield firstname} {mergefield lastname}," and the salutation would be something like "Dear Ms. {mergefield lastname}." This is just an example to get you thinking of ways to structure your main document and data file, because it's impossible to cover all possible situations and data files with a single method.

Creating a Basic Print Merge Application

The main document is the foundation for your form letters and documents. It contains both unchanging text and fields. These fields can contain names that correspond to fields in the data file, instructions for getting data from the user, and include statements for inserting other documents into your main document. This section discusses how to

- Design your main document
- Create and edit the main document and data file or header file at the same time

There are three basic ways to proceed in creating a print merge application. You can

- Enter the merge fields when you are editing the main document and create the data file or header file when you have finished with the main document.
- Create the data file or header file before editing the main document.
- Alternate between adding mergefields to the main document and editing the data file or header file.

If you know the names of the fields that will be in your data file, then create your data file or header file before entering the field codes in your main document. This way, Word validates the field entries as you type, and you can use Word macros to insert the fields. If you don't know the field names of the data file in advance, then go ahead and insert the field codes into your document as you create it. You can either wait until you finish the main document to create the data file, or you can switch back and forth between the main document and the data file, adding a new field to the data file after each new entry you add to the main document.

Inserting MergeFields into Text   The most common type of field that you'll use is the *mergefield*. This field simply tells Word to get the current record in the data file, and insert the text from the column that has the same title as the mergefield. For example, **mergefield name** inserts the text from the **name** column in the current record.

Inserting Merge Fields without a Data file or Header Record   When you insert field codes into a document that is not yet a print merge application, there is no data file or header file for Word to verify your entries. When you insert print merge fields into such a document, you insert the merge fields just like any other field. You may find yourself in this situation when you are taking a specific document, then converting it into a print merge application. An example would be when you develop a cover letter, then decide to go back and replace the variable text in the cover letter with field codes.

The procedure for inserting fields into a document, then transforming that document into a print merge application, is outlined below. Follow these steps to insert a merge field code:

1. Position the insertion point at the place you want to insert the field.

2. From the Insert menu, choose **Field** (**Alt I, D**.)

    Word displays the Field dialog box.

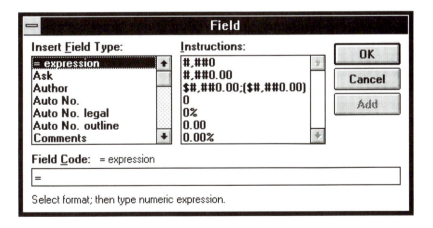

Figure 12.6

3. In the Insert Field Type box, select Merge Field as the field type (**Alt-F**, then select **Merge Fie**

N O T E Make sure Field Codes are displayed. From the View menu (**Alt-V, C**), verify that there is a check mark next to the Fieldcode menu item. If no checkmark next is displayed, click the FieldCode menu item.

Word inserts {**mergefield**} after the insertion point.

4. Position the insertion point to the left of the closing brace, and type the name of the corresponding field in the data file.

   For example, if you wanted to insert data from the column labeled **name**, you would enter {**mergefield name**}.

5. Choose **OK**.

6. Repeat steps 2-5 until you have entered all the mergefields.

Creating a Data File   Now that you have created the main document, you can define the document as a print merge document and create the data file. Follow these steps to create a data file:

1. From the File menu, choose **Print Merge** (**Alt-F, M**).

   Word displays the Print Merge Setup dialog box.

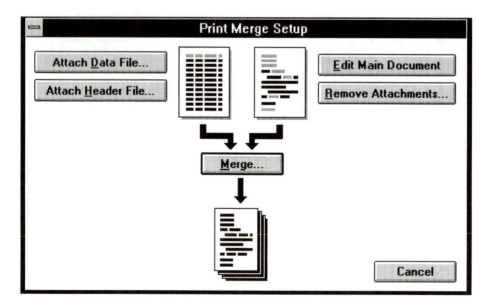

Figure 12.7

2. Select Attach Data File (**Alt-D**).

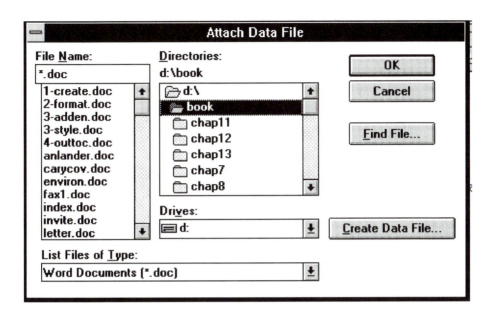

Figure 12.8

3. Choose **Create Data File** to create a new data file.

    Word displays the Create Data File dialog box.

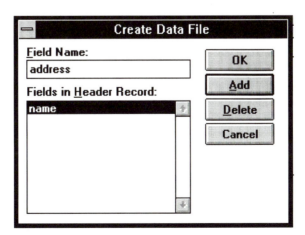

Figure 12.9

4. Add each of the field entries that your main document uses by typing the field name in the **Field Name** box, then choosing **Add** (**Alt-A**).

    In the example menu shown, we've added a field called **address** to the data file, which already has a field called **name** entered. These field names are the names that appear in the mergefield statement ({**mergefield address**} for example) in your main document.

5. After you've entered all your mergefield names, choose **OK**.

Creating a Header File Follow these steps if you want to just define your header file instead of creating an entire data file:

1. From the Print Merge Setup dialog box, choose **Attach Header File** (**Alt-H**).

    Word displays the Attach Header File dialog box.

2. Create a new header file by choosing **Create Header File** (**Alt-C**).

    Word displays the Create Header File dialog box.

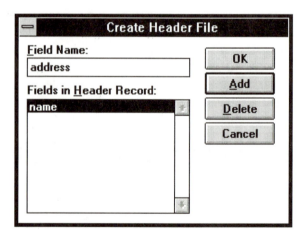

Figure 12.10

3. In the Field Name box, enter the names of the new fields in the header file.

4. Choose Add (**ALT-A**).

    Word adds the new fields to the header file.

Checking the Main Document After you finish creating the header file or main document, Word displays a window, reporting any discrepancies between the field names you used in the main document and the field names in the data file:

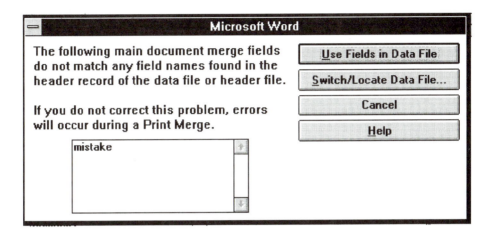

Figure 12.11

The box in the lower left has a list of all the fields in your main document that don't match any field names in your data file. In our example, we entered a field called "mistake" which does not match any field names in the data file. These are errors that you have to fix eventually, so you must take one of the following courses of action:

Table 12-3

If you want to...	*Then choose...*
Ignore the problem now, fix it later	Use Fields in Data File (**Alt-U**)
Fix the problem	Cancel and choose **Edit Data File** in the new option bar (see Figure 12.12)
Use another data file	Switch/Locate Data File (**Alt-S**)

If you don't have any problems, or you do have problems and choose **Cancel** or **Use Fields in Data File**, as described in the table above, you will see that you now have a new menu bar in the document window:

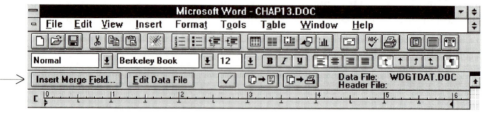

Figure 12.12

This Toolbar gives you some new options. You can

- Insert a merge field with a single button click
- Edit the data file, changing, adding, or correcting field names
- Perform a print merge to a file or a printer

Also note that the name of the data file and header file (if used) are displayed in the right-hand corner of the screen.

If Word identified problems due to name misspellings between your data file header and your main document, then you can correct the merge fields in your main document. If there were problems in the data file, such as a missing field name, then you will need to edit the data file.

Creating and Editing the Data File   When you choose the Edit Data File button, Word opens the data file, and allows you to perform the following operations:

- Add, change, or delete field names.
- Add, change or delete records.
- Number records.
- Sort records.
- Check the data file.

After you choose the Edit Data File button, Word displays the following type of menu:

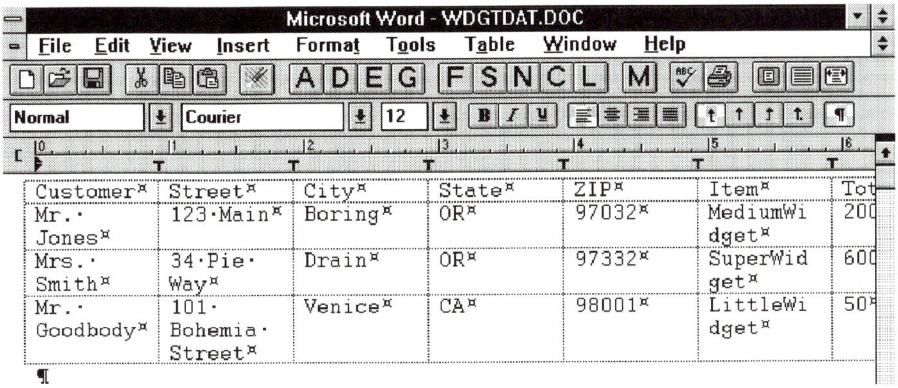

Figure 12.13

The first line of the file is the header record (in the example, this is Customer, Street, City, State, Zip, Item, and Total). The lines after the header record are the actual data (there are three records in the example: Mr. Jones, Mrs. Smith, and Mr. Goodbody).

You also will notice the new icons: **A**, **D**, **E**, **G** and **F**, **S**, **N**, **C**, **L**, and **M**. These icons provide you with quick and easy ways to add or modify information in your data file:

Table 12-4

If you want to...	*Click on...*
Add a new record to the database	A
Delete a record from the database	D
Edit a record in the database	E
Go to a particular record in the database	G
Add a new field to the database	F
Sort the database	S
Number the records in the database	N
Clean up the database (allows several different kinds of checking and reformatting on common database problems)	C
Link to another application's database	L
Switch back to editing the merge document	M

Inserting Merge Fields When a Data file or Header File is Available This section applies when you are creating a new document and the data file or header record exists. Follow these steps:

1. From the File menu, choose **Open (Alt-F, O)** and open your main document.

2. From the File menu, choose **Print Merge (Alt-F, M)** to use it as a print merge application.

   Word displays the Print Merge Setup dialog box.

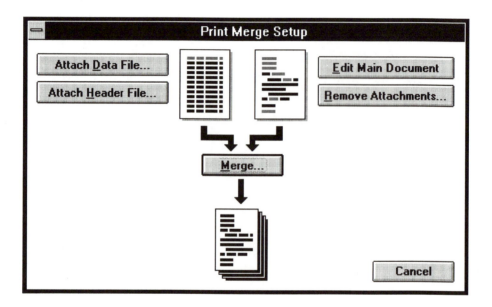

Figure 12.14

At this point, the data file or header file need not exist, but you must create one before trying to use the field commands, as shown in the following sections. The Attach Data File dialog box will give you the option of creating a new data file or header file or using an existing one before continuing. If you don't want to create a data file or header file before continuing, the previous section, "Inserting Merge Fields without a Data file or Header Record" explains the process for doing so.

3. *If you want to define a header file instead a data file*, go on to Step 4.

   If you have an existing data file, or if you want to create one now, follow the steps in the bulleted list below:

   ▪ Select Attach Data File (**Alt-D**).

     Word displays the Attach Data File dialog box, in which you can either attach an existing data file or create a new one.

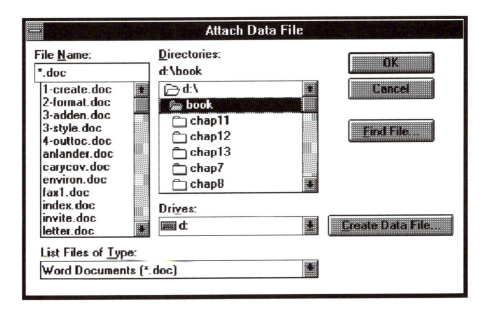

Figure 12.15

   ▪ If you have an existing data file, select the file name from the **File Name** box, and proceed to the section on "Editing Your Main Document."

     or

     a. If you want to create a data file, then choose **Create Data File** (**Alt-C**).

     Word displays the Create Data File dialog box as shown in Figure 12.16.

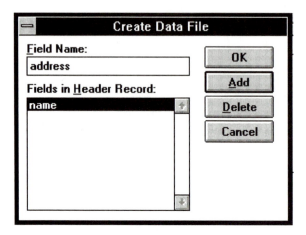

Figure 12.16

This example shows an already created a field called **name**, and a field to be created, called **address**. These field names are the names that appear in the mergefield statement ({**mergefield address**} for example) in your main document.

b. Add each of the field entries that your main document uses by typing the field name in the **Field Name** box, and choosing **Add** (**Alt-A**). Next, proceed to the section "Editing the Main Document."

c. Proceed to Step 5.

4. If you want to just define your header file, choose **Attach Header File** from the Print Merge Setup dialog box.

Word displays the Attach Header File dialog box.

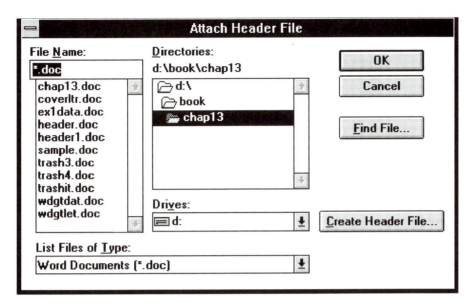

Figure 12.17

5. Next, either:

■ Select an existing header file (by choosing the appropriate file name in the File Name box) and proceed to "Editing Your Main Document."

or

a. Create a new header file by choosing **Create Header File** (**Alt-C**).

Word now displays the Create Header File dialog box.

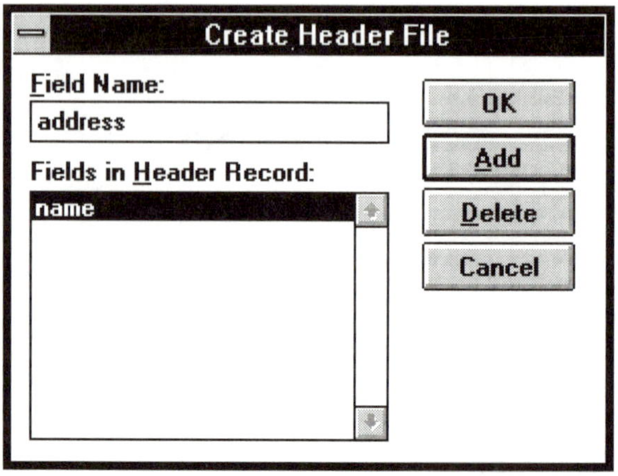

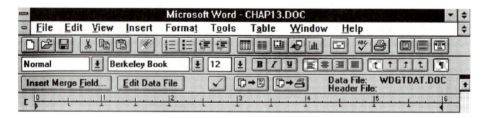

Figure 12.18

b. Enter the names of the new fields in the header file in the Field Name box.

c. Choose **Add** (**Alt-A**) to add it to the header file.

Editing the Main Document After you have finished adding or creating your data file or header file, you will see a new menu bar in your main document window:

Figure 12.19

Whenever you get to a point in the main document text where you want to insert a print merge field, click the Insert Merge Field button to display the Insert Merge Field dialog box. This dialog box shows a list of all the fields in either your data file or the header file, whichever one you chose earlier. In the Print Merge Fields box, select the field name you want to merge.

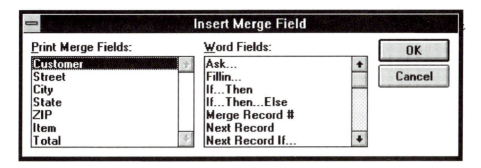

Figure 12.20

Using More Complex Fields for Additional Control

In the previous examples, the mergefield was the only type of field used. That is sufficient for most applications, as Word allows you to choose a portion of the data file if you want to pull only certain records from the data file.

However, there may be times when this is not sufficient. You may need to get additional information from the user at the time you perform the print, to get special comments to insert in the document, or to test to see if records meet conditions that difficult or impractical to specify in the merge menu. You may want to combine several records from the data file into one document.

Getting Data from the User   The **ask** and **fillin** fields allow you to get information from the person who is performing the print merge. There may be information that needs to be in your print merge documents that simply won't be available in the data file. For example, suppose you have a data file of customers, and each month you want to send them mail indicating what items you have "on special" for that month. The information for what you have "on special" changes, but is not the sort of thing you would want to have in the data file (if you had a field called **onspecial**, then you would have to copy the same information over and over for each customer record). Another possibility is that you could have a paragraph in the main document about specials, and simply edit it.

The **ask** and **fillin** fields allow you to avoid editing the main document. By inserting one of these field types, you can print a message to whoever is running the print merge to enter the required information. Word displays a dialog box like the following one when it encounters a field type like **{ask special "Enter the special sale items"}**.

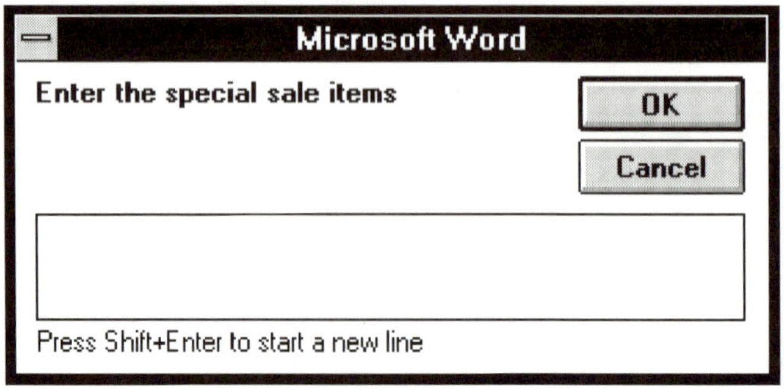

Figure 12.21

The user would enter the appropriate response, like **shoes at 15% off**, and your response would be stored in the label **special**. Now, wherever you want this information to appear in your document, you would simply insert a field with the label "special" in it:

```
Our special for today is {special}
```

If there were only one place in your document where you wanted to insert this information, then you could simply use the **fillin** field instead. The fillin field displays a dialog box, just as the ask field does. The difference is that the fillin field does not store your response in a label. Instead, it inserts your response in its location in your document:

```
The special for this month is
{FILLIN "Enter the special for this month"}
```

Whatever you type in response to the question **Enter the special for this month** will appear at the location of the fillin field in your main document. If you typed **shoes at 15% off**, you would see this in your print merged documents:

```
The special for this month is shoes at 15% off.
```

Using More than One Record at a Time from the Data file There may be occasions when you want several records from your data file to be printed in your print merge document. Suppose you are creating a directory of all your customers and how to contact them. You certainly don't want to print a separate document for each customer, but if you use the mergefield commands by themselves, that's exactly what you'll wind up with. That's where the **next**, **nextif**, and **skipif** commands come into play.

The **next** command tells Word to get the next record in the data file and use that record for whatever field statements follow. Suppose you want to create a document that has five records from the data file, using the name and address field of each record.

You would enter something like:

```
"Directory Listing" {MERGEFIELD name} {MERGEFIELD address}
{NEXT}{MERGEFIELD name} {MERGEFIELD address}
{NEXT}{MERGEFIELD name} {MERGEFIELD address}
{NEXT}{MERGEFIELD name} {MERGEFIELD address}
{NEXT}{MERGEFIELD name} {MERGEFIELD address}
```

This is a somewhat tedious way to proceed, since a directory listing of 100 customers would require 99 {NEXT}{MERGEFIELD..} statements. Still, it gives you an idea of what the **next** command can do.

Now, suppose you just want to print five entries from your data file, but these entries are for customers with sales greater than $500. Assume you've got a field in your data file called "total," where you store the total sales information for each customer. You could use the **nextif** field to select only the customer records that meet your criteria:

```
"Directory Listing" {MERGEFIELD name} {MERGEFIELD address}
{NEXTIF {MERGEFIELD total} > 500}{MERGEFIELD name} {MERGEFIELD address}
{NEXTIF {MERGEFIELD total} > 500}{MERGEFIELD name} {MERGEFIELD address}
{NEXTIF {MERGEFIELD total} > 500}{MERGEFIELD name} {MERGEFIELD address}
{NEXTIF {MERGEFIELD total} > 500}{MERGEFIELD name} {MERGEFIELD ad-
dress}
```

Now suppose you want to send a letter to all your good customers, those who have bought more than $500. Another way of looking at the problem is to say that you want to skip creating a document for any customers who have less than $500 in purchases. You could use the **skipif** field to do this:

```
{SKIPIF {MERGEFIELD total} < 500}
Dear {MERGEFIELD name}
Thanks for your orders this year! We have really enjoyed spending the money
you gave us.
Sincerely
Mr. Widget, Inc.
```

More and More Decisions   The decision-making examples you've seen so far deal with using or excluding certain records from the print merge process. Often, though, you may want to make decisions based on the value of a field and use the results of that decision to determine text to include or exclude from your document. For example, suppose you want to modify the example letter shown above to praise customers who purchased more than $500, and criticize those who didn't (indicating you're not very good with customer relations). You could modify the main document to the following:

```
Dear {MERGEFIELD name}
{IF {MERGEFIELD total} > 500} "Thanks for your orders this year! We
have really enjoyed spending the money you gave us." "Orders from you
were pathetic! Maybe next year will be better..."}
Sincerely
Mr. Widget, Inc.
```

This is an example of an if field—**if** the total is greater than 500, **then** print the first message, **else** print the second.

Comparing Fields with Text Values   You've seen examples of how you can use the if field to see if a line is blank and not print it if it is. You've also learned how to compare against numeric values—**if** a field is greater than some value, **then** print the record.

You can also use if fields with text fields—**if** a field is equal to "Oregon," **then** print the record. You can also use *wild cards*, which make the selection more flexible. For example, you may want to print all employee records whose last names begin with "L." The wild card character * allows you to do this—the statement {IF{MERGEFIELD name} = "L*" "{MERGEFIELD name}"} prints all employee names who have an "L" as the first character of their last names.

Including Other Documents   You can include other documents in your print merge applications and use tests to determine whether to insert the document or not. To *always* include another document, use the **include** field and the document name, like this:

```
{INCLUDE c:\\mydir\\mydoc.doc}
```

Note that Word requires you to use double slashes (\\) instead of the single slash that you commonly use when accessing a DOS file. This example will insert the document *mydoc.doc* from the *mydir* directory in the field location. You can insert the include field by using the Field command from the Insert menu (**Alt-I, D**).

You may find, though, that you need to choose between two or more documents. This is possible by use of the if field. For example, suppose you want to insert a document for patients that are using Medicare, and you have a field in your data file called "insurance" that tells you whether the patient is using Medicare or some other form of insurance. You would insert an include field like this:

```
{IF {MERGEFIELD insurance} = "Medicare" "{INCLUDE c:\\dir\\medcare.doc} " }
```

Refer to the following table for information about defining and using fields.

Table 12-5

If you want to...	Then use the field type...	Example	Result
1) Specify certain conditions for data to be merged	IF	{IF {mergefield amount} > 100 "As your total is more than $100, you are automatically entered in our preferred customer program."}	If the field amount is greater then 100, the text is inserted at the field marker.
2) Prevent blank fields from from being printed		{IF{address}<>"" "{If your application does not have a header record, then you must create one and attach it as a separate header file when you perform the print merge. Header files are discussed in address}"	If the address field is not equal to a blank, then print it at the field marker.
Get information from the user, assign it a label, and use it later in the document in one or more places	ASK	{ASK name "Enter the recipient's name"}	Get the recipient's name from user and assign it to the label "name". No text is printed at the field marker, the response is stored in the label.
Get information from the user and use it in one place.	FILLIN	{FILLIN "Enter the recipient's name"}	Take the user's response and enter it at the current field location.
Define a label as being equal to some string of text, and use it one or more places in the document	SET	{SET tax "={cost}*4%}"}	Evaluate the expression, and assign the result to the label "tax."No text is printed at the field marker, the results are stored in the label.
Insert a string into the document, performing any calculations needed.	QUOTE	QUOTE {={cost*4%}"}	Evaluate the expression and print it in the current field location.
Insert the record number of the record being merged	MERGEREC	{MERGEREC}	Inserts the current record number of the data file at the field location. If the current record is 10. the number "10" is printed.
Get the next record in the in the data file without starting a new document	NEXT	{MERGEFIELD name} {NEXT} {MERGEFIELD name}	Print the name field of the current record, go to the next record in the data file, and print the name from that record.

Table 12-5 (continued from previous page)

If you want to...	then use the field type...	Example	Result
Skip a record in the data file based on certain	SKIPIF	{SKIPIF {MERGEFIELD total<100}	Skip this record entirely if the total field is less than 100, and get the next record from the data file.
Get the next record if certain condition are met	NEXTIF	{MERGEFIELD name} {NEXTIF {MERGEFIELD total}<100} {MERGEFIELD name}	Print the name field of the current record, then, if the total field in the next record is less than 100, get the next record and print the name field.

Creating the Data File Before the Main Document

You may find it necessary or convenient sometimes to prepare your data file without using the built-in macros. This section discusses how you can create a data file or headerfile manually.

Creating Your Data file in Word   To create a data file manually, keep in mind the following concepts:

1. The first line should be the header.

2. The second through the last lines are the actual data.

3. If you're using Word, then consider creating a table in which to store the data file. Otherwise you can separate each field with either tabs, commas, or paragraph marks. If you need more than 31 fields, however, you cannot use a table to store your data. You must use comma or tab-delimited fields.

Using Data Files from Another Application   You are not limited to using just data files prepared from Word. You may have a Lotus 1-2-3 spreadsheet or a dBASE database with the information you need, and you certainly don't want to reenter all this information in another format.

Word supports these products, in addition to Microsoft Excel and WordPerfect versions 4 and 5. Choose the file produced by one of these products as the data file for your print merge. Word will ask you what file format you are converting from.

If Your Data File Does Not Have a Header Record   Word must have a header record to use when using a data file. When you import data from another application, this header file may not necessarily be present. If the application you plan to use does not have a header record, then you must create one and attach it as a separate header file when you perform the print merge. Header files are discussed in the "Creating a Header File" section.

Selecting the Data File Records to Use

There may be many times when you do not want to use every entry in your data file. Suppose you want to send an overdue billing notice to customers whose account balance is greater than $500. The record selection feature for print merge allows you to use only those records from the data file that meet this account balance criteria. This feature of print merge is not limited to just a simple comparison. You can combine many conditions with ANDs and ORs of rules. For example, if you want to use only records from the data file that have San Francisco, CA and Seattle, WA as the city and state, you can specify a rule like "State equal to CA AND City equal to San Francisco OR State equal to Washington AND City equal to Seattle."

This type of record selection is performed after the print merge operation. After you choose **Print Merge** and select the data file or header file, Word displays the Print Merge Setup dialog box, and you can choose the **Merge** button.

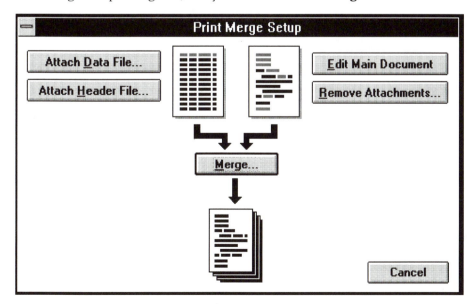

Figure 12.22

After you choose the Merge button, Word displays the Print Merge dialog box where you can choose the **Record Selection** option (**Alt-R**):

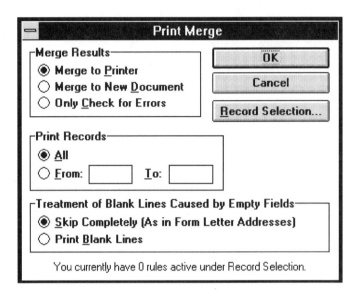

Figure 12.23

After you choose Record Selection, Word displays the Record Selection dialog box:

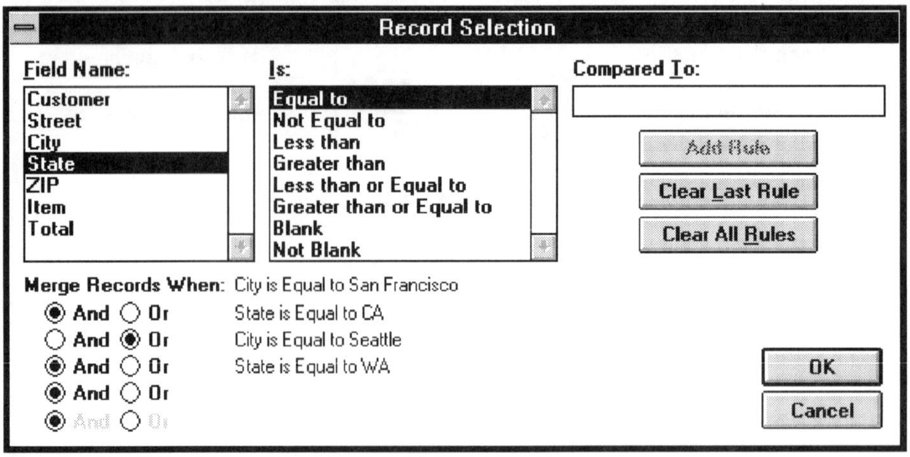

Figure 12.24

In this example, the merge condition is "State equal to CA and City equal to San Francisco OR State equal to Washington and City equal to Seattle." When you are creating the record selection rules, select a field from the **Field Name** box, a condition from the **Is** box, and a value to compare against in the **Compared To** box. Choose **Add Rule** (**Alt-A**) to add the rule to the database. If you have more than one rule, connect them by selecting **And** or **Or** from the **Merge Records When** section.

The Merge Records When section tells Word if the rules are connected by **And** or **Or**. These "and/or" statements are affected by how they are ordered. The **And** conditions are evaluated first, then **Or** conditions are evaluated. If the rules had been rewritten as "City equal to San Francisco or City equal to Seattle and State equal to CA and State equal to WA," the results would be entirely different. Word would look at each record and select it if the city was San Francisco, or the city was Seattle and the state was WA and the state was CA. Records with Seattle as the city would never get printed, since the state would have to be equal to CA and equal to WA—obviously impossible!

PRINT MERGE EXAMPLE

We've created a simple print merge example for you to use and try out. First, make backup copies of the files on your floppy disk. The files you need for this exercise are WDGTLET.DOC and WDGTDAT.DOC, which are the cover letter and data file for a simple print merge application. Copy these two files to a directory on your hard disk. Now, load your copy of the cover letter WDGTLET.DOC. Ensure that the option to view field codes is turned on (**Alt-V, C**). You should see the following text:

Dear {MERGEFIELD Customer}:

Thank you for your recent order of {MERGEFIELD item}. This order will be sent to you within the next few days.{IF {MERGEFIELD total} > 500 "In order to show our appreciation of your business, we are giving you a $25 gift certificate to be used towards your next order"}

{ FILLIN "Enter any special closing comments for {MERGEFIELD Customer}"}

Sincerely,

The ACME Widget Company

Figure 12.25

There is a data file we created manually, by creating a line of header information, and then typing information into the file, using tabs to delimit each record. Attach this file to your main document by performing a print merge (**Alt-F, M, D**), and selecting the file that you copied WDGTDAT.DOC into from the demo disk.

You should be able to edit the data file by clicking EDIT DATAFILE. Word will display a window like this:

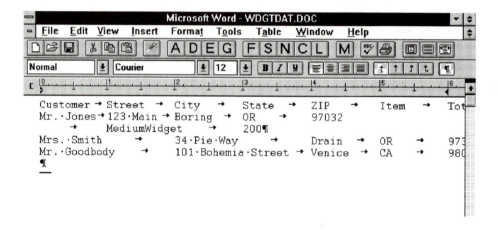

Figure 12.26

The first record is the header record, the second through fourth are data records. Note that the layout is somewhat more confusing than the previous example of a data file, because the fields don't line up in columns. If this bothers you, you can easily convert the text to a table format. Simply select all the text in the data file, then choose **Convert Text to Table** from the Table menu (**Alt-A, T**). Word converts the data file to table format. Now, return to the main document by closing the data file.

Perform a Basic Print Merge

Now that you've attached the data file, it is easy to perform a simple print merge. Click the Print to File button.

Word creates a copy of the document for each record. Since a fillin field was inserted, Word asks you to enter any special comments for each document, and tells you the name of the customer.

Word will print three copies of the document: one for Mr. Jones, one for Mrs. Smith, and one for Mr. Goodbody. Mrs. Smith's total was greater than $500, so the if field conditions were satisfied, and the special message for good customers, promising them a bonus certificate, will be printed. After reading the form letters, close the form letter document.

Select a Subset of Records to Merge

Now suppose you want to print documents only for Oregon customers. You could code this into the document, in the form of nextif or skipif statements, but suppose you want more flexibility than that. In this case, you can use the Print Merge Record Selection dialog box (**Alt-F, M, M, R**). Choose **State**, **Equals**, and **OR** for the compare value. Your menu should look like this:

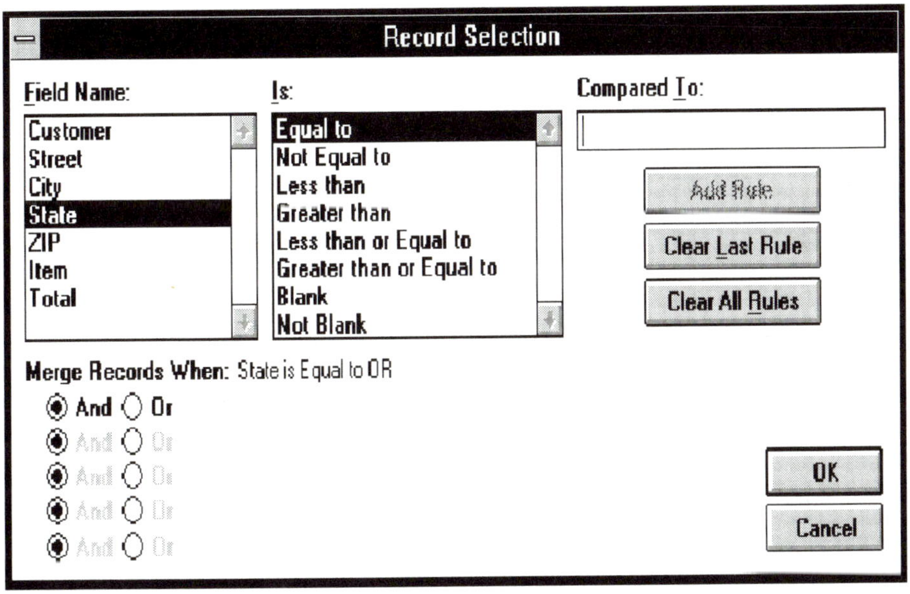

Figure 12.27

Choose **Add Rule** and perform the print merge. Mr. Goodbody will be excluded from the printing because he does not live in Oregon.

Using the SET Field

Imagine you wanted to enter the same comment for all the letters, and you had more than three customers. Entering the same information would be tedious and unnecessary, because you could use the **ask** field instead. Edit your copy of the main document to use the **set** field, in place of the **fillin** field. Put a set field at the beginning of the document, and "special" where the fillin field was. Your document should look like the document pictured below:

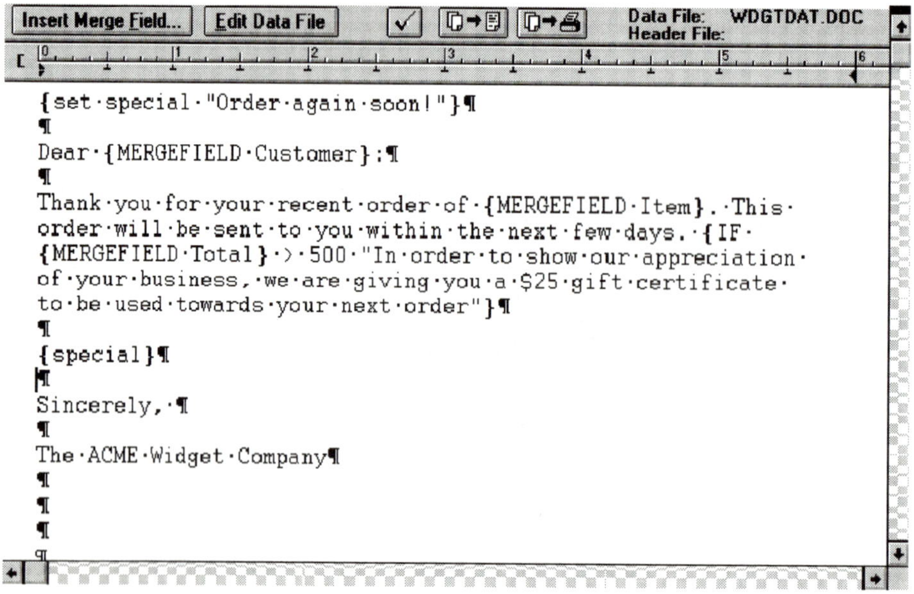

Figure 12.28

Now, when you perform the print merge by selecting the Print to File button, you will see the same text repeated for each copy. Could you have just edited the main document instead, you may wonder? The answer is yes, but by having all the variable information at the beginning of the document, the areas that need to be changed are harder to overlook.

MAILING LABELS

Word provides a convenient way for you to address a large quantity of envelopes by printing mailing labels from a data file, with the same process used in earlier print merge examples. Printing mailing labels is just another application of the print merge process. The difference is that the main document is printed on a sheet of mailing labels, instead of regular paper. Word assumes that you are using Avery mailing labels (or labels that correspond to one of the Avery styles) and formats the document so that the label text will be printed onto the mailing label. Word accomplishes this by putting the label information into cells in a table, and centering the table cells over where the labels will be in document. Word has a special template for the mailing label main document, which calculates how to position the table cells based on the Avery label style you enter.

There are three basic ways to use the mailing label template. You can

- Create a new label data file and print labels from the label data file.

- Print labels using an existing data file from another print merge document. An example would be a print merge document for a form letter. You could use the data file for the form letters to print the mailing labels.

- Print a single mailing label, either manually or from a document, using the letter template

Label printing is an essential part of generating form letters. The convenience of creating form letters automatically would be diminished if you had to manually create the mailing labels. Word allows you to automate both the letter creation and envelope addressing process.

Creating Your Mailing Label Application   Follow these steps to create a mailing label application.

1. Create the main document.
2. From the File menu, choose **New** (**Alt-F, N**).

Word displays the New dialog box.

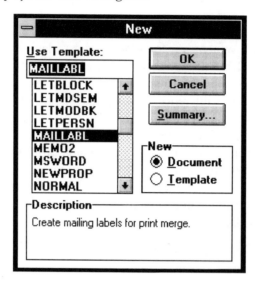

Figure 12.29

3. Select **MAILLABL.DOT** from the Use Template box and choose **OK**. Word displays the Laser Printer Label Sizes dialog box.

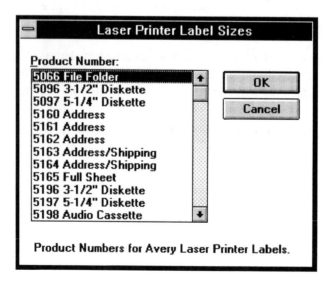

Figure 12.30

4. Select the Avery product number of labels to be printed in the dialog
   box pictured above.

   Next, Word will ask you if you want to print one or more labels:

Figure 12.31

5. Choose **Single Label** or **Multiple Labels**.

   If you just want to print one label, choose Single Label (**Alt-S**).

   If you want to print labels from a data file, then choose Multiple Labels
   (**Alt-M**).

   If you choose to print multiple labels, Word asks you for the name of
   your data file. Choose the name of the data file as you did earlier for
   print merge applications.

Next, Word displays the Layout Mailing Labels dialog box, which allows you
to determine how you want to lay out your mailing labels.

This dialog box allows you to select which fields you want to print on your mailing
labels. As you define your mailing label, you will see how it will appear in the
Sample Mailing Label window. Use the following guidelines when creating your
mailing label:

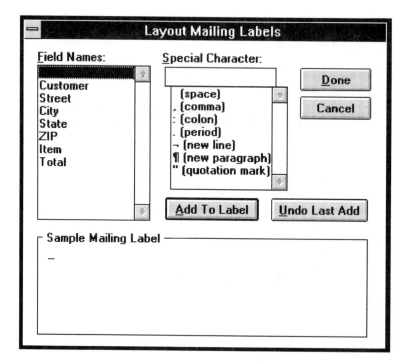

Figure 12.32

■ To add a field to the mailing label, select the field name, then choose **Add to Label** (**Alt-A**).

■ If you want to add a space or a comma, put the next field on a new line, or insert other special characters, select the corresponding special character in the **Special Character** box.

■ If you make a mistake, choose **Undo Last Add** (**Alt-U**). You can choose Undo as many times as necessary, until you remove all fields from the label.

The following is an example of a mailing label layout. Notice that the Customer and Street fields are followed by the new line character, the City and State" fields are separated by a comma, and the State and ZIP fields are separated by a space.

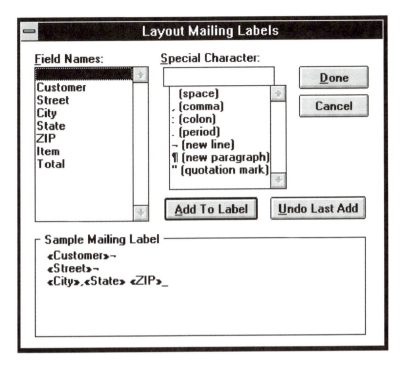

Figure 12.33

After you finish the mailing label definition, Word tells you how to edit the data file or print the mailing labels.

Figure 12.34

Choose **OK** to close the box. Note that you can also print to a file before sending the labels to a printer (use the **Print to File** button).

Word will now create the mailing label main document. Then Word creates a table and inserts a print merge field entry that you made for the mailing labels into each cell of the table.

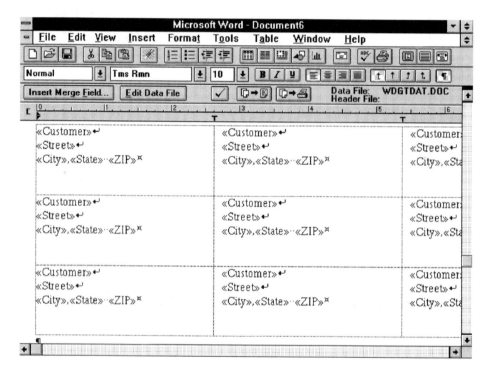

Figure 12.35

After Word fills out the table, you can perform the print merge operation. You may find that printing to a file first will give you some immediate feedback as to whether the print merge operation is set up correctly.

To print to a file, choose the Print to File button to print to the

printer, choose the Print to Printer button .

If you choose the Print to File option, your document will look something like this:

Mr. Jones↵ 123 Main↵ Boring, OR 97032×	Mrs. Smith↵ 34 Pie Way↵ Drain, OR 97332×	Mr. Goodbody↵ 101 Bohemia Street↵ Venice, CA 98001×
×	×	×
×	×	×
×	×	×

Figure 12.36

If this looks correct, you can insert your blank mailing labels into the printer and click the **Print to Printer** button. Since mailing labels are relatively expensive, you may want to print a trial page on a regular sheet of paper, then place this paper over your mailing labels to see if the alignment of the table is correct. If not, then recheck the label type you chose.

SUMMARY

This chapter has presented you with the basic concepts needed to use the Print Merge features of Word succesfully. Now you can use the wide range of Word's Print Merge features, from creating a simple form letter to managing more complex form documents.

CHAPTER 13

WordBasic

This chapter gives you an overview of how to use Microsoft's powerful WordBasic programming language. You will learn

- *how to create your own custom WordBasic programs*

- *techniques for modifying macros you have created by recording keystrokes*

- *some of the basics of programming and debugging techniques*

This chapter also contains suggested review questions and exercises so you can check your understanding of what you have just learned.

WHAT IS WORDBASIC?

WordBasic is a programming language that is very similar to the BASIC programming language. WordBasic, however, is oriented to the Windows environment, providing special features that are needed for applications to work within Windows. In addition to its BASIC-type structure, WordBasic provides access to all of Word's robust text-processing capabilities. WordBasic is a text-processing language for the Windows environment.

WHY USE WORDBASIC?

You might be surprised to learn that, if you've created macros, you've already used WordBasic. Whenever you create a macro, that macro is created in the WordBasic language. But since the macro is stored in a programming-language format, you can easily add features and decision-making capability to your macro that wouldn't be possible if you were restricted to simply entering keystrokes.

Like any powerful programming language, there are many different ways to use WordBasic macros. With WordBasic, you can

- Customize macros of recorded keystrokes to make them more flexible and useful in a wider range of documents
- Perform complicated operations that would not be possible to record as a series of keystrokes
- Create "intelligent" documents, in which selecting a word in the document causes a WordBasic function to execute
- Start and control other Windows applications

You learned from the previous chapter that you can invoke these functions using any combination of special key sequences, Toolbar icons, custom menu choices, and macro lists. This chapter focuses on the fundamental use of WordBasic—creation and editing of macros for text processing.

GETTING STARTED: VIEW AN EXISTING MACRO

There is an easy way to understand some of the fundamentals of WordBasic—create a macro, then list the macro and try to understand how each instruction relates to the action the macro is performing. You can also use this macro to get an understanding of some of the essential concepts of how to create a program.

In the following example, a listing is shown of one of the macros that come with the CHAP12.DOT style sheet in the examples floppy disk—MSGBOXES. It illustrates some of the key concepts of a WordBasic program, but is simple enough to use for an example. Look at the listing of the macro below:

```
Sub MAIN
MsgBox "Mission Completed", "MsgBox with OK Button Demo", 64
a = MsgBox("You can choose YES or NO", "MsgBox with YES and NO
demo", 292)
If a >= 0 Then
    Print "You chose NO"
Else
    Print "You chose YES"
End If
End Sub
```

Simple as this program is, it illustrates several fundamental programming concepts:

- **Functions**: Using other programs, like MsgBox, that are part of the WordBasic function library

- **Variables**: Created and using temporary storage locations, like "a" in this example, to save and manipulate information

- **Decision making**: Controlling program flow by testing and evaluating expressions, such as in the if then else statements

The first and last statements (**Sub MAIN** and **End Sub**) must appear as the first and last statements in every WordBasic program. The second and third statements contain a request to display a message box to the user. A close look shows that there is a fundamental difference between the two statements: one has **MsgBox** at the beginning of the line, the other has **a=MsgBox...** at the beginning. The **a = MsgBox** is an assignment statement—meaning that a variable (which is **a** in this case) is assigned the value returned by **MsgBox**. Note the **if** statement following the **a=MsgBox....** This is a decision statement, which uses the value stored in the variable **a** to determine the appropriate message to print. Don't worry if you don't understand these concepts yet — they are expanded upon in later sections of the chapter.

The point here is to give you an idea what a WordBasic program looks like, so when more definitions are introduced later, it will be easier to relate to how they fit into an actual application. You will run this macro and others and will learn how to use the macro debugging facilities of Word.

WORDBASIC FUNDAMENTALS

This section addresses the most important concepts of WordBasic:

- Ways to get input from the user

- Ways to write results back out

- Basic elements of a WordBasic program.

How to Use the Demo Macros

Before continuing with the rest of the sections in this chapter, you will need to know how to access and use the CHAP13.DOT template on the demo disk. This template contains all the demo macros for this chapter. The following procedure will get you ready to run, examine, and edit the demo macros. Instead of repeating the procedure for each example, you will see it once, in this section.

Copy the CHAP13.DOT template from the floppy disk to your hard disk. You can copy it to the location of your choosing; as an example, you could choose \PWRWord as the directory name.

```
MKDIR \PWRWord
COPY A:\CHAP13.DOT \PWRWord\CHAP13.DOT
```

Now open a new document, and chose \PWRWord\CHAP13.dot as the template (use your pathname, instead of PWRWord, if you chose a different path than the example). You can get a list of the words by selecting Macro from the Tool menu (**Alt-O, M**). Ensure that the **Template Macros** option is selected. To run a macro, select the macro name, then click run. Click Edit to see the macro.

Running, Editing, and Stepping Through the Macros

Now that you've made a copy of the template, feel free to edit and change the demo macros as you see fit. That's the best way to learn and see how WordBasic really works. You're modifying a copy of the demo template, so you can always make another copy of the template from the floppy disk if you've made a lot of changes and want to get back to where you started.

Chapter 11 discussed the macro editor, and how you can use it to modify, single-step, and examine variables. Whenever you see a reference to a macro, use the macro editor to step through the macro to see how it works.

When debugging a macro with the macro editor, be sure to choose Arrange All from the Windows menu (**Alt-W, A**). You want to have two screens when debugging a macro, one with the document in it, and the other with the macro in it. Otherwise, when you step through the macro, the macro will try to access text within itself, instead of your test document. Also note that after you choose Arrange All, you must click on the test document window to make it active prior to performing any single steps, or traces in the macro editor, because (again) the macro may try to access its own text unless the document window is highlighted.

WARNING

Using the Status Bar for Input and Output

Most of the WordBasic routines you will write will require input in some form or another—data entered from a keyboard by the user, or read from a file (like the document on which you want to perform the macro, for example).

Reading from the Status Bar

The simplest way to get information from the user is to input information directly from the status bar, which can be accomplished in a single statement such as the following:

```
Input "Enter your shoe size", size
```

The key word in this statement is **Input**. It tells WordBasic to print whatever follows it to the status bar. Note that there are three parts to the input statement: **Input**, **"Enter your shoe size"**, and **shoesize**.

The text **Enter your shoesize** is printed in the status bar. This is the prompt that the user sees. The word **shoesize** is a variable name that stores the response the user types in the status bar. A *variable* is a temporary storage location for information. In this case, the number that the user enters is stored in **shoesize**, where you can later access it in our program. You will learn more about this later.

First, you need to understand the two basic types of user input: numeric and string. A *numeric entry* is one like **123.5**, or **12**. A *string entry* is something like "**John Doe**" or "**123 Adams**". Basically, a numeric entry contains all numbers (with possibly a decimal point included), and a string entry can be any combination of characters. WordBasic needs to know if you're expecting a numeric or string entry when you use an input statement.

You do this by using the dollar sign (**$**) at the end of a variable name. String variables are distinguished from numeric variables by a dollar sign at the end of the variable name. Suppose that instead of the shoe size, you wanted the user to enter his shoe color. Since this means that you're expecting something like "black" or "brown," you need to use a string variable. The input statement looks something like this:

```
Input "Enter your shoe color", shoecolor$
```

The dollar sign tells Word that the variable **shoecolor** will contain a string, not a numeric value.

Writing to the Status Bar

The next thing you need to know about is how to output data to the user. You can do so easily through use of the **print** statement. Suppose you want to print the shoe size after you read it (OK, so a lot of us have a bad memory, and immediately forget what we typed!). You could print this information through a statement like the following:

```
Print "The shoe size is", shoesize
```

This would print **The shoe size is** on the status bar, but instead of the word **shoesize** appearing at the end of the line, the value of what is in the variable **shoesize** would be printed. You can run the example programs shoesize and shoecolor to demonstrate these principles, using the CHAP13.DOT template (Refer to "How to Use the Demo Macros" for more information).

This is the printed listing of Shoecolor:

```
Sub MAIN
Input "Enter your shoe color", shoecolor$
Print "Your shoe color is ", shoecolor$
End Sub
```

This is the printed listing of Shoesize:

```
Sub MAIN
Input "Enter your shoesize:", size
Print "Your shoesize is ", size
End Sub
```

Using Simple Dialog Boxes

You may have noticed a big difference in how Word presents and requests information from you in the use of the of the status bar for these transactions. Dialog boxes are the boxes that Word displays whenever it communicates with the user and you may have recognized by now that there are many different forms that these dialog boxes could take. Dialog boxes fall into one of the following categories:

- MsgBox
- InputBox
- ListBox
- Combo Box

This section discusses the first two types of dialog boxes, MsgBox and InputBox, in the next section. The ListBox and ComboBox are much more complex, and are best created with a tool called the Dialog Editor. Using the Dialog Editor is discussed in a later section.

MsgBox

The MsgBox is one of the simplest dialog boxes available in Word. You use a MsgBox to either write an informative message to the user, like "Format Completed," or to get a "yes" or "no" answer from the user regarding a question. Unlike the "input" statement, which is easy to overlook because of its location on the status bar, the MsgBox is almost impossible to miss. Load and run "MsgBoxes" from the CHAP13.DOT template. (Refer to "How to Use the Demo Macros," for more information.)

This is the printed listing of MsgBoxes:

```
Sub MAIN
MsgBox "Mission Completed", "MsgBox with OK Button Demo", 64
a = MsgBox("You can choose YES or NO", "MsgBox with YES and NO
demo", 292)
If a >= 0 Then
Print "You chose NO"
Else
Print "You chose YES"
End If
End Sub
```

The example illustrates two basic ways of using the MsgBox: the first prints an informative message; the second asks the user to make a choice, records the choice, and uses it later on in the routine.

Now, look at the demo program in more detail. The first statement after the Sub MAIN header is:

```
MsgBox "Mission Completed", "MsgBox with OK Button Demo", 64
```

Referring to the graphic below, you can see how the different pieces of the "MsgBox" statement affect the displayed result. Since this message box only prints a message and doesn't ask for input, you see the "i" character in the round icon in the box. This stands for "informative" (or "information"), meaning that no response from the user is required other than to choose OK, indicating that the user has read the message. (You need this feature where the user must choose OK, since otherwise you wouldn't know how long to display the message to ensure that the user reads it). This is the first message box you see:

Figure 13.1

This is the second message box you see:

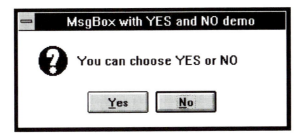

Figure 13.2

Suggestions and Questions

- Single-step through the macros. What do you think the "If" statement does?

- After stepping through the "a=MsgBox.." statement, click the "vars" button in the macro editor. What is the value of the variable "a"?

- Can you predict the value of the next "If" statement?

MSgBox Type Arguments   The last entry in the MsgBox statement is a number. This number tells Word how to construct the MsgBox. There are three parts to the message box that this parameter affects:

- the type of buttons
- the icon symbol that appears to the left of the message
- the default button (the button that is chosen if you simply enter a return after the MsgBox appears)

Word lets you select a combination of these three things by a single parameter. This parameter is the sum of the codes for the button type, the icon type, and the default action. In other words, take the number for the button type you want, add it to the number for the icon type, then add the result to the number for the default action.

Table 13-1

Action	Parameter	Result
Button	0	OK button (default)
	1	OK and cancel
	2	Abort, Retry, Ignore
	3	Yes, No, Cancel
	4	Yes, No
	5	Retry, Cancel
Icons	0	No icon
	16	Stop icon
	32	Question Icon
	48	Attention Icon
	64	Information Icon
Default	0	First Button
	256	Second Button
	512	Third Button

You can try an example to see how this works.

Suppose you want a message box with Yes, No, and Cancel buttons, the Stop icon, and Cancel for the default. From the table you see that 3 is the number for the button type you want. Next, choose the icon number (16) for the Stop icon, and add it to 3. Now take the result (19) and add the code for the third button default to it (512) to it to get the final code of 531 (3+16+512=531).

Load and run the MsgBox2 macro from the CHAP13.DOT template. (Refer to "How to Use the Demo Macros" earlier in this chapter for more information.)

```
Sub Main
n = MsgBox("Choose an action", "MyMacro", 531)
If n =-1 Then
Print "You chose YES"
ElseIf n = 0 Then
Print "You chose NO "
Else
Print "You chose CANCEL"
EndIf
End Sub
```

When you run the macro, you should see a MsgBox like the following:

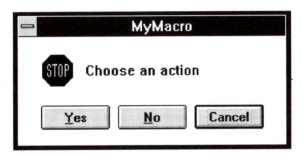

Figure 13.3

Suggestions and Questions

1. Run the macro several times, choosing different buttons, and seeing the messages printed in the status bar. Try *not* choosing a button and just entering a return. You should see a message verifying that "Cancel" was chosen by default.

2. Step through the macro. After executing the **n=MsgBox...** statement, click the **vars** button in the macro debugger menu. What is the value of "n"? Can you predict the next statements to be executed?

3. Choose a different icon, and modify the MsgBox code from 531 to the new value required to display your icon.

Input Box

You've seen how you can display information through the message box and prompt the user for push-button operations. There are many times, however, when you need to get more information from the user, such as the name of the file or a directory.

The InputBox$ provides a means to get more complex information from the user. The InputBox$ statement is used in the following manner:

```
File$ = InputBox$ ( "Question", "Title", "Default")
```

The type of display the InputBox statement produces is like the following:

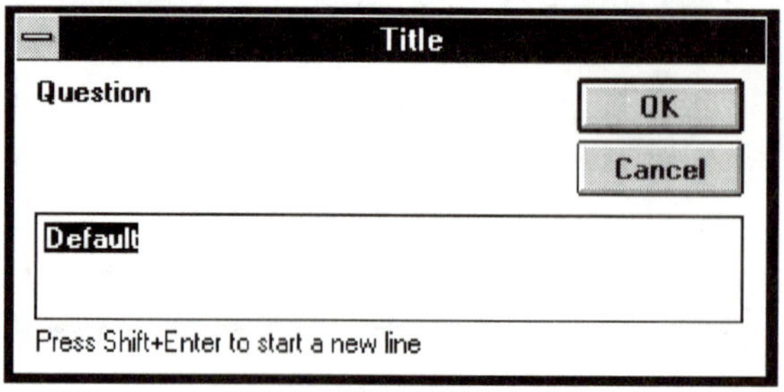

Figure 13.4

The InputBox$ statement works like this:

The InputBox$ statement returns whatever string the user types in response to a question you specify and allows the user to choose a default, also specified by you, by simply selecting the OK button.

You specify the question to be displayed in the first argument (**Question** in the example), the title of the menu as the second argument (**Title**), and the default string to return as the third (**Default**).

The example macro is InputBox, which is in the CHAP13.DOT template. (Refer to "How to Use the Demo Macros" for more information).

This is the printed listing of InputBox:

```
Sub MAIN
a$ = InputBox$("Question", "Title", "default")
MsgBox "You entered " + a$
End Sub
```

Suggestions and Questions

1. Type anything in response to the question, and see it get echoed in the status bar.

2. What is **a$** set to in the example if you simply select OK when the message box is displayed? The answer is Default as the third argument is default; so when the InputBox$ is displayed, and the OK button is chosen without entering any text, the InputBox$ returns the value of "default," and the variable a is set to this value.

3. Change "default" in the InputBox$ statement to something else, and run the macro again. How does the display change? What happens when you choose OK without typing anything else?

Variables

You have gotten a quick look at what variables are and how they are used, in the sections discussing dialog boxes. Without seeing the context of how variables are used, it is difficult to understand the different types of variables and why they are needed. Now that you've covered those basics, read about the variables in more detail.

What are Variables?

Variables are temporary storage locations for information, like numbers or text, that you need to use at different times in your WordBasic program. Variables are really labels or names for locations in the computer's memory. Instead of forcing you to use some complicated scheme to access this memory, WordBasic allows you to give these memory locations meaningful names, like "FileName$" or "NumberOfWords."

Types of Variables

As discussed earlier, there are two basic kinds of variables—numeric and string. A *numeric variable* is a number like 1, 94, or 12.5. A *string variable* can contain text and numbers. Examples of string values are "Title", "My Name is Mike", or "12345 Jacob Ct".

Arrays

So far, you've learned about variables that contain a single value, like a name or number. Often, though, you need to store related information together, and naming a different variable for each piece of information is impractical. WordBasic provides a way to accomplish this, by means of the array structure. An *array* is a group of variables which all share the same name but which are individually accessible with an index.

For example, suppose you want to calculate the average grade of a collection of test scores, and each test score is going to be stored in a variable. If you were forced to name each test score variable a different name, like "Test1," "Test2," and so on, the process of calculating the average would be a tedious painful process (average = (Test1 + Test2 + ... Test100) / 100). Arrays make the process much easier, both to code and modify, since you could instead store the test scores in an array called Test, and access the individual test scores by means of an index, like Test[1], Test[2], and so on. The real power of using an array becomes visible here, because the calculation can the be done inside a loop, instead of by brute force:

```
Dim Test [100]
<some other code here, loading test scores into Test>
Total=0
for i = 1 to NumTests
    Total=Total+Test[i-1]
Next
Print "The average is ", Total/NumTests
```

To use an array, you first must define it by means of the dimension statement. In the example above, Test has 100 elements. When you access the array, however, you do so by using the indexes 0 through 99. There are still 100 elements, but the very first element is accessed with an index of 0. That's why Test[i-1] was in the loop—you are accessing tests 1 to 100 with array elements 0 to 99.

Note that you don't have to use the 0 element; you can always start at element 1 (or any other element). The key is to remember that the last element in your array is one less than the value you have in your dimension statement. If you tried to access Test[100], you would have an error, since the last element of the array is 99.

Here is another point worth noting:

You can dimension string variables as arrays as well—simply dimension them like numeric variables, except for the dollar sign, like this: dim StrVar$[100] You can even use a variable to dimension an array, which is useful when you don't know how big the array needs to be when you write the program. This works just as you might expect:

```
dim Tests [NumberOfStudents]
```

How to Name Variables

WordBasic gives you a lot of flexibility in how you can name variables. There are three basic rules to keep in mind:

- Variable names cannot begin with a number if the variable is a string variable
- End the variable name with a dollar sign ("$")
- Make the variable names meaningful

A valid name for a numeric variable might be "LinesInFile," and "FileName$" might be a valid name for a string variable. Invalid names are names like "1File," since this name begins with a number. Although you are certainly not forced to, it is good idea to make variable names meaningful, as well. For example. a name like "LinesInFile" suggests that it contains a count of the number of lines in a file. Nothing prevents you from naming the variable "L," but you can see immediately how much more difficult it would be to understand what this variable contains if you are reading through a program that you wrote a long time ago, and had forgotten how it worked.

Operations that You Can Perform on Variables

Now that you've read about the two kinds of variables in WordBasic, you're ready to tackle the different kinds of operations that you can perform on them.

Numeric   Not surprisingly, numeric variables are intended for use in mathematical operations, such as addition, multiplication, and so on. The operations you can perform on numeric variables are defined in the following table:

Table 13-2

Operation	*Symbol*	*Action*	*Example*
Assignment	=	Assign the value on the right side of the = to the left.	a = b takes the value of variable b and copies it into variable a.
Addition	+	Adds number on the right of the + sign to the number on the left.	a = b + c adds variable b to variable c and copies the result into variable a

Table 13-2 (continued from previous page)

Operation	Symbol	Action	Example
Subtraction	–	Subtract the number on the right from the number on the left.	a = b - c subtracts variable c from variable b, and places the result in a
Multiplication	*	Multiply the numbers on either side of the * sign.	a = b * c multiplies variable b by variable c and copies the result to variable a
Division	/	Divide the number on the left of the / by the number on the right.	a = b / c divides variable b by variable c and copies the result to variable a.
Modulus	MOD	Take the modulus of the left with the number on the right. MOD converts the numbers to integers, performs a divide, then returns the remainder.	8.5 MOD 2 returns 0 (8.5 becomes a integer (8), 8 divided by 2 gives 4, with 0 as the remainder.
Absolute Value	ABS	Returns the absolute value of a variable.	ABS(-1) returns 1
Signum	SGN	Returns -1 if the argument is less than zero, 0 if the argument is zero, and 1 if the argument is greater than zero.	SGN(-35) is -1 SGN (0) is 0 SGN(123) is 1
Integer	INT	Return the integer portion of a number	INT(12.5) is 12

String   Because string variables are intended for storage of string information, they don't have many of the arithmetic operators available to them. However, there is a large range of string manipulation operators that you can use instead. The following table explains the different types of string operations:

Table 13-3

Operation	*Usage*	*Action*	*Example*
Concatenation	stringa+stringb	Appends stringb to the stringa	b$ = "The" + "cat" b$ will be set to "The cat"
Get ASCII Code for character	ASC(string)	Returns ASCII code for a character	ASC("A") returns 65
Get character for ASCII code	CHR$(num)	Returns character for the ASCII code	CHR$(^&) returns "a"
Find location of search string in target string	InStr(Target string, Search string)	Returns the number of characters into the target string where the search string was found	InStr("Windows", "do") returns 4, since "do" appears four characters into "Windows"
Convert to lowercase	LCase$(String)	Returns a lowercase version of the string	LCase$ ("FILE") returns "file"
Extract characters from string	Left$(string,num)	Left$ returns a string of num characters starting from the left of the string	Left$("ABCDEF",3) returns "ABC"
	Mid$(string, num1,num2)	Mid$ returns a string of num2 characters starting num1 characters into the string	Mid$("ABCDEF",3,2) returns "CD"
	Right$(string, num)	Right$ returns a string of num characters starting from the right of the string	Right$("ABCDEF",3)
Determine the number of characters in a string	Len(string)	Returns the number of characters in a string	Len("ABCDEF") returns a value of 6
Convert a numeric value into its string equivalent	Str$(string)	Returns the string version of a number	Str$(b), if b is set to 4.3, would return "4.3"
Repeat a single character a specific number of times	String$(string, num)	Repeats the first character of string num times	String$("ABC",5) returns 55555

Table 13-3 (continued from previous page)

Operation	Usage	Action	Example
Convert a string to all uppercase	UCase$(string)	Returns a version of string with all uppercase values	UCase$("AbCd") returns "ABCD"
Convert a string to a numeric value	Val(string)	Returns the numeric version of string	Val("123.4") returns 123.4

Placing Document Text into a String Variable   You may often need to copy selected text into a string variable so it can be manipulated and used, so you need to understand some of the WordBasic functions provided for this purpose.

The basic procedure to follow for loading text into a string variable is to use the following steps:

1. Select the text.
2. Assign the selected text to a variable by using the Selection$() function.

You might be tempted to avoid this process and try to use WordBasic's file reading and writing functions on Word documents. This won't work. Word documents are in binary format, which is not compatible with WordBasic file input and output.

To select the text you want to load into a variable, move the cursor to the location where you want to start, then select whatever amount of text you want to load into the variable.

 There is a limit of 32,684 characters that can be loaded into a string variable, so you'll have to limit your selections to be less than 32,684 characters.

N O T E

This section does not discuss the syntax of each function in detail. Instead, there is a table of functions for moving the insertion point and selecting text. To get more information, choose **Index** from the Help menu (**Alt-H, I**), then scroll down and select the WordBasic Programming Reference menu item. From this point, you can select the function on which you want to find more information.

Table 13-4

To move the cursor, with the option of selecting text, from the current location to the...	Use...
Beginning or end of the document	EndOfDocument StartOfDocument
Beginning or end of a window	EndOfWindow StartOfWindow
Next or previous page	NextPage PrevPage
Next or previous paragraph	ParaUp ParaDown
Next or previous sentence	SentRight SentLeft
Beginning or end of a line, or to the previous or next line	EndOfLine StartOfLine LineUp LineDown
Next of previous word	WordLeft WordRight
Next or previous character	CharLeft CharRight
Beginning or end of a column or row in a table, or to the next or previous cell in a table	EndOfColumn StartOfColumn EndOfRow BeginningOfRow NextCell PrevCell

Table 13-4 (continued from previous page)

To move the cursor, with the option of selecting text, from the current location to the...	Use
Next or previous tab stop	NextTab PrevTab
Next or previous object	NextObject PrevObject
Next or previous field	NextField PrevField

The important thing to remember is that these functions allow you to move the insertion point from its current location to the location you specify. You have the option of selecting all the text between the current location of the insertion point, and the place you are moving to. Once the text is selected, you can copy it into a string variable using the Selection$() function.

You may need to search within the document for the appropriate starting point to begin selecting text. If you need to start at a particular word, but you don't know its location, use the EditFind function. This moves the insertion point to the appropriate starting place. If you want to start selecting at a particular line number or word count, use the cursor movement commands combined with the information from SelInfo, described in the table below. Refer to the on-line help for SelInfo, in the WordBasic Reference.

Table 13-5

For the selected text, if you want to find the:	Then the argument to SelInfo should be:
Page number	1
Section number	2
Page in document	3
Number of pages in document	4
Horizontal position of start of selection, relative to the page, Only valid in page view. Returns -1 if the selection is not visible.	5
Vertical position of start of selection, relative to the page. Only valid in page view. Returns -1 if the selection is not visible.	6
Horizontal position of start of selection, relative to enclosing display rectangle. Returns -1 if the selection is not visible.	7
Vertical position of start of selection, relative to enclosing display rectangle. Returns -1 if the selection is not visible.	8
Character column (same as on status bar)	9
Line number	10
Frame status: returns -1 if selection is an entire frame	11
Table: returns -1 if selection is in a table	12
Table row (starting with 1) of start of selection. Valid only if the selection is in a table, otherwise returns a value of -1.	13
Table row of end of selection. Valid only if the selection is in a table, otherwise returns a value of -1.	14
Number of rows in table. Valid only if the selection is in a table, otherwise returns a value of -1.	15
Table column (starting with 1) of start of selection. Valid only if the selection is in a table, otherwise returns a value of -1.	16

Table 13-5(continued from previous page)

For the selected text, if you want to find the:	Then the argument to SelInfo should be:
Table column of end of selection. Valid only if the selection is in a table, otherwise returns a value of -1.	17
Max number of columns in selected rows. Valid only if the selection is in a table, otherwise returns a value of -1.	18
Current zoom factor	19

Selection type:
    0 for normal selection
    1 for extended selection
    2 for block selection
	20

Status of Caps Lock (returns -1 if depressed)	21
Status of Num Lock (returns -1 if depressed)	22
Status of Overtype mode (returns -1 if depressed)	23
Status of revision marks (returns -1 if "on")	24
Location is in the footnote pane/area (returns -1 if in this area)	25
Location is in the annotation pane (returns -1 if in this area)	26
Location is in the macro editing window (returns -1 if in this area)	27
Location is in the header/footer pane or area (returns -1 if in this area)	28
Number of the bookmark enclosing the start of the selection	29
Number of the last bookmark that starts before selection	30

Example of Cursor Movement and Selection Functions   Now that you have learned a lot about different functions for moving the insertion point and selecting text, a few examples can be presented to illustrate how you can use these functions in typical applications. You'll see something new—the "while loop" control structure. See if you can understand what this structure does; it is discussed in more detail in the following section.

A Macro that Finds a Word   This macro illustrates how you can search through a document for a word, selecting the sentence in which the word is found, then displaying the page number and surrounding sentence. This is an interesting example because it is not always possible to display the entire sentence in which the word is found. If the sentence is too long, WordBasic displays an error message when it tries to display the sentence in the MsgBox.

The macro must then determine the length of the sentence in which the text appears and shorten the sentence enough to fit the sentence in the MsgBox. You can run this macro from the CHAP13.DOT template, just like the previous macros. Try changing the value the variable "size" is set to see how it affects the final output.

This is the printed listing of FindWord:

```
Sub MAIN '

This macro searches the document for a user specified string, display-
ing the page'number and sentence the word appears in"

'Start at beginning of document

size= 50        'Set the max number of characters to display
StartOfDocument

'get the string to search for

search$ = InputBox$("Enter the string to search for", "Word Finder", "")

'Position the cursor at the first string

EditFind .Find = search$, .Direction = 2, .WholeWord = 1

'Loop while string has been found
'Note: EditFindFound returns the status of the last EditFind opera-
tion. If it was 'successful, then loop will execute. If not, the loop
will not execute, and the macro 'will exit.

While EditFindFound()
    p = SelInfo(3)      'get the page number
    CharRight
    SentLeft 1, 0       'move to the beginning of the sentence
    SentRight 1, 1      'select the entire sentence
    s$ = Selection$()   'get the string where the match was found
    WordRight           'Move to first word of next sentence, so we
                        'don't select same sentence again on next
                        'EditFind
```

```
'display search result, give option to continue

'make sure the string isn't too big

If Len(s$) > size Then
'string is too big. Figure out how to resize the string
    pos = InStr(LCase$(s$), LCase$(search$))
' find out what character position the matching text is at
    If pos > Int(size / 2) Then
'the matching text is more than halfway into the string.
    s$ = Mid$(s$, pos—Int(size / 2), size) ' make string "size"
    characters, starting ' "size"/2 in front of matching text
    Else
'Can't center the string around the matching text, since there aren't
(size/2) characters
'in front of the matching text. Compromise, and display "size" charac-
ters from the
'beginning of the sentence.
        s$ = Left$(s$, size)
    EndIf
EndIf

    m$ = "Page" + Str$(p) + ":" + s$ ' build a display string
    a = MsgBox(m$ + " —continue search?", "Word Location",
    292)
' if 'NO' was chosen, exit

    If a = 0 Then Goto through

'Search for the text again

    EditFind .Direction = 1

Wend
through:
End Sub
```

Look at some of the key things to see the string, insertion point movement, and input/output operations this macro uses:

StartOfDocument—Puts the insertion point at the start of the document text. If you don't use this, then the search will start at the current location of the insertion point.

**InputBox$()**—Gets the text to search for from the user and puts the result in *search$*, a string variable

EditFind—Positions the insertion point at the first occurrence of the search string. Note that the example uses a variable, *search$*, to specify the text to look for.

EditFindFound—Returns true or false, depending on whether the results of the last EditFind succeeded or not.

SelInfo—Gives you the page number that the match was found on from executing SelInfo with the appropriate argument.

SentLeft, SentRight—Gives you the entire sentence that the text was found in. Use SentLeft to move to the beginning of the sentence and SentRight to move to the end of the sentence.

There's one case where this can cause you problems—do you see where it is? We'll go through a sample debugging session to help identify this problem and learn how to fix it. Note that the arguments to SentLeft are (1,0) and SentRight are (1,1). The second argument tells WordBasic if the text should be selected when moving the insertion point. You don't want to select the text when you move to the beginning of the sentence, as you will be selecting the text when you use SentRight, positioning the insertion point at the end of the sentence. If you try to select the text again, WordBasic cancels the selection.

WordRight—Moves the insertion point one step to the right.

Len(s$)—Finds out how many characters are in the sentence you selected.

pos=InStr(Lcase$(s$), Lcase$(search$))—Counts how many characters there are from the beginning of the sentence in s$ to the beginning of the search phrase search$. The Lcase function converts s$ and search$ to lowercase. This is needed, since the EditFind command (the way the example uses it) is ignoring case.

The InStr function *is case sensitive*—if, for example, you have "The Quick Fox" for our string, and you use InStr to search for "quick", it won't find a match, unlike EditFind. So you convert the search string and the string you are looking for to *all* lowercase, in case there are any differences in capitalization.

**s$=Mid$(s$,pos-Int(size /2), size)**—Replaces the currently selected text in s$ by a smaller string that meets your size requirements. We've done some tests earlier, so we know there are at least size/2 characters to the left of where the matching text is, so we copy "size" number of characters, starting at one half the "size" number of characters from where the matching text starts. This "centers" the text in our string "s$".

s$=Left$(s$, size)—We've found that there are less than "size/2" characters to the left of where we found the search string, so we compromise and start at the beginning of the original string and replace it with a new string of "size" characters in length.

m\$ = "Page" + Str\$(p) + ":" s\$—Here we are building a string that consists of the word "Page," followed by the page number (in the variable p), followed by the string you have the text selected in (the variable s\$). The + signs tell WordBasic to paste all these strings together into one long string. We had to use the Str\$ function on the variable p, because p is a numeric value and must be converted to a string to be included in a string variable.

a = MsgBox(m\$ + " —continue search?", "Word Location", 292)—Presents the results to the user. You can see that you can give the MsgBox both a string variable (m\$) plus text ("—continue search?") to display, pasting them together with the "+" sign. Also note that MsgBox has the "yes" and "no" pushbuttons, selected by the 292 code. The MsgBox returns a code indicating the button pushed (0 if No was pushed), which is assigned to the variable a.

Run the FindWord macro from the CHAP13.DOT template. (Refer to "How to Use the Demo Macros "earlier in this chapter" for more information.). Have two windows open, as explained in the "How to Use the Demo Macros" section, and have your document window contain a document with some text in it (any document will do, if you don't have a document ready, simply enter some text into a new document).

Suggestions

1. There's a lot going on in this macro. Try stepping through the macro, to help you understand how it works.

2. Position the insertion point at the beginning of any command you don't understand, and press **F1**. Read the help text that appears.

3. Think about how differently the macro would behave if you removed the "StartOfDocument" command.

Control Structures

You've seen control structures in some of the previous macros. They're the statements that begin with phrases like "if," "then," or "else." They allow you to alter the flow of your program—bypassing or executing groups of commands only when certain conditions are satisfied. This section discusses all the WordBasic control structures in depth.

What are Control Structures?

Control structures are statements that alter program flow. In WordBasic, they take one of the following forms:

- Call
- For...Next
- Function...End Function
- Goto
- If...ElseIf...Else...EndIf
- On Error
- Select Case...Case...Case...Case Else...End Select
- Stop
- Sub...End Sub
- While...Wend

This section covers some basics of the most-often used structures. For structures not covered, choose Help Index from the Help menu (**Alt-H, I**), then click the WordBasic Programming Language Reference.

Why Use Control Structures?

Control structures are a necessity for all but the simplest WordBasic macros. Whenever you need to test for a condition and execute a special set of instructions based on that condition, you'll need to use a control structure. Although the concept may sound complicated, it really develops quite naturally from the outline you prepare prior to writing the macro.

Types of Control Structures

You can group the different types of control structures together in a few broad categories:

- Controlling loops
- Branching
- Decision Making

After learning about the control structures in this section, you can pick the type of control structure needed to solve a particular programming problem. The examples show programs with each type of control structure, helping you build your understanding of each type and how to use it.

Expressions   Understanding expressions is essential to using control structures such as **if..then** and **while..wend** effectively. For example, "a < b" is an expression. You could use this expression in an **if** statement like this:

```
If a < b then
<some commands>
EndIf
```

Before you learn about control structures in more detail, you need to understand the necessary background information for expressions.

An expression performs a test on one or more variables. This can be a numeric expression, like **a < b** or a string expression like **a$ = b$**. The equal sign (=) and the less than sign (<) are examples of relational operators. The full set of relational operators WordBasic provides are:

=	equal
<>	not equal
>	greater than
<	less than
>=	greater than or equal to
<=	less than or equal to

Using these operators, an expression follows this format (the relational operator is abbreviated with "op"):

(number) (op) (number)	1 < 5
(string) (op) (string)	"a" < "b"
(number) (op) (variable)	1 = a
(variable) (op) (number)	a >= 1
(string) (op) (variable)	"ouch' = a$
(variable) (op) (string)	a$ = "ouch"

You cannot have a numeric variable on one side, and a string variable on the other, as comparing two different types doesn't make sense.

N O T E

You may find that you require a more complex test than just a single expression. WordBasic allows you to combine expressions together with the AND, OR, and NOT statements. For example, suppose you want to make sure that both **A < 10** and **today$ = Sunday**. You would combine the two expressions together like this:

```
(A < 10 ) AND (today$ = "Sunday")
```

You use OR the same way:

```
(A > 10 ) OR (today$ <> "Sunday")
```

You use the NOT operator to change a true expression to false and a false expression to true. You probably won't need to use this very often, but sometimes it makes the logic easier to understand and implement. Suppose you wanted to do something whenever the variable today$ was NOT Saturday or Sunday.

You could test to see if it was Monday or Tuesday or Wednesday, and so on for the rest of the week, something like

```
(today$ = "Monday") or (today$="Tuesday") or (today$="Wednesday") or
(today$ = "Thursday") or (today$ = "Friday")
```

A simpler way, though, is just to test and see if today is NOT Saturday or Sunday:

```
NOT ((today$="Saturday") or (today$ = Sunday))
```

You'll also notice that that there are parentheses around expressions. This is not required by WordBasic, but it's best to do so anyway, since it makes it obvious how the expressions will be evaluated. Without parentheses, WordBasic will use *precedence rules* to evaluate expressions. Instead of trying to remember what these rules are, it is much easier to simply put parentheses around expressions and force WordBasic to evaluate them in the order you specify.

Controlling Loops   Perhaps one of the most common operations in programming is *looping*—executing a series of instructions over and over until a particular condition is satisfied. The macros discussed earlier were a good example—

repeatedly searching through text to find a word, print the sentence in which it was found, find the next word, and so on until the end of the file was reached.

Suppose that the loop structures didn't exist. You would then either have to run the macro each time you wanted to search for a word, or you would have to have dozens of "EditFind" operations in a row, one for each time you expected to find the word. Loops enable you to compress these operations into a few WordBasic statements.

There are two main ways to control loops—through the **For..Next** statements, and through the **While..Wend** statements. The **For..Next** statement executes for a fixed number of times, so use it when you know in advance how many times you want to perform something. You use the **While…Wend** statement when you don't know how many times a loop needs to be executed. The loop is executed until the condition specified in the While statement is satisfied.

For..Next: The syntax of the For..Next statement is

```
For CounterVariable = Start to End [ Step Increment]
    statements
Next [CounterVariable]
```

CounterVariable is a variable that is set to the value in start, and incremented by the value specified in Step (if step is omitted, the variable is incremented by one). Once the CounterVariable goes past the value of End, the loop is exited. Use the following guidelines when constructing the For..Next loop:

- The CounterVariable can be any valid numeric variable name, but if you use it elsewhere in your program, its value may be different after it is used in the For..Next loop.

- You can count up from the value in Start to the value in End by specifying a positive step value. You can count down from Start to End by specifying a negative value for the step increment. Be careful—if you have 1 for a starting value, 5 for an ending value, and -1 for the step, your loop will *never* finish. The counter value will decrement from 1 to 0 to -1 to -2. and so on, and will *never* reach 5, as specified in your end statement.

- When the For..Next loop is exited, the CounterVariable is set to the End value plus the value in for the step increment, if the increment is a positive number. If the increment is a negative number, CounterVariable is set to the value in End minus the increment.

- Each statement between the For and the Next statement will be ex ecuted each time through the loop.

While..Wend The **While..Wend** statement is a useful way to specify control looping when you do not know in advance how many times the loop will need to execute. Its syntax is as follows:

```
While Condition
    Statement(s)
Wend
```

This loop executes all of the statements between While and Wend as long as the condition is false. The condition can be one of the following:

- a function that returns a value of true or false

- a simple or complex expression

- an integer (if the value is 0, then the condition is false, otherwise it is true)

There are some conditions to keep in mind when using the "While" loop:

- Make sure that the condition you are testing for will be set to false at some point. Otherwise, your loop will execute forever (or until you reset your PC).

- Be careful about modifying any variables that are used in the condition statement, since you could inadvertently case the condition to always be true.

The FindWord macro has an example of a While loop, using the value returned from a function (EditFindFound) as the condition:

```
While EditFindFound()
<statements deleted for clarity>
EditFind .Direction=2
Wend
```

This loop executed as long as the EditFind operation was successful. Do you see how we could easily make this into an infinite loop (one that never terminates)? If we put another statement after the EditFind operation which moved the cursor back before the text that was just found, the loop would find the same text over and over and over… and would never terminate! That's why it is essential to check over your condition statements carefully with this kind of structure.

You're not restricted to using just functions like EditFindFound in your While loop; you can use expressions as well. Suppose you wanted to add variable b to variable a repeatedly, until variable a reached a certain value. You could use a While loop to do this, in the following manner:

```
While a<Limit
a=a+b
Wend
```

Also, remember that conditions can be made up of more than one expression. Suppose there were two limits you wanted to check for, instead of just one. You could create a While loop such as the following:

```
While (a<Limit1) and (a<Limit2)
    a=a+b
Wend
```

Branching   Branching statements are statements that change the direction of program execution, for example, causing the program to jump from one location to another. In the case of WordBasic, the branching statement is the Goto statement.

Goto   The Goto statement has a bad reputation in the programming world, and for good reason: excessive use of the Goto statement can make programs almost impossible to follow. However, Goto statements can be reasonable ways to break out of a loop before the loop finishes, as the following example shows:

```
For i = 1 to 10
    if Text$[i]=Match$ then Goto MatchFound
    else <do something else>
Next
Print "Match wasn't found
Goto End:
MatchFound:
Print "Match was found"
End:
<finish rest of program>
```

Note that the Goto statement requires either a line number or a label to go to. In this case, the label is **MatchFound**. The label indicates where program execution resumes after the Goto statement is executed. You must add a colon (:) after the label.

Decision Making   *Decision making* is the process of evaluating a condition to control the branches and groups of statements that your program executes. Suppose you write a macro that does one type of thing to italic characters, and another to bold. You would need a decision structure in your program to determine if the character was italic or bold, then perform the appropriate functions.

If..Then..ElseIf..Else The If statement is the decision-making structure you'll probably find yourself using the most frequently. It does mostly what you would expect from its name: **if** some condition is true, **then** do some action, **else** do some other action.

There are several varieties of If statements, using syntax like the following:

Type 1:

```
If Condition then
    Statement(s)
EndIf
```

Type 2:

```
If Condition then
    Statement(s)
Else
    Statement(s)
Endif
```

Type 3:

```
If Condition1 then
    Statement(s)
ElseIf Condition2 then
    Statement(s)
ElseIf Condition3
(you can have as many ElseIf statements as needed)
Else
    Statement(s)
EndIf
```

As you can see, there is a variety of different ways to express If statements. You can have a single **If..Then**, or an **If..Then..Else**, or an **If..Then..ElseIf..Else**. Next, you will learn how "If" statements work, and how to choose one over another.

WordBasic will evaluate the condition after the **If**. If the condition is true, then it executes the block of statements after the **If**, until it encounters either an **Else, ElseIf**, or **EndIf**. If the condition is not true, then WordBasic checks to see if you have an **Else** or **ElseIf** statement. If you have an **Else** statement, then WordBasic executes the block of statements following the **Else**, until it encounters the **EndIf**.

If you have an **ElseIf**, then WordBasic checks to see if the condition following the **ElseIf** is true. If it is true, then WordBasic executes the block of statements following the **ElseIf**. If the condition is false, then WordBasic searches for the next

ElseIf, evaluates that expression, and takes the appropriate action. If none of the conditions after the **ElseIf** statements evaluate to true, then WordBasic will execute the block of statements following the **Else** statement (which has no condition associated with it).

You should also note that once a block of statements is executed, none of the remaining blocks will be executed. The following example shows an example of program blocks. In the case below, the blocks are the assignment statements (b= some value):

```
if a = 0 then
    b=1
elseif a = 0 then
    b=2
else
    b=3
endif
```

In the example, when the expression **a = 0** is true, then only the statement **b = 1** will be executed. This happens even though the condition following the ElseIf is also true. Only the first block with the matching expression is executed; the rest are ignored. The following table will help you chose the appropriate **If** structure to use:

Table 13-6

To...	Choose...
Perform a single block of statements whenever a condition is true	If..Then
Perform one block of statements when a condition's true, another block when it is false	If..Then..Else
Chose one of several blocks depending on more than one condition	If..Then..ElseIf..Else

Examples will help make this clearer. Suppose you want to print a message whenever the number of words is more than some limit. You would use the If..Then.. format:

```
If WordCount > Limit then
    print "Limit Exceeded for Word Count"
EndIf
```

Now, imagine that you want to print a message for both cases: one when the word count exceeds a limit and another when the word count is OK. In this case, the If..Then..Else.. structure presents the best solution:

```
if WordCount > Limit then
    print "Limit Exceeded"
else
    print "Limit OK
endif
```

The next example shows how you can print a variety of different messages, depending on the value of the word count. Run the IfDemo macro from the CHAP13.DOT template. (Refer to "How to Use the Demo Macros" earlier in this chapter for more information.) This is the printed listing of IfDemo:

```
Sub MAIN
Input "enter your shoe size", v
If(v < 2) Then
    Print "Pretty small, I don't believe it"
ElseIf(v < 6) Then
    Print "How dainty"
ElseIf(v < 9) Then
    Print "Normal"
ElseIf(v <= 10) Then
    Print "Kinda big"
ElseIf((v >= 11) And(v <= 12)) Then
    Print "BIGFOOT"
Else
    Print "No way!"
EndIf
End Sub
```

Note that the examples take advantage of the fact that WordBasic will only execute the first block of statements following a condition that evaluates to true. If you look at the example above, you'll see that when v<2, it MUST be less than 6 as well. But because the condition v < 2 is the first condition WordBasic finds to be true, it ignores the rest of the conditions.

Also note that you can add practically as many "ElseIf" statements as you need. But this can get somewhat confusing to read, understand, and debug. WordBasic provides another structure—the case statement—that provides a cleaner way to proceed.

Suggestions:

1. Try editing the macro and stepping through it with different values for the shoesize.

2. Try to predict the next statements to be executed, after you enter your shoesize.

Case The Case control structure selects a group of statements for execution, like the **if..then..else** control structure. The Case structure is best-suited for situations when you want to evaluate a single expression, then choose one of out of many possible actions based on the value of that expression. For example, if you wanted to evaluate the font size of a word you selected, then select one out of a number of different actions based on the font size, the Case structure might be a good approach.

The syntax of the Case statement is:

```
Select Case Expression
    Case Case_Expression
        statements
    Case Case_Expression
        statements
    (as many case statements as you need)
    Case Else
        statements
End Select
```

Note that there are three basic parts to the case structure:

```
Select Case Expression
    Case Case_Expression
Case Else
```

The **Select Case** expression is the part of the case structure in which you specify the expression that you want to compare against the **Case Case_Expression** statements. For example, if you were evaluating the font size, then this statement would be something like this:

```
Select Case Font_Size
```

where Font_Size is a variable we defined earlier that contains the font size.

There is a **Case Case_Expression** statement for each possible action you want to take, based on the value in the expression following the **Select Case**. The **Case_Expressions** can take the following forms:

- simple expressions, such as "5" or "0"
- ranges, such as "0 To 5"
- relations, such as "Is >10"
- lists, such as "1,2,5"

Continuing with our example, we could have Case statements like the following:

```
Case 1 to 5
    print "very small font, between 1 and 5"
Case 6 to 9
    print "barely readable font, between 6 and 9 point"
Case 10,12
    print "reasonable font size of 10 or 12"
Case Is >12
    print "Big font, bigger than 12 point"
```

The Case Else is the "catch all" statement. Whenever the expression doesn't match any of the expressions in the Case statements, the statements following the Case Else are executed. If there is no match and there is no Case Else instruction, an error occurs.

Try the CaseDemo macro from the CHAP13.DOT template. (Refer to "How to Use the Demo Macros.") You will see two windows, one for the macro, another for the document. Position the insertion point on some text in your demo document, then run the macro.

```
Sub MAIN
WordRight 1, 1
Select Case FontSize()
Case 1 To 5
    Print "very small font—between 1 and five"
Case 6 To 9
    Print "barely readable font, between 6 and 9 point"
Case 10, 12
    Print "reasonable font size of 10 or 12"
Case Is > 12
    Print "Big font, bigger than 12 point"
Case Else
    Print "Weird Font!"
End Select
End Sub
```

Suggestions and Questions

1. Try several different font sizes in your sample document and test each of the possible cases of the macro.

2. Try putting the macro in a loop with a **for..next** statement around the WordRight to the End Select:

```
For i = 1 to 10
WordRight 1,1
<rest of macro>
End Select
Next i
```

3. Can you think of a way to search through your entire document, then list all the fonts you might encounter?

4. What happens if a word has more than one font?

5. Can you change the macro to select a single character at a time?

CREATING COMPLEX DIALOG BOXES

You've seen some of the simple methods for communicating with the user: the status bar, the message box, and the input box. There may be times, however, when you want to create a more complex interface, like presenting a list of file names or elements in an array. The Dialog Editor helps you create these interfaces.

This section explains the process for creating a dialog box and placing it in your program. There are two basic ways of creating a dialog box—by creating the WordBasic function calls yourself, or by using Dialog Editor to create the function calls for you. Using the Dialog Editor is the better of the two approaches for most users, since you interactively design how you want the dialog box to appear, and the correct WordBasic statements are generated for you.

Although nothing prevents you from using the "brute force" approach of manually creating the WordBasic statements, you won't actually know what your dialog box looks like until you run your program. You will then probably want to make some changes to the dialog box, such as changing its size (which means going back into your macro), editing the dialog box statements, then running your program again. The dialog editor lets you do all your adjustments before you write any code, saving you a lot of time and avoiding the need to manually edit, run, change, and run again, repeating the process until it is correct.

What is the Dialog Editor?

The Dialog Editor is a program that creates the WordBasic definitions for inclusion in your WordBasic program. You create a dialog box with the Dialog Editor in the following manner:

1. Use the Dialog Editor to design your dialog box.
2. Exit the Dialog Editor (the results are saved in the Clipboard).
3. Switch back to the Macro editor, and choose **Paste** from the Edit menu (**Alt-E, P**). The commands created by the Dialog Editor are pasted into your WordBasic program.

This process is discussed in more detail in the following sections.

What are the Commands the Dialog Editor Creates?

A complex dialog box requires that you create a dialog structure definition before you can invoke the dialog box. This structure definition contains coordinates, button definitions, text, and any other items necessary to define the dialog box.

Once this definition is created, you can invoke the dialog box by calling the dialog function. You can get a numerical code from the dialog function indicating which buttons were entered. The following example helps make this clearer.

This is a listing of the DialogDemo1 macro from the CHAP13.DOT template:

```
Sub MAIN
Begin Dialog UserDialog 422, 150, "Push Buttons"
Text 132, 20, 158, 17, "SELECT A BUTTON"
PushButton 24, 50, 150, 18, "O&ne"
PushButton 24, 74, 150, 18, "T&wo"
PushButton 24, 98, 150, 18, "T&hree"
OKButton 269, 115, 120, 18
CancelButton 269, 90, 120, 18
End Dialog
Dim dlg As UserDialog
n = Dialog(dlg)
a$ = Str$(n)
If n = 0 Then
MsgBox "The Cancel Button was pressed"
Goto Final
EndIf
If n =—1 Then
MsgBox "The OK Button was pressed"
Goto Final
```

```
EndIf
MsgBox "PushButton" + a$ + " was pressed"
Final:
End Sub
```

Try running this demo from the CHAP13.DOT template. (Refer to "How to Use the Demo Macros," earlier in this chapter.)

Note that the dialog function returns a 0 if the cancel button was chosen, and a -1 if the OK button was chosen. Any other value indicates that one of the three pushbuttons was chosen. The codes for the pushbuttons are 1, 2, and 3, in this case, and the values are determined by the order in which the buttons are defined.

You can invoke the Dialog Editor two ways:

- from the Word program group in the Program Manager (if you installed the macro editor to be in the program group)
- by choosing Run from the File menu in the Program Manager, and typing **macrode.exe**.

This process can be made even easier if you load the NEWMACRO.DOC file, included with your Word for Windows package, and install the LaunchDialogEditor macro. If you use the Dialog Editor frequently, then installing this macro will be a real time-saver, especially if you install it as a menu option, such as on the Tool menu as was shown in Chapter 11, "Macros."

This section steps you through the process of using the Dialog Editor. Assume that you want to have a dialog box that lists several items and lets you select an item from the list.

Open the Dialog Editor using one of the methods described above. You'll see something like this:

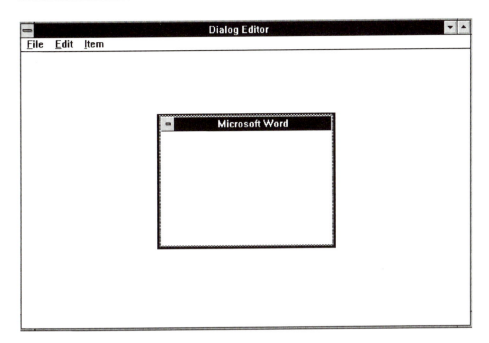

Figure 13.5

The box in the center of your screen is what your dialog box will look like when called by your program. Create a list box with the combo box option and add Cancel and OK buttons. Use the following procedure:

1. From the Item menu, choose **List Box**, then **Combo (Alt-I, L, C)** to create the combo box.

2. From the Item menu, choose **Button**, then **OK (Alt-I, B, O)** to place the OK button in the box.

3. From the Item menu, choose **Button**, then **Cancel (Alt-I, B, C)** to place the Cancel button in the box.

Your dialog box should now look like this:

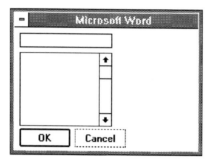

Figure 13.6

You can click and drag any of the buttons to new locations, if the initial placement is incorrect.

N O T E

4. **Exit** the Dialog Editor (**Alt-F, X**).

   The Dialog Editor asks you if you want to save the changes to the Clipboard.

5. Choose **Yes**.

   The dialog definition statements are now stored in the Clipboard.

Now, edit a new macro with the name of your choosing. From the Edit menu, choose **Paste** (**Ctrl-V**) to paste the definition from the Clipboard to your macro. Make your macro look like the following (some of the numbers in the dialog definition may be different; don't worry about these):

```
Sub MAIN
Dim  ComboBox1$(10)
ComboBox1$(0)  =  "Item1"
ComboBox1$(1)  =  "Item2"
ComboBox1$(2) = "Item3"
ComboBox1$(3) = "Item4"
ComboBox1$(4) = "Item5"
Begin Dialog UserDialog 320, 144, "Microsoft Word"
    ComboBox 10, 6, 160, 108, ComboBox1$(), .ComboBox1
    OKButton 10, 117, 88, 21
    CancelButton 109, 117, 88, 21
End Dialog
Dim dlg As UserDialog
x = Dialog(dlg)
Print x, dlg.ComboBox1
End Sub
```

You should be able to run your macro, and get a dialog box like this:

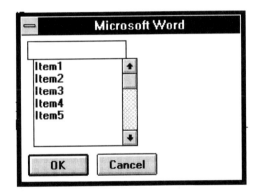

Figure 13.7

You can chose any of the items in the list, and the results of your choice will appear in the status bar. This macro is also on the CHAP13.DOT template as DemoDialog2, in case you have any problems creating your own.

This completes the overview of using the Dialog Editor. Play around with different options in the Dialog Editor, to investigate all the possible variations on how to proceed.

Here are a few additional notes:

- The contents of ComboBox1$ were defined prior to the Begin Dialog statement. Otherwise, the contents of ComboBox1$ would not be displayed, if ComboBox1$ was defined after the End Dialog.

- If you decide to change the combo box in your macro, you don't have to start again from scratch. Copy everything between and including "Begin Dialog" and "End Dialog" to the Clipboard (**Alt-E, C**), invoke the Dialog Editor, then **Paste** (**Alt-P**). Your dialog box will be recreated, where you can change it easily. After you finish editing the dialog box, copy the new dialog statements back to your macro, and delete the old version of the dialog definition.

FUNDAMENTAL PROGRAMMING CONCEPTS

Because WordBasic is a programming language, it is essential that anyone wanting to write their own WordBasic functions understand some key programming concepts. First of all, a program is a list of instructions that the computer executes in the order it reads them. In the case of WordBasic, this list of instructions is simply a list of WordBasic commands. For very simple programs, these instructions may simply be executed once, in the order that WordBasic reads them. For more complex programs, it may be necessary to repeat some instructions many times, or until a certain condition is satisfied. This repetition is known as *looping*, and can be performed in WordBasic in several possible ways, which you learn about later. The order in which the instructions may be executed can also vary. This is known as decision-making, like the "if then else" statements in the first example.

How to Develop Your Macro

The key to success in programming doesn't lie in mastering the programming language. Instead it results from a clear definition of the problem you are trying to solve.

There are many ways to develop programs, ranging from extremely formal, rigidly specified methods, to simply "code and see if it works" strategies. Both have their place—if you're designing software for the space shuttle, then you want to be very careful about the methodology you use. If you are simply trying out a few ideas to see what happens, then there's nothing wrong with "code and go" approach.

For the majority of cases, though, a reasonable compromise is needed. We suggest you take the following steps when creating a macro:

1. Develop a clear, single-sentence description of what the macro is supposed to do.
2. Develop an outline of how the macro will work.
3. Expand the outline of the macro into WordBasic commands.

Developing the Macro Description

Whenever you decide to create a WordBasic function, try to write a one-sentence description of what it does, without using "ands" and "ors" in your description. If you have to use several "ands" and "ors" in your description, you probably should make several macros to do everything you need to do. Note that this is just a suggestion; there is nothing to prevent you from making a complex macro that can't be clearly described in a single sentence. But in doing so, you may wind up with something that is difficult to design and debug.

An example will help clarify this concept. Suppose you need to search through your document and determine on what page a particular word or phrase occurs, so you can prepare an index. A one-sentence description of a macro that does this is: "Lists all page numbers in which a particular user-specified phrase occurs." This clearly defines the scope of the problem you are trying to solve and helps you avoid cluttering up your macro with unrelated functions.

Developing an Outline

The next step after clearly defining your problem is to write an outline of what your macro is going to do in plain English. Imagine yourself describing to someone, step by step, how to perform the function you want to perform, and write down this description in the form of an outline. The page-listing macro will serve as an example of how to begin.

The objective of the macro has been clearly defined:

"Lists all page numbers in which a user-specified phrase occurs."

Think about what Word needs to do to accomplish this. Because Word will be automating steps that you could perform manually, think about how you would perform this operation. The Find command from the Edit menu is the operation that searches through a document for a phrase that you enter, and displays the page number in the status bar each time the phrase is found. Keeping this in mind (there's not much point to introducing functions that don't correlate with what WordBasic offers) you can develop an outline of how the macro might work:

1. Get the word or phrase to search for.
2. Go to the top of the file.
3. Until the end of the file is reached:
   - Find the next occurrence of the word or phrase.
   - Display the page number on which the match occurs.

Statement 1 is where the macro asks for the word or phrase it is to search for. You have to have this step, since the macro must be able to search for any phrase that you want.

Statement 2 means that you want to start the search at the top of the file; otherwise, the search would start from the position of the insertion point to the end of the file.

Statement 3 is a loop—repeat the steps of finding the phrase then displaying the page number over and over, until the end of the file is reached.

Converting Your Outline into a WordBasic Program

Now that you have clearly defined the problem and know how to go about solving it, you can proceed to translate the outline into WordBasic instructions. There are two ways to start: you can start writing your WordBasic program "from scratch," or you can record a macro that is close to doing what you want, then edit that macro to adapt it to your exact requirements. The second approach is a little easier if you are not an experienced WordBasic programmer, so that is the method explained here.

Because the macro involves finding text over and over, you can start by starting the macro recorder, then choosing Find from the Edit menu (**Alt-E, F**) and then Find and Find Next from the Edit menu (**Alt-E, F, F**) to start the macro. You will record a macro, using these commands, then edit it with the macro editor to meet your specific requirements. The following example shows a few Find operations, searching for the word "the," ignoring case and formatting information.

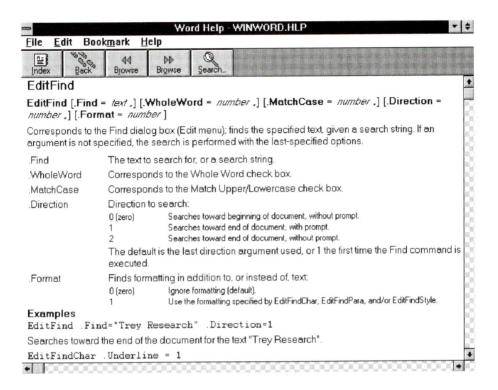

Figure 13.8

To get this display, we simply recorded the macro, then edited the macro with the macro editor. The macro is *not* recorded in a text format that you can edit like any other text file; you must use the macro editor to view the macro.

Recording a macro, then editing it, can be an excellent self-teaching introduction to WordfBasic commands. Suppose you wanted to find out more about the "EditFind" command. Position the cursor in front of "EditFind," then press F1. Word displays a window describing the function, which looks like this:

N O T E

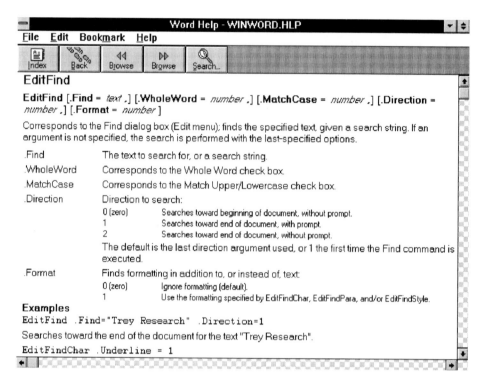

Figure 13.9

This help window describes the WordBasic function, lists its arguments, and provides examples. Sometimes it will have related topics listed at the bottom of the menu. The important concept to understand is that every WordBasic command has arguments, such as **Find** in this example, that tell the function the specifics of what to do. A *function* is a general description of an operation, like **EditFind**, and the arguments are things like ".Find=the," which tells **EditFind** that it is searching for the word "the."

An easy way to keep track of this process is to actually include your outline in the macro being created. Simply precede each line in your outline with the comment sign (the single quote character ') and include it in your document. WordBasic ignores a comment line; it exists strictly for helping programmers remember and document their work. It is also good programming form to have a concise description of your program at the beginning of the program. Since you've already created this description in your one- sentence problem statement, simply put it at the top of your macro file:

```
Sub MAIN
'Purpose: Lists all page numbers in which a user-specified phrase
occurs
end Sub
```

Now, translate each sentence in your outline into the corresponding WordBasic instruction.

```
Sub MAIN
'Purpose: Lists all page numbers in which a user-specified
phrase occurs
'Get the word or phrase to search for
Input "Word to Search for?", search?
'.Go to the top of the file
StartOfDocument
EditFind
'.Until the end of the file is reached:
'Find the next occurrence of the word or phrase
'Display the page number that the match occurs on
<commands to find phrase>
end Sub
```

SUMMARY

At this point, you should have a good working knowledge of Word WordBasic, how to create, edit, and format documents using Word's sophisticated capabilities, and how to edit or create WordBasic macros. While using macros, you are no longer limited to strictly repeated sequences of keystrokes that you recorded manually. Now you can actually go into your macros and edit and customize them to your specific needs.

INDEX

G

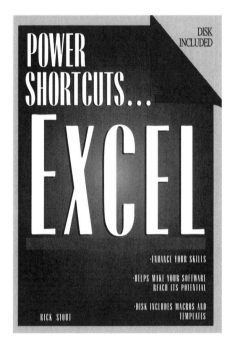

Power Shortcuts...WordPerfect for Windows

by Jerilyn Marler

Even if you're an expert WordPerfect user, WordPerfect for Windows brings you powerful features you've never used before. Get a jump on the best of this latest version with *Power Shortcuts...WordPerfect for Windows*. Using extensive examples and easy-to-follow instructions, author Jerilyn Marler gives you the power edge as you make the transition to Windows word processing. In addition, all programming examples and re-usable macro and merge files are included on disk!

◆ Actual working macro and merge programming files that you can use as templates for your own work.

◆ Use the disk to work through the exercises and learn techniques without having to create the documents from scratch.

ISBN: 1-55828-210-6 $29.95

Teach Yourself...Windows 3.1

by Al Stevens

This powerful book teaches you how to use Windows 3.1 basics, including the desktop, windows, icons, mouse, and keyboard. The book also covers the advanced features, including running programs, organizing data files, managing the system, printing, and running Windows on a network.

With *Teach Yourself...Windows 3.1* you'll learn to:

◆ Master the basics of the Windows operating environment.

◆ Discover the power of Windows 3.1's unique features like the graphical user interface and multitasking capabilities.

◆ Use Windows 3.1 to advance your computer into the converging family of operating platforms.

ISBN: 1-55828-193-2 $ 19.95